DATE DUE

GAYLORD			PRINTED IN U.S.A.

Campaign Crises

CAMPAIGN
CRISES

Detours on the Road to Congress

R. Sam Garrett

LYNNE
RIENNER
PUBLISHERS

BOULDER
LONDON

Published in the United States of America in 2010 by
Lynne Rienner Publishers, Inc.
1800 30th Street, Boulder, Colorado 80301
www.rienner.com

and in the United Kingdom by
Lynne Rienner Publishers, Inc.
3 Henrietta Street, Covent Garden, London WC2E 8LU

Library of Congress Cataloging-in-Publication Data
Garrett, R. Sam, 1977–
  Campaign crises : detours on the road to Congress / by R. Sam Garrett.
    p. cm.
  Includes bibliographical references and index.
  ISBN 978-1-58826-671-2 (hardcover : alk. paper)
  1. Campaign management—United States. 2. Political campaigns—United
States. 3. United States. Congress—Elections. 4. Elections—United
States. I. Title.
  JK2281.G376 2009
  324.70973—dc22

                                                            2009026974

British Cataloguing in Publication Data
A Cataloguing in Publication record for this book
is available from the British Library.

Printed and bound in the United States of America

     The paper used in this publication meets the requirements
 ∞   of the American National Standard for Permanence of
     Paper for Printed Library Materials Z39.48-1992.

  5 4 3 2 1

Contents

Tables and Figures

Acknowledgments

It is impossible to thank everyone who helped complete this book. Those mentioned below deserve special recognition, but the countless others without whom this project would have been impossible are nonetheless appreciated and remembered.

Most of all, the book would be nothing without the enormous generosity of more than eighty political professionals (and a few candidates) who participated in more than one hundred interviews. Many of those sources asked not to be named. Whether named or unnamed, Democrat or Republican, they shared their worlds in extraordinary detail and with great candor. They gave of their time, enthusiasm, and intellect. They voluntarily relived some of the best and worst moments of their careers. They have directly contributed to this research, and I thank each one. Jenny Backus, Paul Curcio, Rich Davis, Rachel Gorlin, Chris LaCivita, Bill Pascoe, Sarah Simmons, Ray Strother, and Tony J. Williams were particularly helpful.

The book would have been equally impossible without its connection to American University (AU) in Washington, D.C. In particular, the Center for Congressional and Presidential Studies (CCPS) was kind enough to host me as an unpaid research fellow while I was revising the manuscript. James A. Thurber, director of CCPS, shared professional contacts and provided generous funding and office space to support my research. His commitment to bringing together scholars and practitioners is the foundation of hundreds of academic and public service careers—including my own. Several other members of the CCPS staff provided moral and administrative support.

Other academic colleagues, at AU and beyond, also supported the book. Candice J. Nelson, the academic director of the Campaign Management Institute and chair of the Department of Government at AU, has been a tremendous resource and friend. She was constantly available during all phases of the research and writing; she was a fair critic and an excellent mentor. Despite Candy's modesty, she is one of the best scholars, teachers, and people I know. Paul S. Herrnson, director of the Center for American Politics and Citizenship at the University of Maryland, is a consummate professional. Paul's work ethic, expertise, and encouragement were particularly valuable during early phases of the research and writing. David A. Dulio at Oakland University has been a wonderful colleague and friend. I thank him for his steadfast support of my research and for his own contributions to the fields covered in this book. Christine DeGregorio's mentoring and work on political context also directly contributed to this project, as did Joe Soss's introduction to qualitative research. Amy Jasperson, Robin Kolodny, Stephen Medvic, and Mark Wrighton shared their expertise and enthusiasm throughout the writing process.

Several other people and institutions provided specific support. The staff at Ace Transcription in Washington, D.C., transcribed most of the interviews. Jay Jennings and Gina Rosen were superb teaching assistants, which allowed me additional time for writing during my year as a visiting instructor at AU. CCPS's Improving Campaign Conduct project, sponsored by a grant from the Pew Charitable Trusts, provided financial support for this and other projects related to political consulting. The AU School of Public Affairs also provided financial support. A grant from the Dirksen Congressional Center covered some transcription costs and other expenses.

Three anonymous reviewers provided helpful insights. One of those reviewers, Michael John Burton, voluntarily revealed his identity and graciously provided substantive and professional feedback. I also thank several other reviewers who read and strengthened previous versions of the manuscript. I thank the staff at Lynne Rienner Publishers for their work.

Others did not have a direct connection to the manuscript but provided an early foundation for my interests in research and writing. In particular, these include Kurt Jacob, Brian Lamb, William Pasternak, and William F. Woo. Pursuing a career in political science would have never occurred to me without the enthusiasm of Professors Alan Levine, Jerome W. Sheridan, and Steven Taylor. Milton Greenberg, my first academic mentor, deserves special thanks. I owe him more than I can repay, although I am sure he keeps the tab running.

This book is a personal endeavor. Any opinions expressed here (unless attributed to others) are those of the author and do not necessarily reflect the views of the Congressional Research Service (CRS) or the Library of

Congress, where I have been privileged to serve as an analyst. Although the book was not part of my official duties, I thank CRS colleagues Keith Bea, Robert Jay Dilger, and Larry Eig for supporting my involvement in the political science community. CRS colleagues Kevin R. Kosar, Walter J. Oleszek, and Harold C. Relyea gave essential advice during key moments in the publishing process.

The book could not have been completed without encouragement from various friends and family members, too many to mention here. My parents, Walter and Martha Ann Garrett, taught me that important things are worth doing, even when it is not clear when or how they will be done. Their love of politics, writing, and learning is reflected throughout the following pages. Jim, Karen, Bridget, and J. J. Owen also deserve special thanks, as does the entire Jansen family.

My wife, Karen E. T. Garrett, has been the most important part of my life since before this project began. During the highs and lows of my research career, as with everything else, Karen has been my refuge. She has allowed my full-time school, teaching, research, and writing to be part of our relationship. She has been patient during late nights and weekends and when I was mentally elsewhere even when we were together. She also made substantive contributions to the book, including being a constant sounding board and providing editing assistance. Our relationship involves no crises and requires no strategy. It is the greatest of adventures and the best of campaigns. I also thank the Trout family for their support.

It is my great hope that political professionals on both sides of the aisle find this work accurate, objective, and interesting. I hope this work does them justice.

1

Campaigns, Crises, and Modern US Politics

There's a tremendous amount of room for research here because this is all done by journeymen politicians who really don't think about what they're doing when we do it. There's no research on this. . . . All of our information is anecdotal, and over the years you just sort of get a feel for it.
— Joe McLean, Democratic fundraiser
and former campaign manager[1]

Within hours of Barack Obama's historic victory in the 2008 presidential election, reporters, political professionals, and pundits considered not only how he had won but also how remarkable it was that others had lost. Just four years earlier, Obama was a little-known Illinois state senator. Hillary Clinton, the presumptive frontrunner, was a prominent US senator and enjoyed widespread name recognition as a former first lady. Many viewed the Democratic nomination as Clinton's to lose.

Even if Obama could overcome Clinton and several other prominent and experienced Democratic opponents, the general election would be hotly contested. Prominent Republicans, including former Massachusetts governor Mitt Romney and former Arkansas governor Mike Huckabee, had lined up to pursue the GOP nomination. Most formidably, Arizona senator John McCain prepared to enter the race. McCain enjoyed widespread popularity and had decades of experience. But McCain's reputation for bucking conservative elements of his party could also complicate the race. His independence meant the potential to appeal to a diverse group of voters but ran the risk of alienating the GOP base.

Against this backdrop, when the presidential campaign began in early 2007—almost two years before Election Day 2008—the odds facing

1

Obama were steep indeed. Obama's victory was described as "among the most remarkable and least probable success stories in the history of American politics," partly for the Democrat's widespread appeal, but also because Obama reportedly "ran a near flawless campaign, one that always seemed to know how to respond to crisis" (NPR 2008). That meant being able to "adapt" to unexpected events, ranging from the grueling primary contest with Hillary Clinton (not to mention several other opponents) to "a sudden jolt of dire news from Wall Street," which replaced the Iraq War as the major issue late in the race (NPR 2008). Despite these challenges, Obama's campaign managed to respond as though the events had been expected. The campaign was widely viewed as one of the smoothest tactical operations in recent political memory.

By contrast, 2008 was less kind to Republican John McCain, who was making his second White House bid (having lost the GOP nomination in 2000 to George W. Bush). McCain's 2008 campaign struggled to respond to the fiscal crisis that shaped the final weeks of the campaign and focused on attacking Obama rather than reinforcing messages about why McCain should be elected (Langley 2008). Nonetheless, his campaign's ability to win the Republican nomination at all represented a monumental shift in electoral fortune. According to media accounts, just months before McCain secured the GOP nomination, his campaign had become a cumbersome organization and was hemorrhaging money. The frontrunner status the campaign expected going into the primaries had not materialized (PBS 2008). A high-profile reorganization managed to salvage the campaign and win the nomination.

Challenging campaign environments and unexpected events were not limited to the 2008 presidential race. Campaigns for US House and Senate seats faced potential crises of their own. The 2008 elections were particularly challenging for congressional Republicans as the Obama campaign gained momentum at the top of the ticket and as public dissatisfaction with the economy and the Iraq War continued. But Democrats, too, were affected. On both sides of the aisle, more than a dozen lawmakers in the House and Senate experienced what the media characterized as "scandals," ranging from continued fallout from a federal investigation of disgraced lobbyist Jack Abramoff to marital, legal, and financial problems that had become public factors in various reelection contests (Yachin and Singer 2008). In some cases, such as Representative Tim Mahoney's loss in a Florida congressional race following his confirmation of marital infidelity (Bennett 2008; UPI 2008), the electoral environment was uniquely affected by individual circumstances. For others, such as the loss of Republican representative Christopher Shays, a longtime incumbent from Connecticut, the defeat appeared to be part of a broader trend that disfavored Republicans, even as they remained largely popular in their own districts. The 2008 (and 2006) congressional races favored Democrats. But Republicans had enjoyed similar advantages during the previous major congressional shakeup, when the GOP won control of the House and Senate in 1994.

The 2008 elections provided fresh examples of pivotal events that shape campaigns. But opportunities to explore how campaigns are won and lost, and how political professionals make strategic decisions in those campaigns, are by no means limited to particular time periods or campaigns. This book examines the decisions and strategies behind key moments in congressional campaigns, including case studies of four Senate races. The lessons learned, however, apply broadly across elections and over time.

Unifying Theory and Practice

A political consultant once advised a campaign intern—this author—that attending graduate school would be a mistake. I would do better, the consultant said, to spend a while working on campaigns first. For the consultant, political scientists spent too little time practicing what they taught.[2]

A few years later, Democratic media consultant Rachel Gorlin suggested that political professionals might benefit from an academic perspective after all. Gorlin recalled a recent campaign scandal full of sensational details—the juicy material that increasingly falls somewhere between tabloid and political journalism. But Gorlin wanted more than salacious anecdotes. She argued that the sensational nature of this particular scandal had overshadowed important tactical lessons that political consultants could not objectively address and, given the hectic pace of most campaigns, did not have time to adequately understand. The case Gorlin described needed a neutral inquiry to understand how the campaigns had reacted and what lessons could be learned for scholars and practitioners alike. As Joe McLean's quotation at the beginning of this chapter demonstrates, sometimes an outside perspective can help practitioners tell, and learn from, their own stories. Scholars help provide an academic forum for those stories among students and researchers. With that perspective in mind, this book explores academic lessons behind practical campaign politics.

These three consultants (Gorlin, McLean, and the unnamed source) had different views on what benefits political science could provide to practical campaign politics. Each was at least partially correct. Political science often remains woefully disconnected from the people, decisions, and events it studies. Fortunately, campaigns and elections research straddles the practical and theoretical worlds better than many areas of the discipline. Nonetheless, important questions and practical connections often remain unaddressed.

Many of those unaddressed questions involve how political professionals—particularly political consultants—do their jobs, how they think about those jobs, and why. Beyond consultants, though, this book speaks to broader themes about campaigns and elections, not only in a theoretical sense but also in a practical one. Especially since the 1980s, political scientists have been laying a solid foundation for understanding how elections are resolved—essentially who wins and loses, by how much, and with what segments of the electorate. And especially since the 1990s, the campaigns and elections subfield has begun to focus on the practical workings of campaigns, particularly by studying the growing importance of political consultants—the independent political professionals who work for a variety of candidates, party committees, and other organizations by providing services such as advertising and fundraising. From theoretical and practical perspectives, however, we still know little about some of the campaigns that make the most headlines through tight races, personal attacks, investigative journalism, and the like. What makes those campaigns so close and so fierce? Sometimes, they are simply hard-fought, tough races. Often, though, some kind of a crisis occurs—a pivotal moment in which a sleepy campaign can become a heated battle. These questions are not primarily concerned with the *outcome* of races, on which most scholarship has focused, or even the *organization* of campaigns, on which the campaigns and elections subfield has focused. Instead, these fundamental questions about campaign crises—the central narrative of this book—emphasize how outcomes *occurred,* who and what shaped those outcomes, and why.

This is not to say that crises explain all wins and losses in campaigns. As the following chapters show, political professionals say that crises are defined in a certain way and that individual circumstances—termed "context" throughout this book—shape campaign responses. In other words, one consultant's crisis might be another's opportunity. That discussion, too, receives attention in the following pages.

The existing work on campaign behavior largely takes root in two schools of thought on strategy and tactics. On one hand, some authors (e.g., Burton and Shea 2003; Bradshaw 2004) and many political professionals contend that campaigns are driven largely by experience and their assessment of on-the-ground conditions. This view might be called the "gut instinct" school. The alternative approach relies on rational-choice theory. The strategic politicians thesis (Jacobson and Kernell 1983) is the classic example of a rational-choice approach applied to congressional campaign strategy.

But candidates and campaigns are not always rational. Those who reject rational-choice approaches to campaign strategy say that a blinding optimism often surrounds even the most hopeless congressional campaigns (Burton and Shea 2003, 162). Similarly, even when national conditions or practical matters suggest that candidates should bow out, relatively few members voluntarily retire from Congress (Wilcox 1987). Personal satisfaction, devotion to single issues, and the faint hope of success also keep repeat losers coming back to the campaign trail (Kazee 1980).

Whether influenced by gut instinct, rationality, or something else, political context plays a big role in campaign decisions. Gary Jacobson and Samuel Kernell limit context to national conditions such as the economy and presidential popularity. They also argue that candidates often take cues from national party organizations.[3] As the book will show, although political professionals say that context can include national conditions, winning and losing elections are more often determined by lower-profile events: internal operations, local conditions, candidate missteps, and other events that might or might not make the evening news.

In addition, political professionals' views don't always mesh with scholarly theories. Consultants and others say that campaign decisions depend largely on experience (the gut-instinct approach). But relationships among different members of the campaign team, and the context surrounding individual events, influence which decisions campaigns make and why. The fact that political professionals' thinking does not fit neatly into existing academic theory should not be disappointing. Rather, it presents an invitation to explore races as the men and women who run campaigns actually see them—as complex. Campaign crises provide a window into that complexity—and a means for understanding how campaigns really work.

Crises help explain why a once seemingly invincible Vietnam-era triple amputee, Senator Max Cleland (D-GA), lost his seat after being criticized for his stances on national defense and homeland security—a scenario that seemed unthinkable early in the race. In this case, the pivotal event was perhaps not the political advertising for which the race became best known, but the fact that many members of Max Cleland's campaign team said they did not recognize that a crisis had occurred until the GOP challenger, Representative Saxby Chambliss, had virtually clinched the election.

Also in 2002, crises mattered for both sides of a contentious US Senate race between Democratic incumbent Bob Torricelli and Republican challenger Doug Forrester in New Jersey. As the campaign unfolded, Torricelli was hounded by a recently concluded federal ethics investigation. Although Torricelli was never charged with a crime, the media feeding frenzy that accompanied the investigation made campaigning untenable. Yet Forrester's campaign was unable to capitalize on an unexpected opportunity when Torricelli abruptly withdrew from the race. Instead of enjoying a planned sprint to victory largely by being an alternative to Torricelli, Forrester's team could not overcome the established reputation of Democrat Frank Lautenberg, who came out of retirement to defeat the Republican and reclaim a place in the Senate.

Senator Paul Wellstone's death in a Minnesota plane crash weeks before the 2002 election was a crisis of epic proportions—most of which had nothing to do with politics. In political terms, though, professionals in the remnants of the Wellstone campaign and Minnesota's Democrat-Farmer-Labor (DFL) Party, along with national Democrats, had to decide, in a matter of hours or days, how to mount a competitive campaign in a radically changed, grief-stricken environment. Republican challenger Norm Coleman also faced a crisis in determining how to continue an effective but respectful campaign in the wake of the tragedy that killed the popular Wellstone along with his wife, daughter, campaign staff, and two pilots. Meanwhile, former vice president Walter Mondale, who was drafted to replace Wellstone, faced the daunting task of jump-starting and finishing his campaign in just ten days.

In contrast to these three cases that clearly involved campaign crises, political professionals disagreed about how, or whether, crises mattered for Democrat Maria Cantwell and Republican Slade Gorton during the 2000 US Senate race in Washington State. Some political professionals argued that the race's narrow margins alone represented a crisis for both campaigns. (Gorton lost by fewer than 2,300 votes of 2.4 million cast; a three-week recount followed.) Others pointed to activities from outside interest groups and Cantwell's unexpected criticisms of Gorton's environmental record. Nonetheless, some political professionals believed that the race was simply a tough one that someone had to lose.

These four races—the 2002 Senate contests in Georgia, New Jersey, and Minnesota and the 2000 Senate race in Washington State—will receive detailed attention. Importantly, however, the discussion is not limited to these cases or even to the 2000 and 2002 election cycles. Rather, this book's primary lesson is about an ever-present facet of American politics: campaign crises.

Why do crises matter? What can the subject explain beyond illuminating sensational cases that occasionally involve sex, drugs, alcohol, or just plain stupidity? In fact, it would be easy to dismiss campaign crises as an anomaly if all or even most crises really involved lurid subjects. The problem with dismissing crises as only sensational or unusual, however, is that most crises are not extraordinary. In short, most *crises* are not *scandals*. Indeed, there is an important distinction between the two.

When allowed to think and talk at length about their world, political professionals' comments establish that although campaign crises are major events, they matter for various reasons that extend beyond winning or losing elections. Crises, how campaigns respond to them, and who inside the campaign makes decisions about crisis management provide a window into critical contests in which Americans choose their elected officials. Although some things about crises are unique—such as the pace of decisionmaking or divisions of labor—much about crises presents broader lessons. Lessons about leadership among political professionals, candidates, and their families, strategic attacks on opponents, negative advertising, and the roles of political parties and "outside" organizations can all be found by studying campaign crises. Although crises often have negative connotations, effective crisis management can help campaigns solidify their standing and turn a challenging situation into an opportunity. Whether positive or negative, crises often mark turning points in campaigns. As examined here, they represent detours (often with an uncertain outcome) on the road to Congress— or any other Election Day objective.

Despite this rich potential, scholarly attention to campaign crises is virtually nonexistent. Even defining what "crisis" means is challenging. Electoral "scandal" is illicit and involves extramarital affairs, abuses of power, financial misconduct, and the like. To paraphrase US Supreme Court Justice Potter Stewart's famous summation of obscenity, scandal is difficult to define, but we know it when we see it.[4] But *crises* are more difficult because there is so little knowledge of what they are or what they mean.

This book broadens the dialogue by asking how political professionals define crises, whether crises are different from scandals, how crises affect campaigns, and what strategies and tactics campaigns employ when managing crises. Crises are intense—sometimes extraordinary—events. But they are not uncommon—and they have more similar characteristics than often seems the case from ten-second sound bytes on the evening news.

The in-depth interviews and case studies presented here demonstrate that political professionals view campaign crises as complex, interactive events. Although popular and scholarly wisdom focuses on campaign scandals as key variables in congressional elections, the findings show that political professionals classify a range of behavior and events beyond scandals as crises and argue that the consequences have broad implications. After categorizing the different ways that political professionals define crises (see Chapter 2), a typology provides an analytical tool for considering crises as internal, external, expected, and unexpected events. The typology is illustrated with examples from the four US Senate races identified previously.[5] This book is, therefore, devoted to building theory about campaign crises. By establishing analytically generalizable (sometimes called "theoretically generalizable"; see Yin 1994, 2003) lessons about what crises are and how they affect campaigns, this book lays a foundation for future research about this unexplored facet of American elections.

Why Political Professionals?

This book relies on insights from those who know campaigns best: the political professionals who run campaigns. Political professionals help campaigns and candidates make strategic decisions. Although consultants' increasing dominance in campaign strategy is well-known, there has been little attention to how decisionmaking and leadership inside campaigns really work. Throughout the book, the phrase *political professionals* refers to political consultants, party officials, campaign managers, and others who make their living from campaigning. The book places special emphasis on political consultants because of their major leadership roles in modern campaigns. Here, too, the book's lessons extend beyond individual cases, consultants, and time periods. In particular, although aspects of who consultants are and what they do have been explored in detail previously, there has been little attention to consultants' detailed responses.

Most previous studies of political consultants rely on surveys or general descriptions to summarize the profession (Rosenbloom 1973; Sabato 1981; Luntz 1988; Johnson 2000, 2001, and 2007; Medvic 2000; Thurber and Nelson 2000; Thurber, Nelson, and Dulio 2000). These works focus on the impact political consultants have on electoral outcomes such as vote-margin or fundraising (Dulio 2004; Herrnson 1992; Medvic and Lenart 1997; Medvic 2001) or provide anecdotal data through case studies (Loomis 2001; Thurber 2001). Few works explore what consultants think, how their thinking influences campaign strategy, or how they behave in critical campaign situations. There is also little understanding about how political professionals think and feel about the evolution of their profession, their role in modern campaigns, and how they and others run campaigns. Comprehensive scholarly discussion about political professionals' perspectives on campaign crises is virtually untouched.

Moving Beyond Scandal

Political science confines its analysis of campaign crises mostly to political scandals, meaning candidates' alleged ethical transgressions. A small body of work emerged mostly in the 1990s, in the aftermath of the House bank scandal, in which dozens of lawmakers were voted out of office after essentially bouncing checks at the chamber's financial institution amid widespread negative publicity. Some works on congressional elections have continued to adopt a dichotomous scandal variable (e.g., scandals were present in a race or they were not). Overall, however, political scandals are a very small subset of the literature on campaigns and elections. The existing scholarly literature lacks a comprehensive, systematic, and theoretically oriented discussion of crises.[6] As a result, scandal has served as a proxy for campaign crises—albeit a narrow one. Furthermore, even the work that discusses crises fails to investigate how the nuances of those events affect campaigns.

The data collected for this book reveal that political professionals view a range of circumstances (beyond the scholarly scandal confines) as crisis situations. More important, political professionals reported that crises can be devastating under the right conditions and in ways not measured by election returns or fundraising. Campaign crises have broad implications not only for the outcomes of particular races but also by providing insight into critical decisionmaking and professional developments in modern American politics.

Context, Crises, and Modern House and Senate Campaigns

Behind all the theory—scholarly and otherwise—political campaigns are human enterprises. Political consultants and their colleagues certainly feel the pressure to perform when crises occur and to prevent them from happening in the first place. According to pioneering Democratic media consultant Ray Strother (2003, 1):

> In political consulting, winning is everything. . . . A win, even a fluke victory over a scandal-ridden opponent, throws the spotlight on the consultant and allows him to prosper. A noble and principled campaign that did not use negative ads and talked about issues of substance turns into ashes if it loses by even one vote. . . . Thus, political consulting becomes a Darwinist, ferocious business in which the law of the jungle rules and the weak are massacred by bigger and stronger predators.[7]

It goes without saying that campaigns matter for candidates, too. The literature suggests that electoral pressures can be particularly complex for Senate candidates. Senate elections are traditionally more competitive than House contests and receive more intense media scrutiny (Abramowitz and Segal 1992). Senators also face unique advantages and disadvantages in constituency size, relative power in funneling pet projects to their states, and in other institutional differences that can affect electoral outcomes (Lee and Oppenheimer 1999). Same-state senators divide and conquer constituencies, media markets, and casework (Schiller 2000), all of which allow them to develop broader constituencies compared to House members.

However, Jonathan Krasno (1994) demonstrates that much of the common wisdom about incumbent senators facing unique obstacles compared with House candidates does not hold up to empirical data. Rather:

> The results directly point to the campaign itself as the source of the different reelection rate of incumbents in Senate and House races. . . . The campaign is the beginning of trouble for senators who face reelection difficulties. This evidence is the last piece of the reelection puzzle: senators' political struggles come about because of their opponents. They do not start off more vulnerable than representatives, but by election day their challengers have made them more vulnerable. (Krasno 1994, 155–156)

Furthermore, "the key point is that elections are contests between two candidates. No senator or representative is actually in danger of defeat until someone runs against him or her" (Krasno 1994, 158). In other words, campaigns matter.

Against that backdrop, and despite *general* differences between House and Senate campaigns, this book does not uncover significant *strategic* differences in how House and Senate campaigns experience or manage crises. Regardless of the type of race, pivotal events such as crises influence how, when, and why campaigns matter to voters. Political professionals play a large role in shaping and responding to those moments. This book emphasizes Senate campaigns, but its lessons about crisis management apply to other kinds of campaigns, too.

Although this book does not focus on public opinion in detail, it is worth noting that campaigns can face mixed incentives when deciding how to manage crises that unfold publicly. Even competitive elections often involve so-called low-information campaigns that focus more on spin and imagery than on substance about policy issues (Thurber 2001a). More generally, public knowledge of Congress and congressional campaigns is frequently lacking, sometimes intentionally so (Gilens 2001).[8]

Therefore, it can be difficult to call attention to a campaign's preferred message—sometimes including attacking an opponent—if the public (or the media) is unwilling to pay attention.

Crises, by contrast, provide events that voters remember. For example, even though the 1990s House bank scandal broke no laws, it "ended many more congressional careers than policy disasters such as the savings-and-loan debacle, which left taxpayers holding the bag for hundreds of billions of dollars." Furthermore,

> members of Congress routinely escape individual blame for major policy failures because the legislative process diffuses responsibility; the action is so complex, the details of policy so arcane, each individual's responsibility so obscure, that it is impossible to figure out who is culpable and who is not. Everyone with a checking account understands what it means to balance a checkbook, however, and each House member's culpability was precisely measured in the count of unfunded checks. (Jacobson 2001, 176–177)

To summarize, crises matter because they shape the electoral environment and often determine the outcome of races for both House and Senate campaigns (and others) in ways that can't be ignored.

Methodological Overview

This book relies on 106 in-depth interviews with seventy-six political professionals based primarily in the Washington, D.C., area. Eight of the 106 interviews were early field tests; the core data included 98 interviews (37 theory-building interviews and 61 case-study interviews). I conducted all interviews in person or by telephone between 2003 and 2005. Most interview subjects were political consultants holding the rank of principal or vice president in major firms actively engaged in providing strategic advice to US House and Senate candidates. I also interviewed experienced campaign managers, party campaign committee officials, and senior congressional staff. Additional information about the interview pool appears in the Methodological Appendix.

This book examines two major themes: (1) understanding what crises are and how they affect campaigns generally; and (2) how crises unfolded in specific campaigns. The thirty-seven first-round interviews are exploratory and theoretically generalizable. They provide a foundation for understanding what campaign crises are, how political professionals think about campaign crises, how they believe crises affect campaigns, and how congressional campaigns manage crises. These interviews establish how experienced political professionals from both parties define crises. This analysis appears in Chapters 2 and 3.[9]

The sixty-one case-study (second-round) interviews provide an in-depth understanding of crises and crisis management in four US Senate races from 2000 and 2002.[10] This analysis appears in Chapters 4–7. The case studies include the 2002 contests in Georgia, Minnesota, and New Jersey and the 2000 race in Washington State. Chapter 4 discusses case selection, introduces the case studies, and reviews the Georgia race. The case-study chapters examine three key elements in each race: (1) how political professionals defined crises; (2) how crises affected each campaign organization; and (3) what strategic and tactical decisions campaign officials made in battling crises. These three themes follow the project's two theory-building chapters (Chapters 2 and 3) developed from the first-round interviews.

To interpret the interview data, the book employs a mixed methodology combining qualitative and quantitative analysis. The interview data are primarily presented in narrative form, highlighting the project's emphasis on grounded theory and descriptive research. Some of the interview data are also coded and analyzed using descriptive statistics. Archival media coverage and political advertising data from the Wisconsin Advertising Project (Goldstein, Franz, and Ridout 2002; Goldstein and Rivlin 2005) supplement the case-study interviews.[11]

Grounded theory, which utilizes practitioner expertise to illuminate an unexplored phenomenon that is theoretically and practically important (Glaser and Strauss 1967; Rubin and Rubin 1995; King, Keohane, and Verba 1994), provides a foundation for the interviews. Especially in unexplored territory—like campaign crises—an "imperfect fit" between research design, theory, and data often emerges (King, Keohane, and Verba 1994, 13). These methodological perspectives (see also Yin 1994, 2003), because they are exploratory, typically do not involve hypothesis-testing; the same is true for this book.

Because of the sparse academic literature specifically about campaign crises, allowing political professionals to think and talk at length creates a better scholarly and applied understanding not only of crises but also, perhaps more importantly, of what those events suggest about campaigns and elections in general. Qualitative interviews are, therefore, essential. The emphasis on "encouraging people to describe their worlds in their own terms" (Rubin and Rubin 1995, 2) is especially important for understanding the relatively closed world of professional politics. This "thick description" (Geertz 1973) is "rooted in the interviewees' firsthand experience [and] forms the material that researchers gather up, synthesize, and analyze as part of hearing the meaning of data" (Rubin and Rubin 1995, 8). To borrow Richard Fenno's (1996, 8) comments on the value of participant observation, the interviews' contribution to the book is essential. Through the inside expertise they reflect, the interviews remind us that "it is, after all, flesh and blood individuals, real *people* we are talking about when we generalize about our politicians" and, in this case, about political professionals.[12]

Overview

Political professionals define crises and explain how they affect campaigns in Chapter 2. Chapter 2 also establishes that political professionals view scandals as one kind of crisis, but not necessarily the most important kind of crisis or the most prominent. Based on the interview data, a typology considers crises as a combination of internal, external, expected, and/or unexpected events. Chapter 2 also provides political professionals' first-hand perspective about why crises matter and how disruptive they are to campaigns. The debate over how frequently crises occur and how they affect campaigns sheds light on important disagreements about the state of modern campaigns and professional politics.

Continuing on those themes, Chapter 3 explores how crises affect campaign organizations, who assumes strategic leadership roles during crises, and how campaigns respond to crises. Despite the focus on crises, much of Chapter 3, and others, highlights the real world of House and Senate campaigns. Political consultants emerge as major leaders during crises. Although this finding is not surprising, the data reveal a distinction between *strategists* and *implementers* that becomes especially important during crises and that signals a largely unexplored transition in professional politics. Much of this discussion highlights the changing relationship between consultants and campaign managers. Here, political professionals also explain strategic decisionmaking during campaign crises. *Context* (individual circumstances) is the key factor behind those decisions. In short, how crises affect campaigns, and the choices political professionals make when responding to crises, depend on individual situations.

Detailed case studies include the 2002 Senate races between Max Cleland and Saxby Chambliss in Georgia (Chapter 4), Paul Wellstone, Norm Coleman, and Walter Mondale in Minnesota (Chapter 5), Bob Torricelli, Doug Forrester, and Frank Lautenberg in New Jersey (Chapter 6), and the 2000 contest between Maria Cantwell and Slade Gorton in Washington State (Chapter 7). All case studies address both sides' perspectives on the race. The Methodological Appendix and the beginning of Chapter 4 provide more information about how the case studies were selected and how they illustrate the typology of campaign crises established in Chapter 2. Chapter 8 summarizes the findings and addresses the implications for previous and future research.

A Note to Readers

Some final points will help readers navigate the text. The political professionals interviewed for this book are identified by name whenever they consented. Those who asked not to be named are identified as agreed during interviews (e.g., as a "senior strategist"). All professional titles refer to the experience that warranted participation in the project, not necessarily the individuals' positions at the time of the interview or now. For example, former National Republican Senatorial Committee (NRSC) political director Chris LaCivita participated in interviews after his tenure at the NRSC. However, because he was interviewed based on his NRSC service, the text identifies him as an NRSC official. The same is true for Max Cleland's 2002 campaign manager, Tommy Thompson, who by the time of his interview was engaged in consulting work for a state party. In many cases, as is common in professional politics, those interviewed have since moved on to other employers. Most political professionals stressed that their comments reflected personal views, not necessarily those of their employing organizations.

Throughout the text, *specific types* of campaign crises are identified by italics when necessary (e.g., *organizational* crises). Specific dimensions of the typology of campaign crises are set off in boldface (e.g., the **internal** dimension of the typology). This identification system does not apply to generic discussions that fall outside the typology. Chapter 2 provides additional details.

Finally and perhaps most important, this book relates political professionals' understandings of, and opinions about, campaign crises, modern campaigns in general, and some specific races. Some of those opinions are blunt. However, I do not draw normative conclusions or make partisan endorsements at any point in the book and hope that those affiliated with either party (or none) find the work to be equally accurate and objective. Any opinions I do express are mine alone.

Notes

1. Joe McLean, personal interview with author, December 1, 2003, Washington, D.C. Throughout this book, all named sources consented to be identified.

2. The consultant's name and identifying campaign references are omitted to preserve the objectivity of presentation.

3. Several works have tested and revised the strategic politicians thesis. One major critique of the model is that it fails to account for important local political context (Livingston and Friedman 1993), which can be especially important in campaign crises.

4. See Stewart's concurring opinion in *Jacobellis v. Ohio* (1964).

5. The book focuses on recent House and Senate campaigns because the limited literature on campaign scandals—the closest existing proxy for crises—emphasizes congressional elections. Limiting the inquiry to congressional campaigns also keeps the project manageable. However, because this book allows political professionals who possess a wealth of experience to define crises and describe their effects, the lessons established here should carry over to other areas of electoral politics.

6. Of course, case studies of single campaign crises do exist. For example, Jasperson (2004) offers a case study of the "sympathy vote" in Minnesota after Paul Wellstone's death.

7. This is not to say, however, that political professionals are unethical—a subject discussed later in the book.

8. This is Martin Gilens's (2001) "rational ignorance" concept.

9. Interviews were solicited until findings became predictable and a rough balance in party and professional specialization was achieved. The thirty-interview threshold also increases reliability in analyzing the data with descriptive statistics.

10. Eight field-test interviews were also conducted. They are not included in the dataset but are reflected in the 106 figure listed at the beginning of this section. Excluding the eight field-test interviews yields a total of 98 sessions (37 first-round interviews and 61 case-study interviews).

11. Use of the 2000 Wisconsin Advertising Project data (Goldstein, Franz, and Ridout 2002) requires the following disclaimer: "The data was obtained from a joint project of the Brennan Center for Justice at New York University School of Law and Professor Kenneth Goldstein of the University of Wisconsin–Madison, and includes media tracking data from the Campaign Media Analysis Group in Washington, D.C. The Brennan Center–Wisconsin project was sponsored by a grant from The Pew Charitable Trusts. The opinions expressed in this [book] are those of the author and do not necessarily reflect the views of the Brennan Center, Professor Goldstein, or The Pew Charitable Trusts." Use of the 2002 Wisconsin Advertising Project data (Goldstein and Rivlin 2005) requires the following disclaimer: "The data was obtained from a project of the Wisconsin Advertising Project, under Professor Kenneth Goldstein and Joel Rivlin of the University of Wisconsin–Madison, and includes media tracking data from the Campaign Media Analysis Group in Washington, D.C. The Wisconsin Advertising Project was sponsored by a grant from The Pew Charitable Trusts. The opinions expressed in this [book] are those of the author and do not necessarily reflect the views of the Wisconsin Advertising Project, Professor Goldstein, Joel Rivlin, or The Pew Charitable Trusts."

12. Emphasis in original.

2
What Crises Are and
Why They Matter

Yeah, if you're attacked, you could define that as a crisis. But I wouldn't define it that way. . . . If you consider that a crisis, you're going to live in a state of adrenalized fear. . . . The only way I look to define crisis is when you have something at risk. A lot of the times your opponent . . . attacks you and/or you attack your opponent, and there's no blood drawn. I think crisis is when blood is drawn—when you draw blood or when you give blood when you're attacked.

—Drey Samuelson, US Senate chief of staff[1]

Well, the truth is, almost every day there's something that someone is calling a crisis because . . . everybody worries that anything you do or don't do right could be that which will eventually lead to enough of a vote loss to lose the election.

—Democratic pollster[2]

Drey Samuelson and the Democratic pollster quoted above demonstrate that political professionals have different views about what crises are and how they affect campaigns.[3] The political professionals interviewed for this book agreed, however, that crises are a major part of modern campaigns. They also warned that sometimes candidates and outside observers are too quick to label any hurdle as a "crisis." Even though crises are unique, fast-paced, and complicated, political professionals routinely reported that crises are more common than scandals. Crises can also offer lessons for campaigning that extend beyond those for narrower scandals. More important, crises are a snapshot of campaigning itself, in which professional relationships, decisionmaking, and strategy are all put to the test in high-pressure and fast-paced settings.

When crises occur, the answers to all kinds of questions matter more, or at least seem to matter more, because political professionals believe it is these key events that often determine the outcome of a race. Good campaign management and professional decisionmaking always matter, but they especially matter when the campaign is on the line. Although the lessons from this inquiry are particularly applicable to crises, their importance does not begin or end there. Indeed, political professionals say that an awareness of crises—and planning for them—is essential in trying to *avoid* crises and minimize damage if they are inevitable. Political professionals are, therefore, always on guard for crises. If scholars and others want to understand how elections are won and lost, crises—or at least the potential for them—cannot go unnoticed.

This chapter analyzes the elements of campaign crises by asking political professionals what the concept means to them. This approach enhances the understanding of congressional campaign politics on three fronts. First, it examines crises from an *internal* perspective by exploring how political professionals define the term and how they believe crises affect campaigns. Second, rather than treating crises as a dichotomous, independent variable (presence of crisis or not), this chapter allows political professionals to fully explore their effects on campaigns. Third, a typology of campaign crises, illustrated by four Senate races, is developed for understanding the variety inherent in campaign crises.

The Existing Focus on Scandal

Political science confines its consideration of campaign crises almost exclusively to political scandals, meaning candidates' alleged ethical transgressions. As long ago as the 1970s, John Peters and Susan Welch (1978, 974) lamented that even though political corruption—which often breeds scandal—is a constant in American politics, it remained a relatively untouched research subject. Susan Welch and John Hibbing (1997, 226) argued more recently that studies gauging the impact of corruption on electoral politics were still "rare." Those authors urged that "given the candidate-centered nature of modern congressional elections, the extent to which the status of the candidates in the race shapes the campaigns, and the importance of the charges of corruption to a candidate's status, the role of corruption charges in elections should indeed be center stage on the research agenda" (Welch and Hibbing 1997, 226). For the most part, subsequent works have nonetheless considered political scandals only as a spectator sport, with minimal attention to sensational detail, but almost none to serious study. Instead, scandal has served as a proxy for campaign crises—albeit a narrow one.

A small body of work emerged mostly in the 1990s, in the aftermath of the House bank scandal in which dozens of lawmakers were voted out of office after essentially bouncing checks at the House's financial institution, which was closed shortly thereafter. Some works on congressional elections have continued to adopt a scandal-specific variable when considering vote tallies on Election Day. Various case studies briefly mention scandals in congressional campaigns (e.g., Bailey et al. 2000; Thurber 2001a).[4] Others focus on waging ethical campaigns (Nelson et al. 2002; Faucheux and Herrnson 2001, 2002). Still more explore whether or not candidates enter or leave races based on their own or an opponent's ethical misfortune (Lough 1998; Groseclose and Krehbiel 1994) or how voters react to politicians embroiled in scandal (Banducci and Karp 1994; Born 1990; Brophy-Baerman 1995; Dimock and Jacobson 1995; McCurley and Mondak 1995; Mondak 1995; Stewart 1994). But these works do not explore the human drama surrounding most crises.

Most works identify political scandal using coded keyword searches of campaign coverage in national publications such as *Congressional Quarterly*, *The New York Times*, and the *Washington Post* (Peters and Welch 1980; Roberds 1997; Lough 1998; Brown 2001); definitions can vary widely. At a basic level, *New Webster's Dictionary* (1992, 336) defines "scandal" as "malicious gossip; disgraceful action; disgrace; injury to a person's character." By contrast, scholarly definitions tend to be amorphous and contradictory.[5] For example, Stephen Roberds (1997, 86) defines electoral scandal as "any issue concerning the candidate that is raised by the media and/or opponent that questions the propriety, morality, or legality of some behavior, action, personality trait, either present or past, and as such is known (or could reasonably be known) by voters in the district and poses the risk of potential divisiveness, disapproval or condemnation by sizeable numbers of the public." That includes events such as drug or alcohol abuse, sexist or racist behavior or speech, financial misconduct, and more.[6] So far, there seems to be little precision surrounding campaign scandals, let alone crises.

Many definitions include a moral element (Miller and Medvic 2002) that implies corruption. Smith (2002, 18), in a broad examination of scandals throughout government, defines the term as "the events following the revelation of possible moral turpitude. This can, but does not necessarily, include illegalities." Smith (2002, 19) also argues that scandals include interactions between three key players: the media, political actors (such as candidates), and institutions (Congress, parties, etc.). Peters and Welch (1978) provide the classic statement on official *corruption*, and code various behaviors as "corrupt," but do not differentiate between "scandal" and "corruption."

Although political scientists disagree about what scandals are, they agree that scandals do matter.[7] Indeed, research consistently demonstrates that scandals of all kinds have a negative impact on electoral outcomes, either in votes, fundraising, or retirements (Peters and Welch 1980; Roberds 1997; Lough 1998; Jacobson and Dimock 1994; Dimock and Jacobson 1995; Bridgmon 2002). Scandals can have the most predictive power of any independent variable on challenger quality, challenger and incumbent expenditures, and incumbent vote share (Goidel and Gross 1994).[8] In other words, at least in some research, scandal has been found to have more of an impact on vote outcome than any other factor. Specifically, scandals cost House incumbents about 7 percent of the total vote share and yield an additional $100,000 in challenger fundraising (Goidel and Gross 1994, 140–142). Scandals also invite "quality challengers," those most likely to unseat incumbents (Roberds 1997; Lough 1998), and can reverberate throughout several elections (Bridgmon 2002).

Most existing scholarship does not consider whether different types of scandals have different effects. However, a few exceptions exist. For example, in their examination of House corruption charges between 1968 and 1978, Peters and Welch (1980, 705) found that morals and bribery charges have particularly damaging effects on incumbents, leading to vote losses of between 12 percent and 22 percent for members of both parties. Relying on Peters and Welch's (1978; 1980) typology, Todd Lough (1998) examines the effect of different kinds of scandals on retirement decisions, vote share, and challenger emergence between 1976 and 1994. His findings were similar to Peters and Welch's (1980), although Lough found that morals charges were likely to be more damaging in primary elections than in general elections.[9]

The data collected for this book reveal that political professionals view a range of circumstances beyond the narrow definitions of "scandal" as campaign crises. More important, political professionals reported that crises can be devastating under the right conditions, and in ways not measured by election returns or fundraising, which most academic work emphasizes. More than that, crises have implications for understanding campaigns in general, whereas scandals are sometimes so focused on perceived ethical issues that political professionals, scholars, and the public apparently believe they have little to do with broader campaigning.

How Political Professionals Defined Campaign Crises

In interviews, political professionals were first invited to think and talk at length about what crises meant to them. They reported that crises are multifaceted and interactive.[10] Across all interviews, political professionals defined crises using a median of three different descriptions; in other words, typical interviewees said that crises were not confined to a single definition.[11] Analysis and coding of political professionals' answers revealed nine distinct categories (frames) of campaign crises: (1) strategic disruptions; (2) candidate scandals; (3) candidate political errors; (4) attacks; (5) organizational; (6) media; (7) fundraising; (8) polling; and (9) constant crises, as shown by frequency of use in Table 2.1.[12] This chapter provides an overview of political professionals' descriptions of each kind of crisis.[13]

The table also reveals that political professionals defined crises similarly across first-round and case-study interviews. This agreement suggests that political professionals had similar understandings of what campaign crises are and how frequently various kinds of crises occur. The most important part of the analysis, however, is the commentary that political professionals provided during interviews.

Strategic Disruption Crises

The vast majority of political professionals (more than 80 percent, as shown in Table 2.1) used what was later coded as the *strategic disruption* frame when defining campaign crises. In a business in which planning is everything, major changes in the strategic environment certainly represent crises—or at least potential crises. *Strategic disruptions* stop campaigns in their tracks and can lead to other crises. These events also interrupt the campaign plan. Even if only for a day (but often much longer), political professionals said that *strategic disruptions* are the essence of campaign crises because they prevent campaigns from doing what they had planned to do, usually in a major way. Examples include candidate deaths, unexpected election recounts, unexpected third-party messages contradicting candidates (e.g., attack ads launched by interest groups), and other events that surprise the campaign and reshape its environment.

Unexpected changes in resources—in time, personnel, and money (some of which are impossible to redirect or replace)—are often the most damaging element of crises. Accordingly, political professionals reported that these strategic disruptions can mark the beginning of the end for a campaign because some battles simply cannot be won due to time or momentum. Accordingly, *strategic disruptions* often have to do with *context* (environmental factors), an all-important element of campaign crises and elections in general.

One Republican pollster explained during an interview:

> The best description of a campaign I ever heard is chaos that is all moving in the same direction. So, I always think of 27 tumbleweeds all rolling in the same direction down the prairie. But when all the tumble-

Table 2.1   How Political Professionals Defined Campaign Crises

	All Interviews			First Round			Case Studies		
Frame	Rank	N	Percentage	Rank	N	Percentage	Rank	N	Percentage
Attack	3	33	43.4	3	23	62.2	5	10	25.6
Candidate political error	5	29	38.2	5	15	40.5	2	14	36.8
Candidate scandal	2	38	50.0	2	25	67.6	3[a]	13	33.3
Constant crisis	7[a]	19	25.0	7[a]	11	29.7	6	8	20.5
Fundraising	8	17	22.4	6	14	37.8	7	3	7.7
Media	6	22	28.9	7[a]	11	29.7	4	11	28.2
Organizational	4	31	40.8	4	18	48.6	3[a]	13	33.3
Polling	9	5	6.6	8	4	10.8	8	1	2.6
Strategic disruption	1	64	84.2	1	32	86.5	1	3	81.6

Total interview N for Question 1 = 76
First-round interviews = 37
Case-study N for Question 1 = 39

Source: Elite-interview data compiled by author.
Notes: Multiple coding allowed, so percentages do not sum to 100.
a. Represents tie rankings.

weeds have to stop and address something, they're not rolling. And a campaign has limited time, limited budget. Everything is limited, and every second of every minute little bit of resources [that are] taken away from what you're supposed to be doing is slowing [and] killing your campaign.

Author: So, the idea of disruption is one of the key elements in a crisis?

Pollster: I would think so. I would think that would be *the* key.[14]

Candidate Scandal Crises

Candidate scandals are the second most common way in which political professionals defined campaign crises in the first-round interviews; they were also frequently mentioned in the case-study interviews.[15] *Candidate scandals* are the most obvious kinds of crises and the focus of existing research. When describing scandals, political professionals offered examples of sensational events such as drug or alcohol abuse, messy divorces, and other personal turmoil. Candidate scandals often imply that the candidate has concealed some personal fault from the campaign team or the public. Democratic media consultant Ray Strother's explanation of crises fits the *candidate scandal* frame: "A crisis event is when something unexpected happens, as [with] the exposure of someone having an illegitimate child or having been arrested for narcotics or having a DUI or [spousal] abuse— some breeches of integrity that have been hidden up to that particular time."[16]

Political professionals said that ethics are the key to crises involving scandals. *Candidate scandals* require the revelation of actual or alleged unethical or illegal behavior by the candidate or, sometimes, a member of the candidate's family or campaign team. Accordingly, these kinds of crises routinely invite other crises, such as attacks from opponents and media feeding frenzies. Importantly, however, even though *candidate scandals* are the most obvious form of crises, political professionals said they are fairly rare. In fact, many political professionals volunteered that they could think of only a few clients—and often none—who had experienced genuine scandal. Therefore, the interviews revealed an important caution against using scandals as a proxy for campaign crises, as the existing literature has done.

Candidate Political Error Crises

Candidate political errors are related to *candidate scandals,* but political professionals described them as distinct kinds of crises. (In fact, 30–40 percent of political professionals described *candidate political errors* when defining campaign crises; see Table 2.1.) *Candidate scandals* allege unethical or illegal behavior. By contrast, *candidate political errors* emphasize candidates' tactical mistakes, such as misstatements that foster attacks or media scrutiny. Often the result of a candidate gaffe or poor campaigning skills, candidate political errors invite unwelcome external scrutiny. As with many crises, candidate political errors might not be particularly damaging in and of themselves, but the poor public image and invitations for attacks they create can be serious.

Recalling biographical advertisements he had produced using interview footage with an incumbent member of Congress, Republican media consultant Tom Edmonds explained:

> [The candidate] had a line that said, "I was born in a tarpaper shack." . . . His family *lived* in a tarpaper shack, like tenant farmers, but he was born in the hospital and went home to the tarpaper shack—a very minor point. It wouldn't have made *any difference* if he hadn't said it. . . . "When I was born, my family lived in a tarpaper shack." That wouldn't have been any different than, "I was born in a tarpaper shack." But it became an issue. And it wasn't major, but it just hurt him.[17]

In Edmonds's example, the candidate probably did not willfully mislead voters (which would be a *candidate scandal*). But the candidate's lack of discretion and careless speech created vulnerability for the campaign. Although the event represented a crisis, it was not detrimental to the campaign—as is far more often the case with candidate scandals. Candidate political errors can also include principled—but politically risky—issue positions.

Attack Crises

The *attack* crisis appeared in more than 60 percent of the first-round interviews. However, as Drey Samuelson's opening quotation shows, defining attacks as crises is controversial. Some political professionals reported that attacks are simply part of the routine back-and-forth between campaigns. Nonetheless, many believed that attacks can be crises under the right circumstances.

Attacks represent each side's attempt to gain advantage by criticizing the opposition. They are the main way that campaigns try to *cause* crises for their opponents. This includes counterattacking to try to distract opponents and the media from a crisis within one campaign (often referred to in the interviews as "turning a negative into a positive"). Former Democratic campaign manager and fundraiser Joe McLean explained:

I did an attorney general's race [in which the candidate] got hit with a negative [ad] that said he was playing a shell game with this campaign money. Now, this is a very complicated issue [but] his opponent was able to say, "Well . . . he had this money here, that money there. He's just doing it to get around the election law." Really simple argument, right? Persuasive argument. [But the charges were] untrue.[18]

Organizational Crises

Many *organizational* crises highlight poor relationships between candidates, consultants, and campaign staff. (Approximately 30–50 percent of political professionals described *organizational* crises during interviews.) If not properly managed, dysfunctional relationships can become campaign disasters by limiting the organization's ability to operate and execute strategy. Even simple staff problems can foster poor decisionmaking that can lead to campaign crises. Former Democratic Congressional Campaign Committee (DCCC) official Jenny Backus explained:

Campaigns that are very tightly disciplined tend to do very well, except for where they can't realize that their candidate has a problem. And sometimes, someone can create a crisis by saying "there's a crisis in the [candidate's] campaign because he's fired three managers." Now, that may not be a crisis. That may be [the] campaign *responding* to a crisis because they had a bad manager and [are] solving it. But the other side can turn that into a crisis in the perception of the media. So there's *external*, perceived crises and there's *actual* crises inside.[19]

In addition to poor decisionmaking, as Backus noted, mental stress and physical exhaustion can cause organizational crises. A Republican election lawyer added: "If you want to know what a campaign crisis is, it's being at a victory party at 12:00 where everybody's drunk and nobody knows whether you won or not. And that is the classic crisis-management situation where [people ask], 'Who's in charge? What's going on?' The candidate's burned out, and you're trying to figure out, 'What do we do now, because this TV station said that we won and this TV station said that we lost?'"[20]

Additional Crisis Types: Media, Fundraising, and Polling

Political professionals also offered three other definitions: *media*, *fundraising*, and *polling* crises. Although these frames were mentioned infrequently, their consequences can be serious. For all the human drama that campaign crises often include, political professionals said that even the best campaigns experience crises if they fail to take care of fundamental issues such as raising enough money, if their messages are not absorbed by the public, or if intense media scrutiny makes what might have been *potential* crises into full-blown public debacles.

Media feeding frenzies (*media* crises), low public support (indicated by polling crises), or insufficient money (*fundraising* crises) can all spell doom if campaigns are unable to recover. Political professionals described each kind of crisis as distinct events but also said that each kind can indicate other crises. For example, candidate scandals spur media scrutiny. Similarly, most long-shot campaigns face fundraising crises, as unknown candidates try to raise enough money to be competitive.

Aren't All Campaigns Inherent Crises?

Most political professionals agreed that crises are distinct events and represent serious threats to campaigns. They also said that crises are fairly common. However, a vocal minority said that crises are so common that they are unremarkable. This *constant crisis* perspective, the ninth and final frame, represents a counter to many of the other crisis categories.

About one-third of political professionals hesitated to define campaign crises and argued instead that the term *crisis* itself can be misleading. Political professionals who held this view said that modern campaigns are always crises or that only poorly managed campaigns should experience crises. Those rejecting the concept of campaign crises argued that what appear to be crises are, in fact, often normal events, even if some candidates and political professionals *believe* they are crises. From this perspective, campaigns are inherent crises—thus the *constant crisis* frame.

For those who hesitated to define crises, *expectedness* was essential. According to a Democratic pollster, "I always say that [our firm does not] use the word 'crisis' very much. We don't think that's a very helpful frame. We would use the frame where, 'this is a serious attack, but we have a plan for it, so let's implement our plan.' If a team is run well and the job of the team has been done well, then we're anticipating the crises."[21]

According to that logic, as long as campaigns properly anticipate crises, they can plan for them and limit their damage. As Democratic communications specialist and former party spokesperson Kiki McLean explained: "[Inoculation is] the most important thing you can do. . . . It's not a crisis when *you* announce it or you can control [the release of information]. It's a crisis when someone else uses it against you."[22] Therefore, the *constant crisis* frame can also include those events that opponents *try* to make a crisis for one's campaign but that political professionals believe are not crises because they are specifically prepared to combat the situation.

Nonetheless, even professionals adopting the *constant crisis* view conceded that some situations are worse than others. Another Democratic pollster suggested:

> Well, the truth is, almost every day there's something that someone is calling a crisis because . . . campaigns are almost constantly . . . in crisis mode, or so it seems. Now, having said that, clearly, there is a difference in the level of crisis that exists when, on the one hand, you're trying to worry about do you use the words "tax breaks" or "tax cuts" when you respond to the reporter . . . versus some discovery that you killed your mother with an ax and that's being revealed for the first time on the evening news.[23]

The *constant crisis* view was controversial. When asked about the *constant crisis* perspective offered by some of their colleagues, many political professionals quickly dismissed the idea. For example, political professionals describing organizational crises said that campaigns should be prepared for potential vulnerabilities, but they also argued that it is ludicrous to believe that crises never occur—or that all of them could be anticipated—given human nature and the fierce competition surrounding congressional campaigns. Even with the best planning, they said, some crises are inevitable.

Professional Demographics and Defining Crises

Do different kinds of political professionals define crises in different ways? In general, no, but there are important exceptions. There were notable cases in which political professionals defined crises differently based on who they are and what they do. Descriptive statistics can help us understand how.[24] Due to the small sample size, however, additional research would be needed to draw firm conclusions. (As Chapter 8 explains, there is also the potential for future research to shed additional light on how differences in experience might affect the answers discussed here.)

In the interviews, more Democrats than Republicans defined campaign crises by describing *attacks* (Tables 2.2 and 2.3). In the first-round interviews, for example, almost 80 percent of Democrats characterized campaign crises as *attacks,* compared with only 44 percent of Republicans (see Table 2.2). The difference between Democrats and Republicans is statistically significant.[25] The same pattern holds when comparing Democrats and Republicans across all interviews (see Table 2.3).

There was also evidence in the interviews that Democrats and Republicans had different conceptions of what *attacks* meant. This is particularly true when distinguishing between *proactive attack* (offensive) and *reactive attack*

Table 2.2   Partisan Differences and Use of the *Attack* Frame: First-Round Interviews

	Did Not Use *Attack* Frame	Used *Attack* Frame	Total
Democrats	4 (21.1%)	15 (78.9%)	19 (100.0%)
Republicans	10 (55.6%)	8 (44.4%)	18 (100.0%)
Total	14 (37.8%)	23 (62.3%)	37 (100.0%)

Notes: Cell values are observed Ns. Percentages appear in parentheses. P-value (using Fisher's exact test) = .045 (two-sided), .033 (one-sided)

Table 2.3   Partisan Differences and Use of the *Attack* Frame: All Interviews

	Did Not Use *Attack* Frame	Used *Attack* Frame	Total
Democrats	19 (43.2%)	25 (56.8%)	44 (100.0%)
Republicans	24 (75.0%)	8 (25.0%)	32 (100.0%)
Total	43 (56.6%)	33 (43.4%)	76 (100.0%)

Notes: Cell values are observed Ns. Percentages appear in parentheses. P-value (using chi-square) = .006 (two-sided)

(defensive) subframes. *Proactive attacks* are designed to create crises for opponents through criticism. By contrast, reactive crises befall campaigns that are under siege from opponents. More so than Republicans, Democrats focused their interview comments on attacks when describing crises, particularly in terms of *reactive attacks*.[26] In the first-round interviews, for example, more than twice as many Democrats as Republicans (35.1 percent versus 16.2 percent; see Table 2.4) described *attack* crises reactively.[27]

In other words, whereas Democrats talked about *being attacked* when describing crises, Republicans focused on *doing the attacking*. This does not mean that Republicans are unscrupulous or that Democrats are inherently unprepared. However, it does suggest that, at least during interviews, Democrats' thinking focused more on being caught off guard by attacks, whereas Republicans considered attacks part of a strategy to create crises for opponents. This finding is not surprising given Democrats' high-profile losses during the 1990s and early 2000s, especially in House and Senate races. (Democrats had not yet regained control of Congress, as they did in

Table 2.4 Partisan Differences and Use of the *Reactive Attack* Frame: First-Round Interviews

	Did Not Use *Reactive Attack* Frame	Used *Reactive Attack* Frame	Total
Democrats	6 (16.2%)	13 (35.1%)	19 (100.0%)
Republicans	12 (32.4%)	6 (16.2%)	18 (100.0%)
Total	18 (48.6%)	19 (51.4%)	37 (100.0%)

Notes: Cell values are observed Ns. Percentages appear in parentheses. P-value (using chi-square) = .033 (using one-sided test)

2006, when these interviews were conducted.) Major cases involving surprise attacks (e.g., Max Cleland's 2002 loss and Tom Daschle's 2004 defeat) are focal points for many Democrats who believe that modern campaigning has become ruthless (see Chapter 4).

In addition to some partisan differences in how political professionals defined campaign crises, some interesting findings emerged surrounding professional specialization. Like Democrats, media consultants were significantly more likely than other political professionals to define crises using the *attack* frame. Table 2.5 illustrates that across all interviews almost 70 percent of media consultants defined campaign crises by describing attacks, compared with only 38 percent of all other professionals.[28] Media consultants' emphasis on *attack* crises is not surprising, because they write and produce the advertisements through which most attacks occur. Professional specialization was not associated with significant differences in use of either the *proactive attack* or *reactive attack* frames.

Table 2.5 Professional Differences and Use of the *Attack* Frame: All Interviews

	Did Not Use *Attack* Frame	Used *Attack* Frame	Total
All other political professionals	39 (61.9%)	24 (38.1%)	63 (100.0%)
Media consultants	4 (30.8%)	9 (69.2%)	13 (100.0%)
Total	43 (56.6%)	33 (43.4%)	76 (100.0%)

Notes: Cell values are observed Ns. Percentages appear in parentheses. P-value (using Fisher's exact test) = .040 (one-sided)

The other difference among professional groups was evident in the *constant crisis* frame. Specifically, pollsters defined crises differently compared with other political professionals. Across all interviews, 60 percent of pollsters used the *constant crisis* frame, compared with less than 20 percent of other political professionals (Table 2.6).

When limiting the analysis to only the first-round interviews (see Table 2.7), the relationship is less robust yet still significant, with almost 70 percent of pollsters using the constant crisis frame compared with only about 20 percent of other political professionals.

It is no surprise that pollsters thought differently about crises during interviews. Their jobs depend on being analytical and dispassionate. Crises involve adrenaline, emotion, and stress. Pollsters' thinking is central to the *constant crisis* frame. Analysts solve problems with research and planning. Pollsters said that campaigns should be able to avoid crises by doing just that. Other political professionals, however, must craft messages and handle worried candidates and their families. Media consultants, campaign

Table 2.6   Professional Differences and Use of the *Constant Crisis* Frame: All Interviews

	Did Not Use *Constant Crisis* Frame	Used *Constant Crisis* Frame	Total
All other political professionals	53	13	66
	(80.3%)	(19.7%)	(100.0%)
Pollsters	4	6	10
	(40.0%)	(60.0%)	(100.0%)
Total	57	19	76
	(75.0%)	(25.0%)	(100.0%)

Notes: Cell values are observed Ns. Percentages appear in parentheses. P-value (using Fisher's exact test) = .013 (one-sided and two-sided)

Table 2.7   Professional Differences and Use of the *Constant Crisis* Frame: First-Round Interviews

	Did Not Use *Constant Crisis* Frame	Used *Constant Crisis* Frame	Total
All other political professionals	24	7	31
	(77.4%)	(22.6%)	(100.0%)
Pollsters	2	4	6
	(33.3%)	(66.7%)	(100.0%)
Total	26	11	37
	(70.3%)	(29.7%)	(100.0%)

Notes: Cell values are observed Ns. Percentages appear in parentheses. P-value (using Fisher's exact test) = .051 (one-sided and two-sided)

managers, and others said that, due to human error or other factors, even with solid research crises can sometimes be inevitable.

Campaign Crises Versus Traditional Scandals

It is clear that political professionals view a range of behaviors as campaign crises. Of course, crises may include scandals (the *candidate scandal* frame), but scandals are only one type of crisis. Political professionals differentiate between crises and scandals and said that the two concepts can be mutually exclusive. Although scandals are usually external, ethical events, crises may be internal and often have little or nothing to do with ethics. In addition, crises can sometimes have even more dire campaign consequences than traditional scandals.

Of the thirty-seven political professionals asked during the first-round interviews whether crises must always involve scandals, only one interviewee answered affirmatively—and even he later voluntarily softened his position. When asked if all crises involve scandals, many respondents answered flatly, "No, not at all," signaling that the separation between the two concepts is obvious. Several political professionals reported that they had never worked for a candidate who experienced a scandal.

Importantly, when political professionals elaborated on the distinction between crises and scandals, they provided crisis examples that could be missed by the existing work on scandals. For example, when asked whether crises necessarily involve scandals, Paul Curcio, a Republican media consultant and former National Republican Senatorial Committee official, responded:

> In fact, I would say that the majority of [campaign crises] do not [involve scandals]. The majority of them are difficult political situations. For example, you take a particularly tough piece of advertising run against you. It may simply be dealing with a particular series of votes or something like that and it's going to be difficult to explain. Or you know you have to deal with it, you have to explain it in some way. A disastrous performance in a debate isn't a scandal; it's a performance question. . . . [Scandals] probably are the juiciest, because of human nature, but I would say they are absolutely not the majority.[29]

Former DCCC official Jenny Backus agreed. When asked whether crises must involve scandals, Backus responded:

> Oh, no, not at all. I mean, most of the time crises in campaigns don't involve scandal. They involve really mundane things like forgetting to fill

out your FEC [Federal Election Commission] reports. Here's the link between crisis and scandal: it's when someone else can characterize a crisis as a scandal. You can have somebody, a first-time FEC filer, who forgets to put the employment of all your donors on [the report] . . . and all of a sudden the other campaign is putting out releases every day saying, "Come clean about your dishonest fundraising." Then that's a crisis. But, initially, it was a crisis because you hired somebody who didn't know how to fill out your FEC reports correctly. So it's *not* a scandal, but if it's characterized as a scandal, it gets out of control.[30]

In the preceding example, the sloppy FEC filing caused what Backus viewed as a traditional crisis, which became a scandal after the opponent exploited the issue.

Other political professionals offered similar examples that suggested important distinctions between crises and scandals. *Crises* affect entire organizations; traditional *scandals*, however, are uniquely personal. Just as the candidate is often uniquely responsible for scandals, the candidate also suffers the consequences. In addition, although political professionals are confident in their abilities to address expected crises, such as attacks from opponents, they reported that scandals can quickly become disastrous. Most other kinds of crises can at least be managed.

To summarize, the major point here is that assuming that crises and scandals are synonymous—or ignoring crises altogether—is a serious omission.

The Typology of Campaign Crises

When crises occur, they are usually multifaceted. Accordingly, various types of crises often interact to shape the campaign environment. Political professionals emphasized that this interactivity makes crises so dangerous. The following typology provides a tool for analyzing different kinds of crises, how they develop, and how they interact. The typology also reveals common links across the nine ways in which political professionals defined crises.

Political professionals discussed crises in **internal** and **external** terms. They also described crises as being **expected** or **unexpected**. These four broad dimensions—internal, external, expected, and unexpected—construct the typology of campaign crises (see Figure 2.1).

Examples from the four case studies illustrate the typology in detail. All these races featured multiple kinds of internal, external, expected, and unexpected crises, demonstrating that even though crises often appear to be isolated to one event, the ramifications can be complex. More important, al-

Figure 2.1   The Typology of Campaign Crises

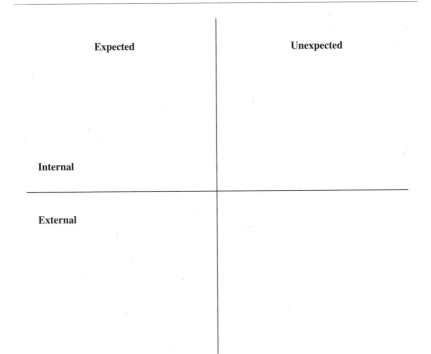

though a major strategic disruption can be spectacular, less public crises, such as organizational or fundraising problems, can be equally damaging.

Finally, it should be noted that the typology is not intended to be a playbook for crisis management in congressional campaigns—something several political professionals warned against during interviews. Rather, it organizes political professionals' descriptions of crises and provides a starting point for considering crises not as singular, obvious events but instead as a complex set of events and circumstances that can change with time and context.

Connecting the Typology Dimensions and the Crisis Definitions

The **expected/unexpected** dimensions of the typology are the most straightforward: either campaigns expect crises or they do not—even though political professionals sometimes disagreed about whether campaigns *should* expect crises before they occur (the *constant crisis* argument). By contrast, unexpected crises surprise campaigns. The *strategic disruption* definition of crises (often a specific event or series of events) is a hallmark of the **unexpected** dimension of the typology because these crises often require drastic changes to the campaign plan—if the plan can be changed at all. Unexpected crises usually originate externally, as with attack crises (launched by the opposition), subsequent media crises (due to journalistic attention), and polling crises (due to loss of public support). Because they are often unknown to, or underestimated by, campaigns, *candidate political errors* and *candidate scandals* (if they have been withheld from the campaign team) are also usually unexpected.[31]

Unexpected *attack* crises are especially important because they can single-handedly reshape the campaign environment. In such cases, the attacking campaign executes its plan by creating internal turmoil for the opponent—usually in a very public way. Meanwhile, the campaign in crisis struggles to adapt to that new environment internally and externally, even while those environments are being controlled by the opposition. Such a "perfect storm" was the case in the 2002 US Senate race in Georgia between Saxby Chambliss (R) and Max Cleland (D). During interviews, both sides reported that the Chambliss campaign experienced no major crises. However, in a significant strategic disruption that represented an unexpected crisis for the Democratic side, the Chambliss campaign aired a controversial ad (representing the *attack* frame) that included pictures of Cleland, Osama bin Laden, and Saddam Hussein while criticizing Cleland's record on homeland security. The Chambliss team vigorously argued during interviews that the ad legitimately criticized Cleland's Senate voting record (a *candidate political error*). By contrast, the Cleland campaign (and other Democrats) vehemently charged that the ad was a direct attack on Cleland's patriotism.

Expected crises are events that the campaign team can reasonably anticipate will present a major challenge. The *constant crisis* frame is the epitome of the **expected** dimension of the typology because political professionals adopting the *constant crisis* view argued that no crisis should be a surprise.[32] Routine research makes many *attacks* expected crises. Similarly, provided that adequate self-research has been performed to check for a candidate's potential political weaknesses, and provided that the candidate has been honest with the campaign team, *candidate scandal* crises also fall into the **expected** typology dimension. Information is the key to the expected typology dimension. The more campaigns know in advance, the better their crisis preparations can be.

The 2000 US Senate race in Washington State between Democratic challenger Maria Cantwell and Republican incumbent Slade Gorton provides an important example of expected events shaping campaign crises. The main attack in the race occurred when the Cantwell team aired an ad late in the campaign criticizing Gorton for shepherding an amendment through Congress that reversed federal restrictions on a controversial mining procedure. Although the Gorton team anticipated an attack, it did not expect the ad to come when it did. When the spot finally aired just before the election, it was too late for the Gorton team to implement its plan to respond (a *strategic disruption*). Nonetheless, because they anticipated some major attack on the mining issue, the Gorton team was able to move forward quickly with the rest of its planned agenda.[33]

External campaign crises are usually public and usually happen *to* campaigns. *Attacks* and *strategic disruptions* are the major crisis frames falling under the **external** dimension because these crises are usually fueled by opponents or third parties (e.g., interest groups). The **external dimension** of the typology also includes media crises—especially damaging pieces of investigative journalism.[34] Candidate scandal crises are often brought to light externally, even if the candidate is responsible for the scandal itself. Fundraising and polling crises are also classified as external because they represent the loss of outside support (e.g., from donors and voters).[35]

The 2002 New Jersey US Senate race illustrates the **external** typology dimension. Throughout the campaign, the Torricelli (D) team was plagued by a high-profile investigation targeting an allegedly corrupt relationship between the senator and a former campaign contributor (a candidate scandal). The Torricelli campaign was never able to control its external environment and wage the campaign on its own terms. Continual attacks from Republican challenger Douglas Forrester inflicted more damage on the Torricelli campaign, as did intense media attention surrounding the senator.

Organizational crises are the major frame within the **internal** typology dimension. All three campaigns in the 2002 US Senate race in Minnesota faced profound organizational crises when Democratic incumbent Paul Wellstone died in a plane crash shortly before the election. The crisis represented a strategic disruption to say the least, not only due to Wellstone's death but also because the tragedy was a major unexpected change for Republican challenger Norm Coleman's campaign and, later, for the replacement Walter Mondale campaign. Internally, what remained of the Wellstone campaign (which also lost staff members in the crash, along with Wellstone's wife and daughter) was in turmoil—personally and organizationally. Meanwhile, Coleman suspended his campaign, as senior advisers quietly huddled to sort out what lay ahead and as Democrats recruited Mondale, the former vice president and senator, to replace Wellstone on the ballot. Once Mondale was nominated, his campaign faced immediate organizational and fundraising crises, all while reintroducing voters and donors to the elder statesman. Figure 2.2 summarizes the connections between crisis definitions, the typology, and the cases.

Conclusion

Defining crises can be complex, but political professionals know crises when they see them. The campaign environment (context) plays a large role in that determination. Understanding how the campaign views that environment—and why some events are considered crises and other are not—requires appreciating how the campaign team perceives the world around it. The campaign context can include a variety of national and local factors (Fenno 1992).[36] It shapes crises and vice versa, but political professionals did not describe the campaign context as a form of crisis in and of itself. Managing

Figure 2.2 The Typology of Campaign Crises and the Cases

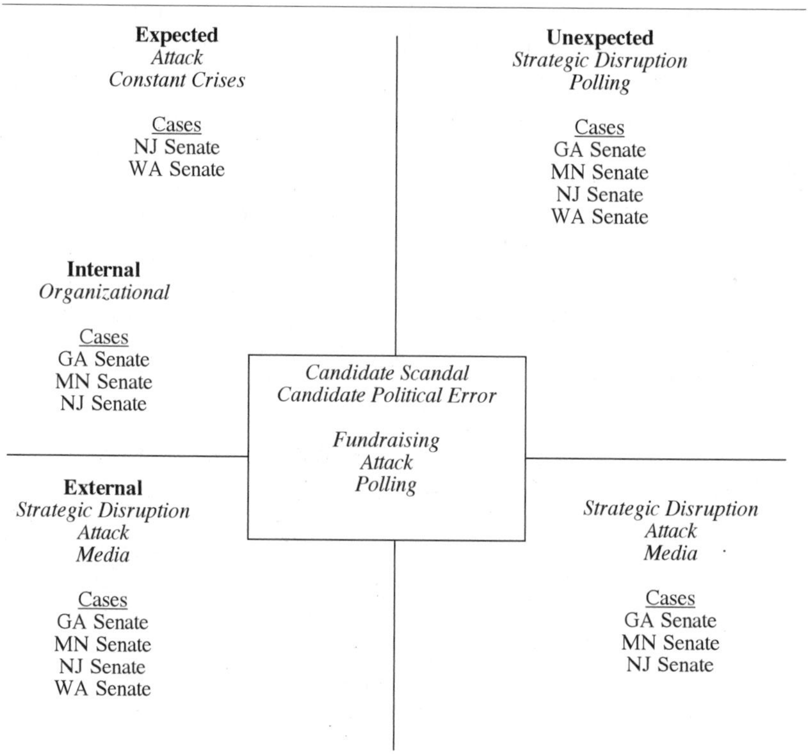

crises—and campaigns more generally—depends on keeping the campaign environment favorable for the candidate and making it less favorable for opponents.

Diagnosing crises without internal knowledge of campaigns can be risky, because crises often occur with little public fanfare even though the consequences can be profound. With political professionals' comments in mind, the following definition of campaign crises therefore guides the rest of the analysis:

> *Campaign crises are interactive events that the campaign team believes represent a significant disruption to the campaign strategy or plan. Campaign crises may be **internal** or **external** and are usually **unexpected**. The full complexity of campaign crises is rarely explained by a single event.*

Studying only campaign scandals—the most obvious type of crisis—misses at least half the diverse portrait of campaign politics. Studying only scandals also fails to consider many of the events that so often make or break campaigns but do not meet the popular, quasiethical notion of what constitutes a scandal. Understanding the complete picture of campaign crises is doubly important because most congressional elections are noncompetitive. During an era when allegedly few campaigns matter, therefore, crises—and how political professionals define and respond to them—are vitally important in understanding what shapes competitive campaigns. Crises are also not limited to a few House and Senate campaigns occurring every two years. As the interview data and typology demonstrate, crises are an ever-present force in congressional races even when campaigns have not yet formally begun. To ignore campaign crises—whether in full bloom or below the public radar—neglects a component of congressional politics that is as fundamental as campaigning itself.

Campaign crises also help us understand how political professionals think about their work and their world. Understanding the multifaceted nature of crises improves the knowledge of how many elements of a campaign have to be managed (or at least anticipated): organization, opponent actions, money, candidate behavior, interpersonal relationships, and more. All these factors are potential breeding grounds for crises. Yet they are also a necessary component of every campaign—including those that experience no crises at all. In short, understanding how political professionals define crises illuminates their priorities in campaigns. If crises represent things that go wrong in campaigns, then they also signal the things political professionals especially want to go right. As the interview comments make clear, a key challenge is to reach consensus within the campaign about which events are crises and which are not and, when crises do occur, how to respond. Chapter 3 explores this all-important debate.

Notes

1. Drey Samuelson, personal interview with author, August 14, 2003, Washington, D.C.

2. Democratic pollster, personal interview with author, July 2003, Washington, D.C. Additional information has been omitted to protect the source's confidentiality.

3. Previous versions of this chapter were presented at the 2003 annual meeting of the Northeastern Political Science Association (Garrett 2003) and the 2004 annual meeting of the American Political Science Association (Garrett 2004b). An abbreviated version appears in Garrett (2006a).

4. The work on presidential scandal is also limited. For an account of Iran-Contra, see Chestnut (1996). On Clinton impeachment, see Bridgmon (2002) and Campbell and Rae (2003).

5. Applying uniform standards to campaign "ethics" is similarly difficult (Miller and Medvic 2002, 30).

6. Despite the broad nature of Roberds's definition, there are two clear components. First, "for the action to count as a scandal it must be publicly revealed and it must be of such a nature that it could reasonably be expected to be controversial" (Roberds 1997, 87). Second, scandal means more than mere "spin" of unpopular positions or even policy reversals; these concerns are considered "politics, not scandal" (Roberds 1997, 88).

7. Most modern scandal analyses build on Peters and Welch's (1980) finding that "corruption" charges result in a 6–11 percent vote loss for incumbents.

8. The Goidel and Gross article is primarily devoted to campaign finance, but scandal serves as a dummy variable in their models. Their method uses a three-stage least squares (3SLS) regression approach, which marks a departure from the two-stage (2SLS) approach traditionally employed. Three-stage least squares allows for estimating an entire set of equations simultaneously.

9. However, Lough's overall finding was that scandals have the greatest impact in general elections. For a summary of his findings with respect to vote share and challenger emergence, see pp. 146–149.

10. This chapter analyzes the first-round interviews focused on theoretical generalizability as well as the case-study interviews designed to illustrate the theory established in the first-round interviews. The data revealed very similar definitions of campaign crises across all interviews. The Methodological Appendix describes the coding. This chapter covers two interview questions. The first asked political professionals how they define campaign crises. The second asked whether crises must always involve scandals.

11. The means were 4.14 frames (first-round interviews), 2.69 frames (case-study interviews), and 3.39 frames (all interviews). Although the same question was used in the first-round and case-study interviews, case-study interviews generally faced tighter time restrictions and focused on a particular case, compared to the open-ended nature

of the first-round interviews. Therefore, case-study interviewees might have been less inclined to elaborate as much as first-round interviewees.

12. Initial coding included more than a dozen frames, which were refined and collapsed to reflect key distinctions in interviewees' answers. For initial coding, see Garrett (2003).

13. For additional discussion of the framing methodology, see appendix C in Garrett (2005).

14. Republican pollster, personal interview with author, July 7, 2003, Washington, D.C. Emphasis in original. Additional information omitted to protect confidentiality.

15. However, there were some sizable differences between the first-round and case-study interviews. This finding presents a possible example of selection bias. Although case-study interviewees were asked to define campaign crises, the main purpose for their selection was work on particular races, only one of which involved a public scandal.

16. Ray Strother, telephone interview with author, July 16, 2003.

17. Tom Edmonds, personal interview with author, November 7, 2003, Philadelphia.

18. Joe McLean, personal interview with author, December 1, 2003, Washington, D.C.

19. Jenny Backus, personal interview with author, July 30, 2003, Washington, D.C. Emphasis in original. This example also displays elements of the *attack* frame.

20. Republican election lawyer, personal interview with author, July 29, 2003, Washington, D.C. This passage is cross-coded with the organization and strategic disruption frames. Additional citation information omitted to protect confidentiality.

21. Democratic pollster, telephone interview with author, August 2003. Additional citation information omitted to protect confidentiality.

22. Kiki McLean, telephone interview with author, July 30, 2003. Emphasis in original.

23. Democratic pollster, personal interview with author, July 2003, Washington, D.C. Additional citation information omitted to protect confidentiality.

24. In most of the crosstabs generated for this chapter, at least one cell frequency is below 5, making large-N difference-of-proportions tests such as confidence intervals and chi-square inappropriate because the small-N sampling distribution does not resemble the normal distribution required for large-N methods (Agresti and Findlay 1997, 224). Instead, the analysis turns to Fisher's exact test for comparing groups within the coded interview data. Fisher's exact test is appropriate only for two-by-two crosstabs. Rather than the normal distribution, Fisher's relies on "hypergeometric" distribution (Blalock 1979, 292). For additional discussion, see Agresti and Findlay (1997, 224–225).

25. The case-study interviews alone also produced a highly significant distinction between Democrats and Republicans in their characterizations of attack crises (P-value = .007, two-sided). At first, it is tempting to believe that this finding is unduly influenced by the case-study interviews, which include two prominent cases in which Democrats believe their candidates were attacked unfairly (the Cleland and Torricelli campaigns). However, additional significance testing did not support this claim.

26. Some of the results discussed in this section are not displayed in the tables.

27. In the case-study interviews, 12.8 percent of Democrats used an *offensive attack* frame, while no Republicans did so (P-value = .037 using a one-sided test). In all

interviews, 23.7 percent of Democrats used the frame, compared to only 7.9 percent of Republicans (P-value = .040 using a two-sided test).

28. The significant relationship did not hold up when examining only the first-round interviews. Nonetheless, in the first-round interviews, 75 percent of media consultants used the *attack* frame, compared with 56.8 percent of other political professionals.

29. Paul Curcio, personal interview with author, July 16, 2003, Washington, D.C.

30. Jenny Backus, personal interview with author, July 30, 2003, Washington, D.C. Emphasis in original.

31. Fundraising crises and subsequent organizational crises are also often unexpected.

32. From this perspective, a failure to reasonably expect crises represents professional incompetence, falling under the *organizational* frame and classified in the **internal** typology dimension.

33. Importantly, however, there was disagreement within the Gorton team about whether the Cantwell ad represented a crisis at all. Some members of the consulting team viewed the ad as the extension of a fierce campaign in which the Gorton campaign simply lost. This logic is consistent with the constant crisis view of campaign crises. See Chapter 7 for details.

34. In such cases, the media attention may be due to the media's own work or by opponents providing damaging information to the media (or internal leaks).

35. However, both frames may also be classified as internal if poor decisions cause polling or fundraising crises.

36. Fenno (1992, 215) uses "context" to refer to the campaign environment. Although he does not focus on crises, the description of campaign context as a background factor is similar.

3

Campaign Leadership and Strategy During Crises

Just because you're a campaign manager doesn't mean you can't be involved in crisis management. . . . The titles become less relevant these days. I think in the [2000] presidential round . . . being "the strategist" became the big deal. . . . What happens in campaigns is there tends to be a small cadre of people who are decisionmakers. Sometimes it's two or three. Sometimes it's five or six. When you get beyond that . . . it's unwieldy. In a Senate race, it better be two or three or you're going to be in big trouble. Pollsters, consultants, media consultants tend to play a big role.

—Tad Devine, Democratic media consultant[1]

One of the first things [successful campaigns] do is good opposition research on themselves. It is a difficult expenditure for a campaign to make, but it's a fine investment. Most of the time, the candidates themselves resist it like crazy. But hiring the toughest, meanest son of a bitch you can find to do opposition research on your candidate, so that you know what's coming before it hits you, is one of the best investments campaigns can make in avoiding crises.

—Whit Ayres, Republican pollster[2]

Campaign leadership and crisis management depend more often on needs that develop from particular circumstances and less on universal norms. Tad Devine, in the opening quotation, explains that there can be important divisions between campaign *managers* and campaign *consultants*, with a premium on "strategists." This dynamic is largely unexplored in existing scholarship, but it suggests a notable step away from candidate-centered campaigns of recent decades and toward increasingly consultant-centered campaigns (see Shea and Burton 2006, ch. 1). The analysis below provides one of the few empirical accounts of which political professionals lead and

41

influence congressional campaigns. Although it emphasizes leadership and decisionmaking during crises, many of the findings also apply to routine campaign settings.

To summarize, political professionals reported that consultants dominate campaign strategy for two reasons: first, because many junior campaign staff lack the experience and judgment to know when not to panic or what strategy to employ; and second, because candidates and families often lack the objectivity to make tough strategic decisions that are best for the *campaign* but perhaps painful for the candidate. Campaign crises can accentuate professional divisions and make them insignificant, depending on the type of crisis. Strategic choices can also depend on campaign leadership.

Whereas *strategists* make most campaign decisions, those described as *implementers* carry out those decisions. Much of the distinction between strategy and implementation reflects recent changes in the political consulting industry and professional politics. Campaign managers and other regular campaign staff—those employed full-time by the campaign (or, in a low-budget campaign, full-time volunteers), such as schedulers, press secretaries, researchers, personal assistants,[3] and field organizers—are usually those closest to the candidate. They see the candidate daily and become employees, teammates, and friends. These political professionals were often characterized in interviews as implementers. Political consultants can also form close relationships with candidates, but consultants usually handle multiple clients at once. Consultants' relationships with individual campaigns might also be more transient than other political professionals, as consultants develop strategic expertise over many years and with various campaigns. Overall during the interviews, political professionals said that consultants' diverse experience, age, and (sometimes) more measured judgment create a division between those making strategic decisions (strategists) and the staff implementing those decisions (implementers).

In addition to exploring the division of labor among official campaign actors, much remains to be learned about unofficial advisers, particularly candidates' friends and families. Personal advisers are largely ignored in campaigns and elections research, but their influence over candidates and campaigns can be substantial. As Whit Ayres's opening quotation makes clear, political professionals believe that candidates and their personal confidants are sometimes poor strategists, especially during crises.

The Evolution of Campaign Leadership

Historically, the division of labor inside campaigns was straightforward, as parties dominated virtually every aspect of electioneering. Even today, there is little guidance in the existing literature on the internal divisions of labor, especially between consultants and regular campaign staff. Clearly, however, political parties and their loyal supporters played significant roles in orchestrating House and Senate campaigns until the middle of the twentieth century, but that party influence on campaign decisionmaking has declined in recent decades.[4]

During the so-called golden age of political parties "an individual candidate's 'organization' was often little more than a loyal following within the party" (Herrnson 2004, 69). By the 1950s, however, few candidates could depend on parties alone to win nominations and elections, and more candidate-centered campaign staffs began to emerge. Candidates, experienced managers, and some party officials represented the small strategic team in most campaigns through the 1960s and into the 1970s (Goldenberg and Traugott 1984; Herrnson 2004; Sabato 1981).

During that time, campaign managers emerged as strategic leaders in House and Senate campaigns, especially after party dominance faded. For incumbents, the campaign manager was often the chief of staff from the House or Senate office (Herrnson 2000b, 68–70; Goldenberg and Traugott 1984, 20).[5] However, dominant campaign managers did not last long. By the 1980s political consultants had become major strategic players in campaigns at every level (Dulio 2004; Herrnson 2004; Johnson 2007; Sabato 1981; Strother 2003; Thurber and Nelson 2000). "As political parties lost control of campaigns, the essential nature of modern campaigns changed. . . . When candidate-centered elections became the norm, campaigns had to focus on selling the candidate to a wide group of potential supporters," who were not necessarily partisan loyalists (Hrebenar, Burbank, and Benedict 1999, 6). Persuading those voters meant emphasizing mass media through political consultants' technical expertise (Herrnson 1988). Consultants therefore became the key actors responsible for campaign strategy, theme, and message (Dulio 2004; Dulio and Nelson 2005; Johnson 2007; Johnson 2001; Johnson 2000; Medvic 2001; Thurber, Nelson, and Dulio 2000; Thurber and Nelson 2000; Thurber 2001).

Some observers worry that consultants' influence has dangerous consequences, as candidates allegedly become increasingly removed from their constituents. According to Mark Petracca (1989, 12), "We have witnessed a major shift in who controls, guides, and implements the campaign. Formerly campaigns were run by a candidate's closest and most loyal supporters. While still a part of the campaign process, these individuals have been displaced by professional political consultants." Furthermore, "candidate campaigns are now the episodic organizations of professionals and experts that political parties once were" (Hrebenar, Burbank, and Benedict 1999, 6).

Until recently, those concerned about consultants' influence could take some comfort in the fact that most consultants confined their work to technical specialties. For example, media consultants made commercials; pollsters handled polling; and general consultants formulated campaign strategy. Opposition researchers and others provided even more specialized services.[6] This compartmentalized division of labor is clear from early descriptions of the consulting industry (Sabato 1981; Napolitan 1972; Nimmo 1970). Modern profiles still say that political consultants are mostly a segmented group (Dulio and Nelson 2005; Thurber and Nelson 2000; Thurber, Nelson, and Dulio 2000). However, during interviews for this book, political professionals said that strategic power is shifting away from generalists, especially campaign managers and general consultants, and toward media consultants and pollsters. As a result (and somewhat ironically), media consultants and pollsters, whose work was previously specialized, are increasingly responsible for providing *general* strategic advice along with technical products (e.g., advertisements and polls).

Distinctions among types of political professionals have not been entirely lost on existing work, although much of it still lumps all consultants into one group. In an important exception, Dennis Johnson describes "three fairly distinct tiers" among consultants.[7] The top tier—strategists—includes general consultants, campaign managers, pollsters, media consultants, and direct-mail consultants (Johnson 2000, 39–41). The second tier includes "specialists," such as fundraisers, research consultants, media buyers, field/get-out-the-vote (GOTV) staff, and lawyers. Finally, vendors design websites, sell voter data (voter files), and supply other tangible services, often to "anyone who will pay for them," regardless of party (Johnson 2000, 40).

However, Johnson emphasizes:

> Not all political consultants are alike, and not all contribute the same value of services to a campaign. In campaign studies, this elemental fact is sometimes lost and, as a consequence, consultants of all stripes tend to get lumped together in the same category and are then added together. When social scientists fail to make critical distinctions about the work of professional consultants, they often end up with simplistic and unrealistic conclusions about the role and impact of consultants. (Johnson 2000, 39)

Johnson is correct. By exploring distinctions between groups of political professionals, this analysis extends his discussion of a hierarchy among political professionals.

Strategic Decisionmaking Teams

The interviews confirmed Johnson's analysis, but political professionals pointed out some important exceptions to his strategic hierarchy. The research presented here confirms that general consultants, media consultants, and pollsters are strategic leaders during campaign crises, just as they are during routine campaign settings.[8] Nonetheless, the intense political and personal pressures present during crises mean that key strategic decisions often fall to those whom the candidate trusts most regardless of that person's professional title. In addition, most political professionals' views of campaign managers' strategic roles did not support the powerful strategic *decisionmaking* roles that scholars such as Edie Goldenberg and Michael Traugott, or Dennis Johnson, attribute to managers.

Political professionals described modern campaign organizations as a microcosm of the changes that have occurred in American elections since party dominance began to subside in the mid-twentieth century. Overall, campaign leadership and decisionmaking revolve around small groups that are loyal to, and hired by, candidates.[9] The party-dominated organizations of old are far from common in the modern era.

During the first-round interviews, political professionals, when asked to describe typical strategic decisionmaking teams during crises, listed an average of five positions, two of which are filled by political consultants.[10] Campaign managers and candidates were mentioned in more than 80 percent of the answers. However, political professionals did not assign great strategic decisionmaking responsibilities to candidates and campaign managers. Virtually all political professionals (more than 90 percent) cited at least one consultant, and the majority cited two, three, or four consultants as strategic leaders during crisis decisionmaking. In other words, although the average decisionmaking core includes about five people and almost always includes the candidate and campaign manager, political professionals said that consultants within those groups heavily influence strategy. Media consultants (mentioned in almost 80 percent of interviews) and pollsters (almost 60 percent) are especially prominent.

Table 3.1 lists the strategic decisionmakers that political professionals identified during interviews and the frequency with which they did so.

Political professionals mentioned candidates and campaign managers most frequently when asked to describe the strategic decisionmaking team (both are discussed in more detail below). When it comes to consultants, it is no surprise that although the context of a particular crisis determines the individual skills needed, media consultants and pollsters occupy a prominent role. General consultants are also intimately involved in crisis management. These three groups of players—general consultants, media consultants, and pollsters—are the major strategic decisionmakers not only during campaigns in general but also during crises because of their broad experience and knowledge. During crises, consultants can also take on duties outside their areas of expertise.

Table 3.1   Strategic Decisionmakers During Crises

Professional Specialization	N	Percentage
Campaign manager	32	86.5
Candidate	30	81.1
Media consultant	29	78.4
Pollster	22	59.5
Press secretary	17	45.9
Spouse	16	43.2
Kitchen cabinet[a]	13	35.1
General consultant	11	29.7
Research staff	7	18.9
Chief of staff (incumbents only)	4	10.8
Direct-mail consultant	4	10.8
Fundraiser	3	8.1
Party officials	3	8.1
Other official staff (incumbents only)	2	5.4
Campaign policy staff	2	5.4
Nonspecific reference to consultants (refuse to specify types)	2	5.4
Interest-group representatives	1	2.7

Note: a. Interview subjects characterized the "kitchen cabinet" as personal advisers to the candidate. Although these individuals may hold political positions, they are primarily family and friends.

Interviews also revealed changing roles inside the political consulting industry, especially greater strategic power among media consultants and pollsters than in the past. Political professionals rejected historical stereotypes portraying pollsters as specialists who provide information without strategic advice. Many of these comments occurred voluntarily, suggesting that political professionals regarded changing dynamics among consultants as a particularly important topic.

When asked about changing relationships between media consultants and pollsters, for example, longtime Democratic media consultant John Franzén responded:

> [Pollsters have] a lot more direct involvement and a lot more day-to-day involvement in the decisionmaking process of the campaign [than in the past]. It's one of the gripes that media consultants very often have, which is, I think, in some cases, an over-involvement, an over-controlling of the message by pollsters these days. And a lot of what you see on the air reflects that. A lot of ads look like they were written by pollsters [because] in effect, they were. . . . And don't get me wrong. I wouldn't want to run any campaign in a significant, competitive level without good survey research and other public-opinion information.[11]

As with defining campaign crises (see Chapter 2), party affiliation and professional specialization had a modest impact on how political professionals defined the strategic decisionmaking team during crises. Nonconsultants (party officials, congressional staff, and members of Congress) were more likely than consultants to include campaign press secretaries as strategic decisionmakers.[12] More Republicans than Democrats included general consultants as part of the strategic team during campaign crises.[13] This finding is consistent with the conventional wisdom that general consultants are less common in Democratic circles than in Republican ones (Thurber and Nelson 2000). Overall, however, political professionals agreed about which of their colleagues make up the typical decisionmaking team during crises.

Strategic Reasons for Keeping the Decisionmaking Team Small

More important than who is on the decisionmaking team are the choices that team makes. The rest of this chapter explores how the organizational structure described above is designed to preserve effective strategy and decisionmaking. Campaigns turn inward during crises, relying on a smaller group of decisionmakers than they would during routine campaign decisionmaking. In particular, political professionals described organizational structures that separate strategists from implementers. The main objective behind doing so, political professionals said, is to preserve what Michael John Burton and Daniel Shea (2003, 5) call "strategic thinking," which is "the capacity to relate the knowledge of political terrain and campaign rules, often by combining a forward-looking plan with a reverse-engineered vision of electoral success."[14] Put simply, this means determining what tactics the campaign will employ to win the election and to anticipate how to prevent opponents from doing so. Although developing strategy based on individual tactics is an obvious component of elections, political professionals say that the ability to remain calm and to make analytical, proactive decisions (rather than simply reacting to opponents' behavior) requires experience and reasoned judgment. Most of the time, strategy is left to consultants rather than to regular campaign staff.

According to a senior staff member to a Republican congressman,

> The key point in a crisis, a developing crisis, is to keep the players to a minimum, those that are aware of what's happening until you can get a hold of the situation. Many times, campaign volunteers in campaign offices aren't aware of what's happening. There's no reason for those who are doing the

sort of grassroots [work] to really know the details of something [a crisis].
Then the fact is you just don't want information to get out there.[15]

An experienced campaign staffer and press secretary to a member of Congress agreed:

> [During crises, campaigns] circle the wagons, get a few people in,
> make sure others don't realize that there's a potential problem so that
> you don't slow the business of the campaign. You don't want the
> fundraising to stop. You don't want fieldwork to stop. . . . [If] you go
> out and tell the whole campaign that there's a problem, then you lose
> some momentum that you might have had [without wide knowledge of
> the crisis].[16]

Political professionals reported that separating strategy from implementation is not about class or hierarchy but rather about efficiently dividing labor and preserving effective decisionmaking. During crises, it is especially important to try to prevent a panic mentality from overtaking the entire campaign, particularly if, for example, the crisis concerns only a limited constituency. In other words, it is important to guard against a "sky-is-falling" attitude among overzealous and inexperienced campaign staff. Andrew Duke, a Republican chief of staff and former campaign manager to a member of the House of Representatives, explains:

> It's when the wheels fall off that you really see [people's true character].
> And a lot of people, you know, they really, they sort of panic, and [strategic thinking from experienced political professionals] is a function of
> making sure that people *don't* panic. It's making sure that they stay focused on doing what's needed and don't just become sort of mesmerized
> and paralyzed by the situation. And it's making sure that everybody
> keeps a perspective on the big picture and the ultimate goal.[17]

To prevent impulsive strategic errors, political professionals said objective analysis of the crisis should be the first step in deciding how to manage that crisis. More important, many political professionals emphasized that strategic decisions about how to manage crises should already be included in the campaign plan. Sticking to that plan requires having experienced political professionals in place. Similarly, although crises can force major changes in the strategic environment, political professionals said that successful campaigns cannot allow crises to consume the environment. Here again, leadership matters. Saving the rest of the campaign sometimes means simply isolating implementers from strategists so that rank-and-file campaign staff are not distracted from their jobs by trying to manage the crisis.

A Democratic direct-mail consultant who asked not to be identified explained:

> Well, you know, speed kills . . . and that's why I think managers in a lot of well-run campaigns don't involve themselves in crisis situations because, regardless of what's going on in the crisis, money still has to be raised, field stuff still has to get done. There are tasks—you know, there's politics that have to be done. There [are] issues rollouts and other stuff that needs to get done, and their job is to make sure everybody who has line responsibility for those functions is still doing their jobs, regardless of what's going on [during the crisis].[18]

Relationships Between Consultants and Campaign Managers

The greatest differences between the professional categories that Johnson (2000, 41; see above) identifies—a strict hierarchy of strategists down to vendors—and those political professionals described during interviews concern campaign managers. When it comes to crisis management, political professionals generally did not include campaign managers as independent strategists (as Johnson does), but they also elevated the research team to a more strategic role than Johnson's specialist category implies.[19] Political professionals said that most campaign managers are *part* of the strategic decisionmaking team but do not lead strategy as consultants typically would. Campaign managers and the regular campaign staff reportedly "keep the trains running" but largely take strategic direction from consultants.[20] However, views on the strategic relationship between consultants and managers can vary widely.[21]

Republican media consultant Paul Curcio explained:

> I would say [the view of managers as implementers is] probably more true than not. And the reason is that the [manager's job] is to make sure that trains are run on time as opposed to [figuring] out where to lay the tracks and what direction it's going to go in. . . . If they have the experience to be sort of strategic thinkers, [managers] would have gone off and done that already. [Having said that] . . . I'm very appreciative of campaign managers in [the] *very* difficult job that they have.[22]

The campaign manager's status as implementer or strategist can also vary depending on the relationship with the candidate. As Republican pollster Whit Ayres explained:

I have worked in campaigns where the campaign manager was almost a peer with a candidate. On the other hand, I've been involved in campaigns where the campaign manager was an enthusiastic, but exceedingly inexperienced, young man or young woman in their twenties. . . . And in that case, a campaign manager is more of a person who makes the trains run on time, but doesn't have a whole lot to say about the direction the trains are running in. In that case, the consultants are the ones who have far more influence on where the train is going and how the train is going to get there. . . . But it differs *dramatically*, really dramatically, from campaign to campaign.[23]

As Ayres suggests here, campaign managers' being able to retain strategic influence is particularly likely among those with experience who, for all practical purposes, fulfill the same duties as general consultants. In many interviews, political professionals described these managers as "adults," as opposed to a recent college graduate who is managing a long-shot campaign more for experience than salary (often described as "kids"). Adult campaign managers are a far different breed than their younger counterparts: they are experienced political professionals who are often the candidate's closest strategic (and, in some cases, personal) adviser—especially during crises. These individuals are often chiefs of staff or other trusted employees from official House and Senate offices who are on leave for the campaign.

Nonetheless, interviews revealed two important crisis situations in which younger campaign managers might hold an advantage over more experienced political consultants. First, like families and so-called kitchen cabinets, even inexperienced campaign managers are likely to have unusual levels of access to the candidate. Many candidates form bonds, which can be strengthened by crises, with junior campaign managers. According to former DCCC official and media consultant Jenny Backus:

Oftentimes the campaign managers become marriage counselors, divorce lawyers. . . . It's sort of like becoming a teacher in a school that . . . has kids whose parents work. Teachers end up becoming more than just teachers: they're coaches; they're parents. It's the same sort of thing with a campaign manager: not a lot of resources, a lot of spare time, you end up . . . doing a lot more than what you bargained for. A lot of times, campaign managers, especially the newer ones, form these bonds with these candidates that are never split.[24]

Second, throughout these interviews political professionals also pointed out that younger campaign managers—and younger campaign staff in general—have the physical energy necessary to keep working when others, including consultants, cannot. This ability to keep going and to believe in the campaign against all odds is essential in maintaining organizational morale and executing campaign strategy. A former chief of staff and campaign manager for Republican senator Slade Gorton, Tony J. Williams, explained:

> The key between the split [in] the strategic and the tactical side [is] the campaign staff: young people [versus consultants]. Because who has the energy to do this for sixteen hours a day? And so, you need a bunch of twenty-six-year-olds. And then the consultants, the reason they're strategic is they're all forty or older. . . . It's age and experience, but there just aren't a lot of people in their forties who are willing to go devote the hours to running these darn things. One, it's physically hard; and two, you know [consultants and strategists are usually] married and [have] kids and it's not a real good environment.[25]

Finally, despite the emphasis on strategy versus implementation among consultants and campaign managers, some political professionals warned that it is a fundamental error to keep any campaign manager out of the strategic loop and that doing so can exacerbate existing crises or create new ones by preventing the campaign team from having complete information. According to Republican general consultant Carlyle Gregory Jr.:

> We have this phrase that we used to use [referring to consultants], "You've got a problem; I've got a plane to catch." . . . I can come in and tell you the sixteen things you ought to be doing, but I don't have to do them. So, the guy on the ground's got to do them. Having a campaign manager that has a good strategic sense is very, very valuable for a campaign. So [the] bottom line is, most campaigns don't have a campaign manager that is capable of making strategic decisions. But some do. Those are great guys. I try to find them when I can and hire them when I can. So, I don't systematically exclude campaign managers from strategic councils.[26]

One of Gregory's colleagues was even more direct. When asked to comment on the characterization of campaign managers as "implementers," a Republican direct-mail consultant and former campaign manager replied:

> That is just pure, unadulterated bullshit. . . . It is important that things be implemented in a campaign—absolutely critical. And it is important that the campaign manager handle that implementation. . . . You've got to

have the person who's dealing with the day-to-day acts—the day-to-day crises and management role—involved in that strategic decision or else you're making decisions in a vacuum. It *can't* work any other way. What happens in these larger campaigns is that, typically, you have a media consultant who wants to argue for media. You have a direct-mail consultant who wants to argue for direct mail. You have a polling consultant that wants to argue for [polling]. . . . And you've got to have someone that pulls all of this together, extracts the best information, and keeps everyone on focus, and that's the campaign manager. Consultants don't like it, but that's truly the person that it ought to be.[27]

Candidates, Families, and the
Personal Side of Campaign Strategy

Although the literature on campaign management emphasizes the official side of campaigning and political professionals' services, the personal stakes for candidates are enormous. Accordingly, the distinction between strategists and implementers can extend beyond paid political professionals. Spouses, family members, and friends can be *personal* leaders in campaigns, especially during crises. The more personal the crisis, the more invested candidates and families become in campaign decisions. Although disagreements can arise among political professionals about how to best manage crises, the stakes are uniquely personal for candidates and their families. During the most trying times, consultants and regular staff often take a backseat. This is especially true during **internal** crises such as *candidate scandals, candidate political errors,* and **external** *attack* crises launched by opponents. As a Republican election lawyer explained, "It's real personal whether people vote for you or vote against you. People take it personally. . . . And most of the crises involve something personal [so] it's hard not to be personal. You don't raise money, 'Well, they didn't give me the money because they don't like me.' All politics are personal."[28]

The competing priorities and loyalties of consultants and families can cause tensions within campaigns, especially during crises. Democratic fundraiser and former campaign manager Joe McLean explained:

It's very difficult for candidates to see the strategic ramifications of tactical decisions. Candidates want to stand up and defend themselves, and their wives want them to stand up and defend themselves, and their kids—and there's a tremendous amount of pressure on the candidate, not only internally, but from his family and close supporters and people around him. [Families will] say, "Well, Billy Bob, just stand up and tell them you didn't do it!" You can't do that lots of times. It's exactly the wrong thing to do.[29]

More specifically, political professionals warned that strategic input from families can also be problematic because candidates face competing strategic and emotional loyalties. McLean continued:

> Candidates are prone to make bad decisions because they live inside their own skin and not out in the world where voters live. . . . They have so much invested. . . . If Pepsi doesn't beat Coca-Cola, it's okay because the board and the president and the stockholders still go home rich. But if you don't beat your opponent, you are crushed. . . . So the pressure on candidates is unbelievable, because it's really about their whole worth as a human being. . . .
>
> And I'll tell you something, the candidates who are really successful in fundraising and in message delivery are the candidates who aren't personal, right? It's not about them. It's about what they want to do. . . . And it also helps them make strategic decisions in the campaign, because now it's a campaign about issues and not about a person.[30]

Nonetheless, depersonalizing strategic decisions can be especially difficult when candidates are attacked personally. As McLean's comments suggest, political professionals argued that relying on experienced professionals to make strategic decisions is essential when candidates and their families are caught up in the emotion of campaigns' give-and-take.

Despite the emphasis on separating strategists from implementers and, sometimes, isolating the influence of candidates and families, political professionals stressed that strategic decisions must ultimately consider candidates' wishes and well-being. According to Republican media consultant Paul Curcio: "If your reputation is destroyed or your family is destroyed, or your family is publicly humiliated. . . . No elected office is worth that. None. And, so, as a philosophical thing, the first thing that I would want to know is what the candidate feels is right for his or her personal integrity and reputation, and equally important, for the families."[31]

Indeed, many interviewees emphasized the importance of candidates setting the tone for strategic decisionmaking, even if actually making those decisions often falls to consultants. This distinction, too, can cause tension within campaign organizations. A former Democratic member of Congress confirmed that sentiment when explaining an extraordinary step that many political professionals might well argue leaves the campaign open to crises by giving away campaign strategy:

[During] my first run for Congress . . . I had said I was not going to run a negative campaign. . . . And then my campaign team [asked], "How do we get even with [the opponent]?" One of the suggestions, and one that we ended up using, was [the opponent's] change of position on several key issues. And we ended up doing a spot about that. It was a *terribly* difficult decision for me. "Is this going negative in a sense of getting personal?"[32] . . . That turned out to be the occasion for me to establish a rule for myself, which helped me feel better about it and I also think was a good rule, which was whenever then and in the future I did a campaign spot that was critical of my opponent in some way, I gave him or her a copy of it in advance. . . . It really didn't give them an opportunity to do a whole lot other than to know what was coming at them—not that I intended it as such, but I think it may have been disarming in a way.[33]

Campaign Organizations and Preventing Crises: The Role of Research

As the preceding comment suggests, one of the most challenging areas of the relationship between candidates, consultants, and families often concerns negative information about the candidate. Although heart-to-heart talks between candidates and campaign managers sometimes pass for "self-research" (political professionals' term[34]) to identify potential vulnerabilities that opponents could exploit, professional research is often necessary. That research explores common vulnerabilities, including unpaid taxes, public divorce records (*candidate scandals*), and unpopular policy positions (a *candidate political error*). Perhaps because of resistance from family members and the candidates themselves, many political professionals said that campaigns pay too little attention to researching their own candidates—in addition to the obvious need to conduct research on opponents.

Political professionals emphasized that campaign research should not be amateurish. Rather, they said, professional political consultants—or perhaps campaign staff dedicated to research—should investigate their own candidate and the opponents. Echoing Republican pollster Whit Ayres's opening quotation, Democratic fundraiser and former campaign manager Joe McLean explained:

[Candidates] think they're good people, and they are, mostly. . . . Sometimes they've done things in the past that, at the time, looked like it was honest and straight and right. But with the benefit of 20/20 hindsight and a shifting moral playing field, it doesn't look as good as it did when they did it. . . . It's why you always do opposition research on your own candidate first. It's the first thing you do, and frankly, it's a rule I have. If the candidate won't allow opposition research on himself, I won't take the campaign. And I mean real, in-depth, professional opposition research, not just, "Well, Earl Ray my lawyer will tell you what all you need to know." No, hire [professional opposition researchers], pay $25,000, $30,000, have a real, in-depth, professional opposition research team go over [the candidate's] record.[35]

Research, therefore, is a method for understanding and controlling the **expected/unexpected** dimensions of the crisis typology and demonstrates the importance of open communication within the campaign organization, particularly between candidates and strategists. Getting candidates and families to agree to opposition research, however, can take hard bargaining that emphasizes the strategic importance such research can play in winning and losing elections. Making the case for opposition research often falls to experienced consultants.

External Players: Campaign Relationships with Parties and Interest Groups During Crises

The distinction between the campaign team and outside actors—parties and interest groups—can be even starker than divisions of labor inside campaigns. Although it is no surprise that outsiders have lost influence over campaigns given recent history's increasingly candidate-centered operations, little is known about the thinking behind internal-external relationships. This section discusses how political professionals feel about their relationships with outside entities. Often, they don't feel positive.

Several scholars suggest a symbiotic or "allied" relationship between consultants and parties (Abbe and Herrnson n.d.; Kolodny and Logan 1998; Kolodny 2000; Dulio 2004; Dulio and Nelson 2005; Dulio and Garrett 2007; Dulio and Thurber 2003; Monroe 2001). According to the allied view of consultant-party relationships, both sides divide tasks for greater efficiency. Management of individual campaigns, as well as other strategic duties, are often left to consultants; parties focus on tasks such as voter mobilization and some types of fundraising, which consultants can also choose to do (or not) (Abbe and Herrnson n.d.; Kolodny 2000; Dulio and Thurber 2003; Dulio and Nelson 2005).[36] Although conventional wisdom suggests that consultants forced parties out of the strategy business and otherwise potentially weakened parties as political institutions (Agranoff 1972; Petracca 1989; Rosenbloom 1973; Herrnson 1988; Sabato 1981;

Magleby, Patterson, and Thurber 2002), there has always been a strategic division of labor between parties and consultants. Indeed, "the parties have made a conscious decision to look to consultants to provide certain electioneering services," especially those relating to media and strategy, while the party focused on fundraising and opposition research (Dulio and Nelson 2005, 38). Overall, according to the existing literature, relationships between campaigns and outside actors is sometimes beneficial but often ambiguous. Political professionals were generally less charitable when describing outside involvement during crises.

The interviews confirmed that parties and consultants also divide labor during crises, but political professionals suggested that although parties or interest groups can provide important support, their *strategic* input is often unwelcome.[37] Only about 20 percent of political professionals said that parties play major strategic roles in crisis management.[38] The strategic split between campaigns and parties is pragmatic and ideological. On the pragmatic side, political professionals—including many with substantial experience working for and with parties—reported that parties are simply not strategic players in most campaign decisionmaking, including during crises. These data confirm a peripheral "party service" role in modern campaigns.

From a more ideological perspective, some political professionals (about 10 percent) even described genuine frustration with party involvement during crises. According to veteran Democratic media consultant Ray Strother:

> I'm always terrified when the political party, the Democratic Party bureaucracy, gets involved in crisis management. First of all, they lack the experience. Second, they're not *in* the campaign; they're looking in from the outside. Third, it broadens the group and makes it more difficult to make decisions. . . . But it also spreads a problem through Washington. . . . See, in my perfect world, the political parties would raise money and stay out of the way. . . . Usually people right at the top [of the party] have had a lot of experience, but [not the rest of the party staff]. . . . I just don't want them around. They get in the way, cost extra money, and I'm just not interested.[39]

Republicans generally agreed. Republican media consultant Tom Edmonds explained:

> I think political parties are close to being a useless entity. . . . Political parties in America in the last twenty years—their importance has been diminished and diminished and diminished. And there's no institutional

memory. They're an unreliable ally at best. . . . The rise of consultants is part of it. . . . You don't have party bosses in the streets of Chicago rounding up the votes and telling you how to vote. People are all independent agents—both the voters and the candidates.[40]

Nonetheless, and consistent with a continuing allied relationship between consultants and parties, political professionals said that parties can exert substantial power in some narrow circumstances. For example, parties have the potential to make a major strategic impact by deploying special teams of experienced staff (particularly senior field operatives) to assist campaigns in crisis. These operatives also serve in important field capacities before crises strike. Former DCCC official and media consultant Jenny Backus explained how the committee's crisis teams, made up of experienced party field staff and campaign managers, worked in 2002:

> They traveled all the time. . . . They recruited candidates, they got campaigns up and running and then they watched candidates and floated. In the end, each one of them was assigned to a campaign in crisis, basically, or a campaign that we really wanted to win, to pull over the finish line. Then we also supplement that, as you get closer in the cycle, by pulling experts out of offices [in Washington] and sending them in for the last two months. . . . [The crisis teams are] like campaign managers. They're like uber-super-campaign managers that come in, that can serve as your liaison to Washington and the campaign in crisis.[41]

Parties and interest groups can also maintain strategic influence by providing funding, as both Strother's and Edmonds's comments suggest. (However, federal election law and Federal Election Commission regulations on coordination limit the amount of financial and, arguably, strategic support that parties and interest groups can provide to campaigns.) Ironically, even though party money can play an important role in bailing campaigns out of crises, political professionals said that this can foster additional crises by requiring campaigns to make strategic decisions, at the party's behest, that compromise what the regular campaign staff and consultants believe is best.[42] According to Republican general consultant Carlyle Gregory Jr.:

> The party, in a lot of campaigns, is still the biggest funding source. They also have expertise. So, if you're having a crisis in your [voter] turnout, it just looks like it's going to be terrible and you've got a problem there, then the party, you pull those guys in there and you say, "Help us." Or, they say, "We're going to give you money, but we want to spend it on a talking-dog

spot." That's a crisis. But they've got a seat at the table because they're the big funders. They have an organization. They've earned it.[43]

Political professionals reported that interest groups, as with parties, play virtually no role in campaign leadership, tactics, and strategy. However, parties, interest groups (including political action committees [PACs]), and 527 groups (named for the relevant section of the Internal Revenue Code) often provide cover (i.e., validation) for campaigns in crisis and when counterattacking the opposition. Political professionals said they welcome validation when it supports the campaign's message. Indeed, within legal boundaries, parties and interest groups can be surrogates for campaigns, sparing them time and resources and protecting campaigns from having to directly address charges that do not reflect well on the candidate.[44] An experienced Democratic campaign manager and Senate chief of staff explained:

> Often [party committees] will [go] on television to provide some air cover for you to get you to respond to allegations or almost always to attack back for you to see if they can switch the subject for you. And that's always helpful. And [party] committees are often very effective at starting crises for your opponent. [When serving as a campaign manager] I almost always never do the really ugly stuff. . . . The party can send that message, but it's too politically dicey for the candidates.[45]

At the same time, however, political professionals also complained that outsiders' messages often are inconsistent with campaign needs and desires. Particularly when outside groups independently launch attacks meant to create crises for an opposing candidate, the political environment can become chaotic as each campaign and various independent groups try to spread their own messages. In these cases, political professionals complained that Federal Election Campaign Act (FECA) restrictions on communications coordinated between campaigns and outside actors can make it difficult to ask groups (over which campaigns have no control) to change their messages. Political professionals also fear that voters do not distinguish between actual campaign messages and negative messages from outside groups.

Democratic media consultant John Franzén explained:

> We have all these groups now that are running independent-expenditure campaigns—many of them trying to be helpful who completely mess up your campaign by bringing up issues that you don't want to talk about or attacking the opponent very ineptly and maybe in an offensive way. And the voters, of course, very often cannot distinguish between your message

and this interest group's message and they simply assume that message is from you. So, any backfire of that message goes right to the candidate. So the interest groups are creating crisis. . . . I can't recall a single situation where an interest group helped to *resolve* a crisis. . . . We're not supposed to talk to them. We're supposed to have firewalls. If they talk to us, then it's no longer an independent-expenditure campaign. We cannot coordinate [under federal campaign finance law]. You can say things publicly in the press: "I wish these people would get out of our state, and let us run our own show here." But it's a free country. You can't shoot 'em.[46]

Conclusion

Political professionals' comments about how they do their jobs, how they think about those jobs, and their relationships with colleagues and candidates provide insider accounts of changes in professional politics that have gone largely unnoticed beyond the small community of those who make their living running campaigns. Yet those relationships and changing professional norms affect the kinds of campaigns that candidates (or consultants) run and, ultimately, shape the relationship between politicians and the citizens they seek to represent. Important divisions between *strategists* and *implementers* are the organizing principle behind campaign leadership during crises. Political consultants—especially pollsters and media consultants—assume a leading role during campaign crises. Consultant power represents important challenges to campaign managers, parties, and interest groups. When it comes to campaign crises, political professionals say that strategic decision-making is not really candidate-centered, but consultant-centered.

Involvement with the inner circle during crises is ultimately about having knowledge that other people do not. This means that strong campaign managers—or even weak ones who forge close relationships with candidates—can be called into the strategic circle if they have particular skills to offer. Although party and interest-group officials are generally not included in the strategic decisionmaking team during crises, they sometimes play vital supporting roles. Political professionals also said that candidates are not major strategic decisionmakers during crises, although candidates and their families are more involved in strategic decisions surrounding personal crises. Families' concerns sometimes inhibit campaign research, although political professionals say rigorous self-research and opposition research are essential.

At first glance, some of these findings might seem paradoxical. After all, the interviews suggest that political consultants take the lead in decision-making "except when they don't."[47] Political professionals, in fact, reported that consultants are the major strategic decisionmakers during campaigns, especially during crises. But they were also quick to point out that congressional campaigns ultimately revolve around candidate needs and preferences. Especially during trying times, candidates count on support from those whom they trust most, which doesn't necessarily mean turning to strategists. The dichotomy between *strategic* decisionmakers and *personal* supporters does not necessarily fit into a neat division of labor, as is somewhat true for the strategist-versus-implementer dichotomy for consultants and regular campaign staff. But the finding is nonetheless important. One of the chief lessons from all the interviews is that campaigns must be agile to be competitive. Political professionals believe that, even though there are trends in campaign behavior, campaigns that always followed a single playbook would fail quickly. It is, therefore, no surprise that there are exceptions to the general pattern of consultant leadership.

It is also possible that a different interview pool would have produced different results. The interviews relied on input from consultants, party officials, campaign managers, and others—all of whom largely agreed that consultants are the major strategic leaders during crises. The prominent role attributed to consultants is consistent with decades of scholarship. Nonetheless, it is certainly possible that a study focused primarily on party officials or regular campaign staff would uncover a greater role for other professional groups. The debate on whether parties and consultants are allies, adversaries, or something else also continues. Although this book is not focused on that relationship, it helps lay the foundation for others to examine the virtually untouched questions about how nonconsultants view their colleagues.[48]

Regardless of who makes strategic decisions, political professionals said that managing campaign crises is best done proactively as a matter of habit. Tough, professional research, clear communication among staff members, and honest relationships between candidates and top strategists are essential. At the same time, campaigns must be decisive. Although some tactics can make crises less likely to occur, political professionals were quick to warn that campaigns would certainly fail if they constantly lived in fear of crisis and never departed from their plan under any circumstances. Experienced campaign leadership can help determine what plans should be made, when the plan should be rigid, and when it should be flexible. For the most part, that means political consultants. However, the interviews also revealed a rare glimpse into the personal side of campaigns. Political professionals, including consultants, said that they take their personal and professional ethics seriously when advising candidates. Ultimately, they insisted that despite consultants' *strategic* expertise, campaigns are still primarily about candidates and their families on a *personal* level.

Notes

1. Tad Devine, personal interview with author, July 22, 2003, Washington, D.C.

2. Whit Ayres, telephone interview with author, July 16, 2003. Emphasis in original.

3. Most campaign staffs include a personal assistant for the candidate and perhaps the candidate's spouse. These staffers are typically known as the "body man," although both men and women can fill the role. Regardless of title, these staffers, although not generally strategic players, can spend tremendous amounts of time with the candidate while serving as organizer, driver, and assistant with other personal tasks.

4. On variations in parties over time, see, e.g., Aldrich (1985) and Herrnson (1988).

5. Goldenberg and Traugott (1984, 21) note that the term *volunteer* as applied to campaign managers can be misleading. For incumbents, many volunteers are actually experienced congressional staffers who cannot be paid for campaign work while on the official payroll. (However, House and Senate rules do allow some political work by a limited number of designated employees.) Goldenberg and Traugott draw a distinction between these experienced political professionals serving in volunteer capacities, who usually work for incumbents, and the inexperienced amateurs who often truly volunteer for challengers.

6. On opposition research, see, e.g., Johnson (2007, 71).

7. For a related discussion of the evolution of professional lobbyists, see Loomis and Struemph (2003; 2004).

8. It is possible that consultants' strategic influence was inflated in the interviews due to the sampling methodology, as discussed in the Methodological Appendix. Because the first-round interviews relied mostly on political consultants, it is not surprising that they might have a skewed view of their own importance, as a few nonconsultants pointed out during the interviews. Although selection bias is a legitimate concern, it is not a terribly compelling argument in this case given the substantial scholarly and applied literature establishing consultants' leadership roles in campaign strategy. More important, the entire interview pool agreed with the characterization of consultants' key strategic roles, even though some subjects, including many consultants, offered qualifying statements.

9. Of course, some campaigns are small organizations anyway. This is particularly true of challenger House campaigns.

10. The range was between two and nine positions. "Averages" are medians. The median consultant ranking was based on aggregating the major consultant functions cited: media (distinct from press secretary), polling, general, fundraising, and direct-mail consulting.

11. John Franzén, personal interview with author, August 14, 2003, Washington, D.C.

12. Almost 46 percent of nonconsultants (N=17) cited the press secretary as a strategic decisionmaker, compared with about 8 percent (N=3) of consultants who did so. This result is highly significant (exact P-value using two- and one-sided test = .003).

13. About 22 percent of Republicans (N=8) included general consultants in the strategic decisionmaking team, compared with just 8 percent of Democrats (N=3). Using a one-sided test and Fisher's exact test, the P-value = .060. Previous analyses with slightly different sample sizes revealed significant differences below the .05 level. For additional discussion of strategy and tactics during crises, see Garrett (2005, ch. 5).

14. In a related work, political consultant Joel Bradshaw (2004, 28) defines strategy as "simply a definition of how the candidate will win." He operationalizes strategy along four dimensions: (1) dividing voters into supporters, opponents, and undecideds; (2) using research to analyze these groups geographically; (3) making supporters and targeted undecideds the focus of campaign strategy; and (4) after identifying how to win, formulating a strategy to do so.

15. Senior staffer to a Republican congressman, personal interview with author, August 2003, Washington, D.C. Additional information omitted to protect confidentiality.

16. Press secretary to a member of Congress, personal interview with author, August 2003, Washington, D.C. Additional information omitted to protect confidentiality.

17. Andrew Duke, personal interview with author, November 23, 2003, Washington, D.C. Emphasis in original.

18. Republican direct-mail consultant, telephone interview with author, November 2003. Additional information omitted to protect confidentiality.

19. Political professionals also said that direct-mail consultants more often play major roles in House races rather than Senate contests because broadcast media budgets for House campaigns are usually much smaller than for Senate campaigns.

20. The author cannot claim credit for the train analogy. It was common throughout the interviews—so common that it appeared in about one-fifth of all first-round interviews.

21. The first-round interview instrument did not include an explicit question about the roles of campaign managers. Because this became such a prominent theme in the early interviews, an informal probe question was added to most first-round interviews. This probe question asked interview subjects to comment on the managers-as-implementers perspective offered by previous interviewees.

22. Paul Curcio, interview with author, July 16, 2003, Washington, D.C. Emphasis in original.

23. Whit Ayres, telephone interview with author, July 16, 2003. Emphasis in original.

24. Jenny Backus, personal interview with author, July 30, 2003, Washington, D.C.

25. Tony J. Williams, personal interview with author, October 21, 2003, Washington, D.C.

26. Carlyle Gregory Jr., telephone interview with author, July 21, 2003.

27. Republican direct-mail consultant, telephone interview with author, October 16, 2003. Emphasis in original.

28. Republican election lawyer, personal interview with author, July 29, 2003, Washington, D.C.

29. Joe McLean, interview with author, December 1, 2003, Washington, D.C.

30. Ibid.

31. Paul Curcio, personal interview with author, July 16, 2003, Washington, D.C. These views are consistent with previous work (Nelson, Dulio, and Medvic 2002; Gar-

rett, Herrnson, and Thurber 2006) establishing that political consultants rate campaign ethics seriously and argue against unethical behavior in campaigns.

32. In this example, the candidate determined that the ad drew legitimate contrasts on policy positions.

33. Former Democratic member of Congress, personal interview with author, December 2003, Washington, D.C. Additional information omitted to protect confidentiality. Emphasis in original.

34. "Self-research" is sometimes also called "counter-opposition research."

35. Joe McLean, personal interview with author, December 1, 2003, Washington, D.C.

36. The "allied" perspective is similar to Richard Skinner's (2005; 2007) work on "party networks," which emphasizes various political professionals' collaboration toward advancing party goals, regardless of individual professional duties.

37. Party influence in campaign strategy is also generally unwelcome during routine campaign operations (Dulio and Thurber 2003; Dulio and Nelson 2005); the interviews suggested this is particularly so during crises.

38. This question was distinct from the campaign leadership data reflected in Table 3.1. A separate interview question asked interview subjects how common it is that political parties play strategic roles in crisis management. Although the question wording is somewhat narrow, voluntary comments expanding on party roles were common. Therefore, there is no evidence that question wording inhibited broader discussion of parties' roles in crisis management. There was little significant evidence that party affiliation or professional specialization affected political professionals' views about party roles during crises. The only exception was a significant finding that Democrats were more likely than Republicans to cite examples of parties providing "validating" messages to campaigns in crisis; for example, the party might air an advertisement vouching for a candidate's record on a particular issue. Given Republicans' electoral successes between 1994 and 2004, it is perhaps surprising that Republicans did not place a higher value on party services during crises. However, Republican campaigns might also have suffered fewer crises due to their extensive so-called farm team, which consistently produced quality candidates in the 1990s (Peters 1999).

39. Ray Strother, telephone interview with author, July 16, 2003. In addition to professional specialization (e.g., being a consultant), gender might explain interview subjects' disregard for party involvement in campaign crises. The interview sample was largely male, reflecting the political consulting industry as a whole (Thurber and Nelson 2000). Constantini (1990, 763) finds that women exhibit more loyalty toward political parties. There were no obvious disagreements between men and women over campaign crises and decisionmaking during crises. Differences could emerge with a larger women's sample. Nonetheless, Sarah Brewer (2003) finds that there may be few notable differences in how male and female political consultants view their duties or relationships with political parties.

40. Tom Edmonds, telephone interview with author, November 14, 2003.

41. Jenny Backus, personal interview with author, July 30, 2003, Washington, D.C.

42. This claim reflects the adversarial view of party-consultant relationships.

43. Carlyle Gregory Jr., telephone interview with author, July 21, 2003.

44. Nonetheless, much about the relationships between campaigns and 527s and 501(c)s remains unknown because these organizations have only recently become seriously involved in campaign politics.

45. Democratic campaign manager and chief of staff, telephone interview with author, November 2003. Additional information omitted to protect confidentiality.

46. John Franzén, personal interview with author, August 14, 2003, Washington, D.C.

47. The comment comes from Stephen K. Medvic, whose feedback on this project and others has always been appreciated, particularly on a previous draft of part of this chapter (Garrett 2006b).

48. Some survey work addresses this area in general terms. See, e.g., Dulio and Nelson (2005) and Dulio and Garrett (2007).

4

Recognizing and Creating Crises: The Cleland-Chambliss Race

Chapters 2 and 3 established general findings about what crises are and how they affect campaign organizations. With that theoretical foundation in mind, how do crises unfold in specific campaign settings, and what general lessons can crises offer about broader issues, such as professional dynamics within campaigns and strategic interactions with opponents and outside groups? Four case studies presented in this chapter and Chapters 5–7 address those questions. The case studies are not intended to be comprehensive reviews of each race. Rather they focus on crisis management inside each campaign. This includes three key elements that emerged during the more general first-round interviews: (1) how strategic decisionmakers within the campaigns perceived whether crises occurred and, if so, how they defined those crises; (2) how crises affected campaign organizations; and (3) what strategic and tactical decisions campaign officials made to address crises. The case studies do not, however, draw normative conclusions about what went right or wrong or assign blame to individuals. The Methodological Appendix provides additional information about case selection.

The case studies focus on US Senate races because they are typically more professionalized than House campaigns and, because they are regularly contested, contain more potential for crises. Data about Senate races are also more voluminous than for some House races. And finally, during the first-round interviews political professionals cited Senate examples most often. The emphasis on Senate races does not mean that the typology or other findings do not apply to House races, but as a practical matter, Senate races are better equipped to establish a baseline understanding of campaign crises.

The case studies reveal that political professionals inside each campaign defined crises in ways that were consistent with the general lessons of the first-round interviews (see Chapter 2). However, there can be significant disagreement over which events represent crises for particular campaigns. No case represents this disagreement better than the Cantwell-Gorton race in Washington State, in which political professionals reached different conclusions about whether crises occurred and, if so, why. But even in cases in which there was clear agreement that crises occurred—such as the Georgia or Minnesota races—political professionals had different perspectives on which particular events represented crises and why. Many of these comments are consistent with the findings in Chapter 2, which suggest that political professionals not only have varying understandings about what crises are; perhaps more important, they have different perspectives on how crises affect campaigns.

As previously discussed, separating strategy from implementation is important for effective crisis management. Political consultants' strategic leadership can be elevated during crises even more than in routine campaign settings. However, the case studies also present races in which strong campaign managers remained influential. Indeed, virtually all the campaigns profiled featured "strong" campaign managers, each of whom also had substantial professional experience. Despite being called "campaign managers" in these races, for all practical purposes most of them performed at least some general consultant duties.

The case studies also reflect on the more general findings regarding strategy and tactics. When considering that most scholarship on strategy and tactics emphasizes rational-choice decision rules, the finding that political professionals rely so heavily on gut feeling and individual circumstances is important. Therefore, even when held against the theory developed thus far in this book, the case studies offer some unexpected insights. No case study demonstrates the importance of context in directly affecting campaign crises like the Minnesota contest between Norm Coleman, Paul Wellstone, and, after Wellstone's death, Walter Mondale. Although not nearly of the same human toll, Doug Forrester and Bob Torricelli's campaigns in New Jersey both suffered crises that made controlling the strategic environment virtually impossible.

The Case Studies and the Typology of Campaign Crises

As Table 4.1 shows, all the races profiled in the case studies were competitive, suggesting the potential for campaign crises. However, the results can also make those contests look deceptively simple.

Close elections do not necessarily mean that crises occurred. In addition, some margins in the four contests (10 percentage points in the New Jersey

Table 4.1 Election Results for the Case Studies

Candidates	Votes Received	Percentage of Vote Received
Saxby Chambliss (R)	1,071,153	53
Max Cleland (D)	931,857	46
Doug Forrester (R)	928,439	44
Frank Lautenberg (D)	1,138,193	54
Bob Torricelli (D)	—	—
Norm Coleman (R)	1,116,697	50
Walter Mondale (DFL)	1,067,246	47
Paul Wellstone (DFL)	—	—
Maria Cantwell (D)	1,199,437	49
Slade Gorton (R)	1,197,208	49

Source: Data compiled by author from Michael Barone and Richard E. Cohen. 2003. *The Almanac of American Politics 2004*. Washington, DC: National Journal Group.

contest, for example) suggest that the races weren't actually terribly close on Election Day. Indeed, some of the final vote margin was determined by how each campaign had handled crises before voters went to the polls. Therefore, although final results are obviously the most important aspect of any campaign, they are not necessarily an indicator of how those campaigns developed. In fact, crises made each campaign rich and complex.

Each of the case studies was selected to illustrate different dimensions of the typology. The Georgia and New Jersey races are the most complex, offering a variety of crises. Both races involved prominent **external, unexpected** crises in the form of attacks from outside forces. For Max Cleland, political professionals reported that crises included prominent political advertising criticizing the senator on homeland security, even though the Cleland campaign felt homeland security was perhaps its primary strength with voters. Meanwhile, the Saxby Chambliss team reportedly suffered few, if any, notable crises and maintained intense message discipline. The Chambliss team also made inroads in areas of the state that had previously supported Cleland, leading to unexpected vote losses for the incumbent among previously loyal constituents.

In New Jersey, the Torricelli and Forrester teams both suffered **unexpected, internal** and **external** crises. Most notable, Torricelli unexpectedly withdrew from the race shortly before the election, creating a strategic void (and major external crisis) for the Forrester team. An external but expected crisis of negative media coverage and alleged ethical scandal plagued the Torricelli campaign throughout the race, which came on the heels of a US Justice Department investigation. Torricelli was never charged with criminal wrongdoing, but political professionals on both sides said the fallout from the investigation and its accompanying media feeding frenzy created an untenable situation for the incumbent. As the external environment grew more chaotic, both the Torricelli and Forrester organizations encountered internal crises. Although there was comparatively less evidence of organizational problems within Cleland's campaign, members of his team said the campaign was never able to successfully control its strategic environment. In both cases, campaign insiders argued that external crises could have been avoided or mitigated with better crisis management.

The Minnesota and Washington cases are comparatively simple, offering more compartmentalized examples of campaign crises than the Georgia and New Jersey contests. To classify the death of Paul Wellstone, family members, campaign staff, and fight crew as an **external, unexpected** campaign crisis is far too clinical to adequately portray the human tragedy for those affected. But in a theoretical sense, the plane crash that killed Wellstone does represent a major external, unexpected crisis as discussed in this book. The political world was far quieter in Washington State in 2000. The Cantwell-Gorton race exhibited unusual disagreement between political professionals about whether crises occurred at all and, if so, what those crises were. Most notable, members of the Cantwell team said they perceived a last-minute attack on Gorton's involvement in shepherding a controversial mining provision through Congress as a major blow to his campaign. Some members of the Gorton team regarded the attack as an external crisis, even though they expected the attack would come. Other Gorton insiders disagreed that crises occurred in the race, saying it simply represented a hard-fought, but ultimately unsuccessful, effort.

The 2002 Georgia Senate Race

No race explored in this book embodies more passion and heated disagreement than the 2002 Senate contest between Republican challenger Saxby Chambliss and Democratic incumbent Max Cleland. Cleland, a Vietnam veteran and triple amputee, was first elected to the Senate in 1996 after serving as Georgia secretary of state and leading Jimmy Carter's Veterans Administration (VA). At the outset of the 2002 campaign, Cleland's being defeated at least partially on homeland security issues seemed unthinkable. But Chambliss, a GOP congressman from middle Georgia, had established his own defense credentials through his membership on the House Armed Services Committee. Republicans also believed that Cleland's record was not as conservative as the state's political culture suggested it could have been. The contest that followed was one of the fiercest in recent political memory.

In terms of campaign crises, the race is also the most complicated of the four contests studied here. In-depth interviews with both sides revealed that although the race fostered bitterness for many Democrats, Republicans largely regarded it as a well-run campaign based on policy issues and successful campaign tactics. Some Democrats who worked in and around the Cleland campaign reported that they agreed with the Republican assessment, yet they disagreed with some Republican tactics. The interviews offer one of the most thorough published accounts of how decisionmakers inside each campaign felt about the race, what events they believed represented crises, and why each team made the decisions they did. The clearest lesson from the interviews is that Democrats and Republicans had very different—and apparently very genuine—beliefs about what events in their campaigns represented crises, why those events became crises, and what the 2002 Georgia Senate race means for modern campaign politics.

Crises on the Horizon?

Democrats' frustration surrounding Cleland's loss to Chambliss can perhaps be best summed up by Cleland himself. Long before research for this book began, Cleland described feelings of victimization from the 2002 campaign and what he regarded as a broader Republican conspiracy to defeat him. Cleland echoed those same themes in interviews for this book. Many Democrats felt similarly, alleging that Republicans mischaracterized Cleland's voting record on homeland security and rallied white racism through the 72-Hour Task Force, a get-out-the-vote (GOTV) effort designed to mobilize conservative voters favoring gubernatorial candidate Sonny Perdue (R), with the added benefit of defeating Cleland. Most of all, many Democrats said that some television advertising aired against Cleland—and one ad in particular—distorted Cleland's record and represented unethical campaigning. Republicans reported very different perspectives on those events.

As David Mark (2006, 132) explains, Chambliss television advertising represented one of the first major campaign attempts to grapple with homeland security messages following the terrorist attacks of September 11, 2001: "As the [Georgia Senate] race heated up in summer 2002, Chambliss sought to paint Cleland as a liberal Democrat out of touch with Georgia voters." A controversial ad criticizing Cleland's record on homeland security was a major part of that effort. The ad, which began airing in October 2002, stemmed from Senate debate over what form the proposed Department of Homeland Security (DHS) would take. Cleland joined other Democrats in blocking President George W. Bush's "version of the Homeland Security Department plan because it did not include a provision guaranteeing labor rights for federal workers. . . . Cleland's decision to side with the majority Democrats [in the Senate] gave Chambliss an opening to declare his opponent more interested in the fortunes of labor unions than in standing with Bush and beefing up homeland security" (Mark 2006, 133).

Titled "11 Times"[1] for the number of Cleland votes cited, the ad began with images of Osama bin Laden and Saddam Hussein. A voiceover called both "'terrorists and extremist dictators' faced by the United States today" (Kinnard 2002). The ad went on to feature excerpts from Cleland's advertising and emphasized his tagline, saying Cleland was "'claiming he has the courage to lead' but has voted 'against the president's vital homeland security efforts 11 times since July'" (Kinnard 2002). After a transition to "a grainy black-and-white picture of Cleland," a narrator continued, "'Max Cleland says he has the courage to lead, but the record proves he's just misleading'" (Mark 2006, 134). With those closing lines, a large, red "misleading" descends diagonally over Cleland's photo.[2] After prominent Democrats and some media organizations sharply criticized the ad, the opening sequence that featured pictures of Hussein and bin Laden was removed during subsequent airings.

In interviews, Democrats argued that Republicans misled the public about Cleland's voting record and portrayed him as unpatriotic. Those portrayals, Democrats said, were egregious because Cleland's commitment to national security was obvious from his military service and obvious wounds suffered during that service.[3] Members of the Chambliss team and other senior Republicans vigorously refuted these and other Democratic claims.

For Republicans, the "11 Times" ad did not accuse Cleland of being unpatriotic; instead it suggested that his legislative votes on homeland security were irresponsible policy choices. Republicans made similar claims about Cleland's voting record on social issues, highlighted in a hard-hitting series of ten-second ads that aired late in the campaign. Ending with the tagline "Why would he do that?" the ads reinforced the notion that Cleland's positions were allegedly flawed. Republicans argued that Cleland created his own political problems by being out of step with increasingly conservative Georgia voters.

As for the 72-Hour Task Force voter mobilization effort, Republicans acknowledged that high voter turnout in the gubernatorial election helped Chambliss, but they rejected some Democrats' claims of race-baiting. From the Republican perspective, the Chambliss campaign simply pointed out a discrepancy between Cleland and his constituency, which they said had grown worse during Cleland's Senate tenure and which had been previously overlooked during his long service as Georgia secretary of state.

During background research (described in Chapter 2 and the Methodological Appendix), all these events presented themselves as *potential* crises. However, did those inside the campaigns in fact regard them as crises? Were there other events below the public's radar that political professionals described as internal crises? How did these events affect each campaign, and which players inside the campaigns emerged as strategic leaders? What decisions did those leaders make in attempting to manage campaign crises? Below, political professionals from both campaigns answer those questions in their own words.

The Cleland Decisionmaking Team and Organization

In interviews, political professionals in and around the Cleland campaign agreed about who constituted the strategic decisionmaking team. Tommy Thompson held the title of campaign manager, but for all practical purposes he executed the strategic responsibilities of a general political consultant. Karl Struble of the political advertising firm Struble Eichenbaum served as chief media consultant, while Geoff Garin and Fred Yang of the research firm Garin-Hart-Yang shared polling duties. Longtime Cleland confidant Steve Leeds was the campaign chair and a regular participant in strategy sessions. Ray Strother, a consultant for Democrats Zell Miller and Roy Barnes, was responsible for producing Cleland advertisements aired late in the race, in which Miller came to Cleland's defense over homeland security. (Zell Miller was then Georgia's junior US senator and a former governor and enjoyed widespread popularity in the state; Roy Barnes was the sitting governor and was running for reelection in 2002.) Campaign insiders reported that fundraising consultant Carl Chidlow had some of the most regular personal interaction with Cleland. Research director Matt McKenna, deputy campaign manager Sujata Tejwani, and press secretary Jamal Simmons were also sometimes mentioned during interviews as part of the strategic decisionmaking team. Political professionals reported that Cleland, an experienced candidate, was also involved in strategic decisionmaking.

Campaign Crises: The Cleland Team's View

Democrats said they knew that Cleland could face an uphill battle from the beginning. Even before Chambliss officially announced his candidacy, Cleland kicked off his reelection campaign with a prominent tour of the state and $1 million in the bank in April 2001—more than eighteen months before the general election (Baxter 2001; Eversley 2001). Going into the campaign, Republicans conceded that Cleland enjoyed widespread popularity, but they also sought to contrast him with conservative Democrat and fellow senator Zell Miller. In addition, although Cleland was personally popular, some of his policy positions contrasted with those of Georgia voters. Cleland had barely won his first Senate election (Baxter 2001).

The Cleland team focused on three events when asked whether they believed crises had occurred. First, but not necessarily foremost, Democrats identified the "11 Times" ad as a crisis for their campaign. Second, that crisis, said Cleland insiders, was related to a broader crisis undermining support for Cleland's Senate votes on homeland security and social issues. Overall, the impact was to make Cleland appear out of step with the electorate. This included the unexpected decision by the national Veterans of Foreign Wars (VFW) to endorse Chambliss over Cleland.[4] Third, many working in and around the Cleland campaign regarded the gubernatorial race between Barnes and challenger Sonny Perdue, and the massive Republican turnout effort accompanying that race, as a crisis for the Cleland campaign by extension. Overall, however, there was an undercurrent in the interviews suggesting that the greatest crisis for the Cleland campaign might have been that potential crises were not recognized until irreversible damage had occurred. As one senior Democratic insider mused when asked about crises in the Cleland campaign, "Is there such a thing as a crisis when nobody knows there's a crisis? I don't think that there was a good recognition of a crisis [for the Cleland campaign] and so I don't think they operated as if there was a crisis."[5] This sentiment suggests evidence of *organizational* crises for the Cleland campaign, especially strategic differences among Democrats.

The Cleland Campaign's Perspective on Political Advertising as Crises

Political professionals associated with the Cleland campaign cited the "11 Times" ad as a crisis for two reasons, although not all interviewees supported both points. First, several political professionals regarded the ad as the ultimate **unexpected, external** crisis because they believed Republicans waged an unethical attack on Cleland's patriotism by beginning the ad with images of Saddam Hussein and Osama bin Laden, followed shortly by unflattering pictures of Cleland's face, combined with voiceovers implying that Cleland had cast irresponsible votes on homeland security. Democrats favoring this view said they believed that Cleland's commitment to defense and homeland security was obvious due to his physical injuries sustained in Vietnam and by his later service at the Veterans Administration.

Second, many Democrats argued that the "11 Times" ad was factually misleading. Although Democrats acknowledged that Cleland voted against one version of the bill creating the Department of Homeland Security, they also emphasized that Cleland sponsored an alternate version of the bill. Importantly, they said, Cleland's version of the bill preserved DHS employees' ability to join unions, whereas President George W. Bush's preferred version of the bill did not. In either case, the interviews established that most Democrats did not initially believe that Cleland was vulnerable on homeland security. Even if attacks on the issue did occur, Democrats did not expect them to take the form of the "11 Times" ad, or they expected such attacks would not resonate with voters.

According to a Democratic source inside the Cleland campaign, "11 Times" represented a dual crisis for the campaign. From the crisis-typology perspective, the ad represented a classic *strategic disruption* (almost always external and unexpected, as was the case here) because it fundamentally caused the Cleland campaign to stop in its tracks and devise an unexpected plan to manage the crisis and to counterattack. In addition to the mental shock many Democrats said they felt in the aftermath of the ad, the source explained that the campaign also had to devise an unexpected "mini campaign" to assemble surrogates to validate Cleland's record on homeland security and draw media attention to the case in an effort to counterattack.

At the same time, however, many Democrats said that the ad represented a crisis for the Chambliss campaign because of the negative press it generated. Even if the Cleland team could not win the battle, political professionals inside the campaign hoped to blunt the attack with support for Cleland from nationally prominent Democrats. Nonetheless, some Democrats said that even if the Chambliss team suffered a crisis in responding to the negative publicity surrounding the ad, the challenger's campaign responded well. According to the source inside the Cleland campaign:

> Certainly, this was a crisis on [the Chambliss] side as well because whether you agree that it was right or wrong to do it, they had to respond about it. Everyone was calling [the Chambliss campaign asking], "Why did you do this?" "How could you put those two faces in the same ad?" So, that was a crisis on both sides. I think [that] both sides actually handled it pretty well. In the end, we got enough people talking, including [Republican senator] Chuck Hagel [Neb.], threatening to run an ad for us in response to get . . . them to stop the ad. [The Chambliss campaign] did a lot of focus on their message. They never admitted that they were wrong, although pulling [the ad] was an admission.[6] But they never admitted they were wrong. They kept on saying [that they were not criticizing Cleland's patriotism, but his voting record]. And that was their message and they never, ever went off of it. I think it was wrong, I think it was incorrect, but they never went off of it.[7]

Also on homeland security and defense issues, the interviews revealed that the Cleland team was surprised (another **unexpected** crisis) by loss of support among some veterans. No event publicized this crisis more than the national VFW's decision to endorse Chambliss over Cleland on October 9, 2002.[8] Although the endorsement was a surprise to many, and Democrats played down the endorsement as that of a Washington-based group rather than that of individual Georgia veterans, the event accentuated Cleland's complicated relationship with former service members. Although Cleland enjoyed unconditional support from many veterans, others contended that he did not do enough while in the Senate to support Georgia military installations. Some also objected to his alliance with Bill Clinton and with his performance as VA administrator during the Carter administration (Tharpe 2002). Cleland campaign manager Tommy Thompson explained:

> The VFW PAC endorsement of Saxby Chambliss to me was a moment of crisis within that campaign because it was portrayed in the media as the VFW, Veterans [of] Foreign Wars organization, endorsed a candidate who had never served in the military versus one who had a very high profile due to his disabilities and injuries in Vietnam. [In the minds of swing voters] it changed a perception that they had believed to be a truism of Senator Cleland, which was that he was "the veteran's best friend" by virtue of his prior career with the Veterans Administration and his service to his country and so forth. And that endorsement I thought was critical in casting some doubt in [the] persuadable voter's mind. . . . "Is there something else there that is different than what we had believed?" . . . That was a real crisis for us, I thought. . . . This one just seemed to really cut into Max.[9]

Some political professionals also regarded the Chambliss campaign's series of ten-second spots asking about various Cleland votes "Why would he do that?" as crises for the Democrat's campaign. Social issues were especially prominent in those ads. Two of the more potent ads cited Cleland's votes on the so-called morning-after pill and in support for needle exchanges for drug users. As with the "11 Times" ad, Democrats countered that the commercials mischaracterized Cleland's record. As the section on Chambliss's strategy discusses, these ads were a central element in portraying Cleland as out of touch with Georgia voters.

Unlike many campaign crises, the interview data revealed that the Cleland campaign knew that some of these attacks were coming. It had even been provided with scripts of some opposition ads in advance by a source whose identity was unknown even to some inside the Cleland decision-making team.[10] Yet even with an expected crisis, some inside the Cleland campaign said that not enough was done to prepare to counterattack. According to a Democratic source inside the Cleland campaign,

We knew they [the ten-second ads] were coming. But we also knew that when they did come, it'd be a very, very tough thing to overcome because it's a very conservative state. Even the suburban women who like Max generally . . . freak out about [some of the issues cited in the ads]. Frankly, for something that we knew was coming, we didn't prepare for it. So, in that situation, it was a crisis in that we knew it was coming and [did not adequately] respond to it.[11]

Two other advertising and message issues suggest possible crises for the Cleland campaign. First, the data revealed potential message problems for Cleland when the Chambliss campaign used Miller's image and voting record against Cleland. Second, Cleland also said during an interview that the memorial service for Paul Wellstone and others killed in a Minnesota plane crash shortly before the election contributed to Cleland's defeat. According to Cleland, the national media attention on the Wellstone memorial provided another reason for conservative voters, even in Georgia, to bolt from Democrats. (Chapter 7 reveals that even many Democrats believed that the memorial was politically damaging for the party, at least in Minnesota and perhaps beyond.) Most Democrats were undecided in interviews about whether the Wellstone memorial hurt the Cleland campaign specifically. Many Republicans agreed with Cleland that the political fallout from the Wellstone memorial represented a crisis for the Cleland campaign and other Democrats. In general, however, political professionals exhibited less agreement on these points than with their views on the "11 Times" and the broader homeland security issue—at least from the Cleland campaign's perspective.

The Cleland Team's Perception of the 72-Hour Task Force and the Flag Issue

Max Cleland, and many who worked for him, said during interviews that they believed the Chambliss campaign represented a much larger effort than one Senate campaign. For many Democratic political professionals, the 72-Hour Task Force GOTV effort and the attacks on Cleland's record on homeland security were dual crises that distorted Cleland's record in voters' minds and created an untenable strategic environment. They believed these crises resulted from unethical tactics employed by the Chambliss campaign. Specifically, Cleland argued that the Chambliss campaign was orchestrated by the White House via political consultant Karl Rove and Georgia Republican Party chairman Ralph Reed. Cleland and other Democrats also argued that the 72-Hour Task Force tacitly rallied white racism around Barnes's decision to change the state flag by replacing a fifty-year-old version featuring the Confederate battle emblem with one that featured a blue field and small images of all the state's previous flags. The larger controversy over the flag issue, some Democrats said, was a major factor in the gubernatorial campaign and, by extension, in the race between Cleland and Chambliss. Republicans, whose views appear later in this chapter, strongly disagreed.

Cleland was vocal on both points:

> [The race] turned out to be a disaster from the top of the ticket down. . . . Visibly, there was a defining moment in that ad campaign [the "11 Times" ad] . . . [but] I had actually volunteered to fight the war against terrorism . . . and lost a good part of my body [in Vietnam, for] which I'm decorated for valor, against the man who got out [of going] to Vietnam. . . . And yet, [President George W.] Bush came down and laid it on [for Chambliss]. . . . So that was the public side, that was [what] people perceived around the nation. But underneath all that was Ralph Reed's organization that had taken maximum advantage of the white backlash accruing from the Barnes change of the flag and taking away the Confederate emblem, and Reed translating that into, "Democrats [are] trying to take away Georgia's culture." So you had the maximum extent of fraudulent advertising and fraudulent messages at work funded by millions of dollars, basically out of Washington. That's how the White House won, and it was the White House that won.[12]

Members of Cleland's campaign team were generally more moderate than the senator during interviews, but they agreed with most of his sentiments. Even those who did not accuse Republicans of race-baiting said that the connection between conservative whites on the flag issue and Republican turnout was undeniable. According to campaign manager Tommy Thompson:

> It was the issue that generated the enthusiasm within that group of voters that when they were communicated [to] often enough with that message of, "Governor Barnes is after our heritage—those people in Atlanta." Rural Georgia sort of views itself almost separate from Atlanta. And that "those people in Atlanta" [sentiment], I think that has racial overtones to it as well. . . . And Roy Barnes was the king of "those people" and, therefore, he was the one "trying to take away our heritage." I think that that message was articulated to those particular people [white conservatives] often enough and in a manner that was very effective with getting them energized. And in doing so, the president coming in and grabbing Saxby Chambliss and Sonny Perdue by the hand and tying those two races together, it made it important then for those voters to get out and turn out for those two candidates.[13]

Ray Strother, a central figure in the Barnes campaign and adviser to the Cleland campaign on its commercials featuring Zell Miller, expressed similar sentiment. When asked to respond to staunch Republican denials of race-baiting, Strother answered:

> It was a campaign that no one would be terribly proud of, to tell you the truth. Mechanically, it was a beautiful campaign. But philosophically . . . I don't care what they say, and I respect them very much, but the way they used race in that campaign was pretty insidious. And what they did about patriotism. And part of that patriotism problem was ours in that we should have attacked that and we should have attacked our opponent. "The only patriotism is military service"; we should have gone right at him and we didn't. . . . They knew they had an advantage going in and they used it.[14]

Similarly, Cleland media consultant Karl Struble responded to Republican rebuttals that the flag was an issue in the gubernatorial campaign, not the Senate campaign:

> Talking about the Confederate flag is racial. . . . To say that somehow or another, "Well, we only did it in the governor's race. We didn't do it in the Senate race," is like saying, "I'll tell you what, I put my hood on for the Klan; I only singled out the blacks, not the Jews." It's almost the same thing. You are fanning the flames of racial prejudice when you do that. They know it. . . . Sure [the Chambliss campaign] didn't [use the flag in their campaign]. They may not have used it in their campaign. They benefited from the party doing it. They are part of the party. They have some responsibility for what the party's doing. They were responsible for putting us next to Osama bin Laden. So, we're [characterized as] an un-American [candidate] that wants to trample the rights of God-fearing, white voters. Tell me it's not part of the whole thing.[15]

However, even Struble argued that the impacts of the "11 Times" ad and the 72-Hour Task Force were not the biggest obstacles that the campaign faced. In fact, some Democrats also believed that the media overplayed the impact of the Cleland team's campaign crises, including the "11 Times" ad and the 72-Hour Task Force, in determining the outcome of the race—even though Democrats rejected the Chambliss campaign's tactics as allegedly unethical. For these few (yet influential) political professionals associated with the Cleland campaign, homeland security and the 72-Hour Task Force exacerbated Cleland's loss but did not cause it per se. Indeed, a source familiar with Cleland's polling agreed with the Republican claim that even though the 72-Hour Task Force created helpful context for Chambliss, it did not cost Cleland the election: "If we had [lost] by one point, I would argue more. Yeah, given the margin [Chambliss] won by, I think that's a fair point."[16]

Strategic Differences Among Democrats

The interviews also suggested potential *organizational* crises for the Cleland campaign. As noted previously, some inside the Cleland campaign were frustrated by an alleged failure to strongly counterattack the Republican characterization of Cleland's positions on homeland security. These and other comments suggested significant strategic differences within the campaign and at least the potential for organizational crises. Some Democratic sources reported that they had doubts about Cleland's ability to win the race from the beginning because of his comparatively liberal voting record. One Democrat complained that far too much money was spent on political advertising, with virtually no attention to field efforts. Others complained that Roy Barnes's alleged failure to secure strong backing from typically Democratic constituencies, such as teachers, hurt Cleland by extension.

Cleland manager Tommy Thompson conceded that the campaign could have been more aggressive, but he added that Cleland's loss sent a warning to future incumbents seeking reelection:

> What [the Chambliss campaign] did was, I thought, in many ways, predictable. . . . Traditionally, incumbent-type campaigns are analogous to a football game. It's the fourth quarter and you got a two-touchdown lead and so what you're doing is protecting that lead. In my mind, at least professionally, if I ever were in a position to manage again a race like an incumbent-protection campaign, I would not approach it the same way and I would run a much more aggressive challenger-type race.[17]

Struble agreed:

> I think that we were not quite as aware of the enormous amount of money that was sent in and the organization that was put together, that was built out of motivated, Christian conservatives and rural, white interests. That meant that you had skewed turnout. If you would have told me from the very beginning that there would have been that turnout model that [occurred] . . . then we would have probably conducted the campaign differently.[18]

Democrats also said that Cleland faced strategic obstacles long before the campaign began. During interviews, campaign staff complained of legislative staff allegedly doing too little to establish a notable policy record for Cleland during his Senate tenure. Although they did not explicitly blame the Senate staff for Cleland's loss, political professionals said that during Cleland's Senate tenure the legislative staff missed important opportunities to cast Cleland as a moderate Democrat and to shore up constituencies that the Chambliss campaign later converted to the Republican side. Political professionals also charged the Senate staff with being politically unsophisticated and the victims of groupthink that reinforced a perception that Cleland did not need to build a policy portfolio that he could later translate into campaign issues.[19] (In fairness to the Senate staff, however, because they were not identified as members of the strategic campaign team they were not solicited for interviews.)

In addition to strategic differences among many Democrats, interviews suggested concerns about the Cleland campaign's strategic data. At least three political professionals associated with the Cleland campaign reported concerns about the validity of the team's polling data. One political professional suggested that the polling team underestimated turnout among conservative voters in Cleland tracking polls, although the source was quick to add that the methodology was consistent with modern polling practices:

> Let me say that I saw things in the polling that were never completely, adequately described to me. When I look at polling and I see that we're being attacked, let's say on education, I expect that my numbers might go down on education. But if I'm being attacked on education, but my numbers are going down in standing up for strong defense, on the economy, on a whole bunch of other things, then there's something more. . . . The image . . . of Max Cleland had been taking hits. It wasn't explained by the media [coverage] that I was being told about. And there was a second thing that was happening in the polling. . . . What we came to find out [was] we were having a situation where there were more people that were identifying themselves [in polls] as Republicans than traditionally you find [so polling data was being weighted to portray a more typical sample].
>
> *Author:* So, what essentially the polls were reflecting [was] a sample that did not reflect the [population] that turned out on Election Day?
>
> *Cleland insider:* Exactly. That's what most pollsters do. Do I say it's poor polling? No. That's what most pollsters would have done. It doesn't mean that's what served Max right or it should be the way you do it in the future.[20]

Some political professionals also said that because the polling data allegedly overestimated likely support for Cleland, the Democratic Senatorial

Campaign Committee (DSCC) did not provide sufficient financial resources to the campaign. In the words of one political professional, "The DSCC committed malpractice" with respect to the Cleland campaign.[21]

However, a political professional familiar with Cleland's polling refuted claims that the polls paid too little attention to conservative whites: "As a matter of fact, two or three polls that [polling firm Garin-Hart-Yang] did do for the Cleland campaign after Labor Day . . . [the firm] did those polls among white voters and not just all voters. And so, [the firm] looked pretty specifically at white men, white women, older whites, whites by area," including the areas in which Chambliss did well.[22] In addition, this political professional noted that the Cleland team was relying on polls commissioned by the gubernatorial campaign, not those conducted by Garin-Hart-Yang, for daily tracking in the Senate race. Indeed, pollster Geoff Garin explained that because of Barnes's substantial fundraising, the Cleland campaign commissioned few of its own polls, relying instead largely on Barnes polling that included questions about the Senate campaign. Garin also reported that the polling team made the Cleland campaign aware of potential difficulties with conservative whites targeted by Chambliss well before the election:

> [Polling] was important. We did a poll early in the summer. I remember meeting with Senator Cleland and others in the campaign [and concluding that] . . . as soon as Chambliss started to define himself, we needed to [be] more aggressive in defining him. I think the greatest failing and lapse in the campaign was in not doing that in a meaningful or effective way . . . the Senate campaign committee was doing issue advertising. I don't think the issue advertising carried as much of the burden of defining Chambliss as we hoped it would. I think in retrospect, we should have been much more focused defining Chambliss as our most important task in the campaign. We just didn't do that.[23]

The Chambliss Decisionmaking Team and Organization

The interview data suggested the presence of a small decisionmaking group within the Chambliss team. Tom Perdue served as general consultant to the campaign and, by all accounts from the Republican side, was the major strategist.[24] At different points, the Chambliss campaign had two managers. During the primary, longtime Chambliss aide and congressional chief of staff Rob Leebern managed the campaign. After the primary, Republican operative Bo Harmon replaced Leebern as manager. Leebern continued to be heavily involved in the Chambliss campaign's field efforts even after his departure as manager. Gene Ulm and Neil Newhouse of Public Opinion

Strategies served as pollsters for the Chambliss campaign, while Scott Howell and Company served as media consultant. Political professionals said that Tom Perdue also played a significant role in the Chambliss campaign's message strategy. According to Ulm, Chambliss provided an overall vision for the campaign but relied on Tom Perdue to turn that vision into strategy. Nonetheless, several political professionals reported that Chambliss was personally involved in all major campaign decisions.

Republicans in and around the Chambliss campaign flatly denied Democratic charges that Ralph Reed, Karl Rove, or national Republicans ran the Senate campaign. According to Ulm, "I never talked to Karl Rove or Ralph Reed about this race. I doubt that either one of them could pick me out of a lineup of one." He added flatly, "Tom Perdue ran that campaign."[25]

National Republican Senatorial Committee (NRSC) political director Chris LaCivita concurred:

> Ralph [Reed] had no role in the [Chambliss] campaign. None. . . . As chairman of the party, [the NRSC] basically ran our ads through him. But Ralph deserves some credit for building the party and building the grassroots. But he had no role in the campaign. . . . Did the White House play a role? Of course they did. You know, the president went down there, campaigned for Saxby . . . [but the] day-to-day strategic decisions weren't being made from the White House. That's absurd. They were being made by the campaign. . . . The millions that [the NRSC] spent in issue advocacies wasn't being dictated by the White House. They were being driven by polling data. We just had a better team in place and a better candidate and a better message at the end of the day. Yet the Democrats are always looking for the bogeyman.[26]

LaCivita also noted that the NRSC "didn't really become fully engaged" until a few weeks before the end of the campaign when it became clear that Chambliss had a legitimate chance to defeat Cleland.

Campaign Crises: The Chambliss Team's View

Political professionals on both sides said during interviews that the Cleland team never saw many of its crises coming—or at least not in the way they came. Conversely, although causing crises for the Cleland team was apparently central to the Chambliss victory strategy, the Republican team suffered few, if any, crises of its own. Specifically, some Republicans associated with the Chambliss campaign said that their side did, in fact, suffer crises, but they described those events as minor compared with those the Cleland campaign expected. For example, Ulm reported that the

Chambliss campaign lacked a clear plan to effectively spend the massive amounts of money it had raised leading up to the primary.[27] However, the political impact from such events pales in comparison to the perpetual crises affecting the Cleland campaign.

Discussion of Chambliss's crises also lacked the consistency exhibited in interviews with members of the Cleland team; the latter displayed broad agreement that crises occurred for the incumbent. From a crisis-typology perspective, the interviews suggested that the Chambliss team intended to cause multiple **unexpected, external** crises for the Cleland campaign, especially on Cleland's voting record and all it allegedly represented to conservative voters. From a practical perspective, the Chambliss campaign might or might not agree that it intended to cause crises per se but instead intended to execute a solid strategy to win the election. In either case, the strategy worked. Therefore, the Chambliss team—and even most of the Cleland team—agreed during interviews that the challenger's campaign suffered few, if any, crises of its own. Indeed, mitigating organizational problems before they became crises, and controlling the external environment at Cleland's expense, may well explain why Chambliss won. As Ulm said during one interview, some campaigns are less about strategy and more about which side "screws up least" in executing that strategy.[28]

In contrast to Chambliss's smooth sailing, the Cleland campaign, most Republicans said during interviews, represented the epitome of a *constant crisis,* with one crisis perpetually creating others. LaCivita, for example, replied when asked about the Cleland campaign:

> I think their campaign was an ongoing crisis. [It was] just their inability to really sense what was going on in the state. Nineteen ninety-four finally caught up with Georgia [in] 2002.[29] They [the Cleland campaign] did not sense that. And they made the assumption that because their candidate was a decorated war veteran who left three limbs on the battlefield that that would be a strong enough reason to reelect him. And it wasn't— especially when you're able to point out that he had a [poor] record on national defense.[30]

The Chambliss Campaign's Perspective on Political Advertising as Crises

Republicans flatly rejected Democratic charges that the "11 Times" ad criticized Cleland's patriotism. Instead, they said the ad took issue with politically irresponsible votes. Political professionals inside the Chambliss campaign also said that the challenger's political advertising reflected an important contrast between the two candidates. Many Democrats, and some Republicans, regarded the Chambliss team's decision to air the "11 Times" ad as a crisis for the potential public backlash it might (and in some cases did) create. However, even Republicans who grudgingly acknowledged that the ad represented a potential crisis for their campaign said the risk was relatively small and short-lived. For example, even though LaCivita said the ad "approached" a crisis for the Chambliss campaign, it also accomplished an important strategic goal by reaffirming contrasts between Chambliss and Cleland. Although the ad "generated an awful lot of controversy" in media coverage, it reportedly did not hurt Chambliss's polling numbers.[31] In any case, LaCivita and many other political professionals on both sides asserted that the ad did not, in and of itself, cause Chambliss's win or Cleland's loss. According to Chambliss's Senate chief of staff, Krister Holladay:

> I think there were some who believed [the ad] was a crisis. There were people who wanted to make it a crisis. I think the overreaction to the ad by some folks was over the top—the Democratic reaction. It certainly made some of our folks nervous because of that overreaction. But, again, we stuck to our game plan. It didn't distract us. We stayed on message and focus. What they claimed, [that] we compared Senator Cleland to Osama bin Laden and Saddam Hussein, is incorrect. So, from our standpoint, that was factually incorrect. Because of the response, we took those pictures out. But the rest of the ad was still the same. They didn't come back at that point.[32]

Chambliss general consultant Tom Perdue also reportedly rejected Democratic claims that the ad represented an attack on Cleland's patriotism. According to author David Mark (2006, 135), who interviewed Perdue, although the campaign initially did not intend to focus on homeland security issues,

> what changed that political calculus, Perdue said, was a Cleland ad showing himself with Bush, saying he had voted with the president on homeland security issues eleven times. Some of those votes had taken place in committee and some on the Senate floor (the picture of Bush and Cleland together was taken during tax cut negotiations in 2001). Chambliss' campaign felt the senator's claim dramatically misrepresented his real voting record; so now homeland security issues were back on the table. . . . Perdue said the ["11 Times"][33] spot was entirely fair and accurate, since it was based on Cleland's votes. . . . As for the commercial's controversial images, the pictures of Saddam Hussein and Osama bin Laden were never intended to draw a comparison with Senator Cleland, Perdue said.

Nonetheless, the Chambliss campaign does appear to have suffered a near-miss in the form of an **unexpected, external** crisis surrounding the backlash to the "11 Times" ad. Several sources associated with the Cleland campaign reported during interviews that Senator Chuck Hagel (R) like Cleland, a Vietnam veteran, took offense at the ad and was negotiating with the Cleland campaign to publicly condemn the spot. According to Tommy Thompson, "I actually had conversations with Senator Hagel and sent some suggested scripts for an advertisement that he was going to produce at his own cost to run and disavow what the Republicans were doing to Senator Cleland."[34] Chambliss campaign manager Bo Harmon confirmed during an interview that the campaign agreed to drop the opening segment featuring images of Saddam Hussein and Osama bin Laden after Hagel threatened to publicly side with Cleland. However, Harmon also added that the decision came only after substantial debate within the campaign in which it was determined that the opening segment distracted attention from the campaign's intended message that Cleland's votes were allegedly irresponsible policy choices.[35]

These and other comments suggest that "11 Times" was the central issue dividing Democratic and Republican political professionals' assessments of the Cleland-Chambliss race. While Democrats viewed the ad as a distortion of Cleland's record, Republicans viewed it as a factual contrast based on public positions. In addition, while Democrats took offense at what they believed was a comparison between Cleland, Saddam Hussein, and bin Laden, some political professionals associated with the Chambliss campaign said that uniting the three figures never occurred to them when the ad was in production. Instead, some Republicans said they were concerned about the language in the ad rather than the imagery. As Harmon explained:

> The pictures in the ads [were] just [saying], "This is who we're facing. We are up against Saddam Hussein and Osama bin Laden." . . . I was nervous that we were going to be accused of questioning [Cleland's] courage to do that, by using his tagline [which emphasized "the courage to lead"]. But [Democrats] took an entire different tack and said we were questioning his patriotism, which was never the case, and then also comparing him to Saddam Hussein and Osama bin Laden [was] just certainly never the case. [Inside the campaign we] talked about it with several people. We had a fairly extensive internal conversation about whether or not we should use his tagline. And it turned out that that wasn't the issue that anybody even noticed.[36]

Chambliss press secretary Michelle Hitt agreed:

Here's what's really funny about that ad. I saw that ad before it went out. Tom Perdue had to have it and would let us preview things. He wanted just cold reaction to know what you thought. I never even saw those pictures [the opening segment with bin Laden, Saddam, and Cleland] in there. It was up and down so fast. I remember the day we started getting calls about it. I said, "Wait a minute. Where's the tape? Somebody get the tape. I don't remember seeing that in there." We played the tape again and we paused it. We were like, "Oh, yeah, it is. It's right there." We didn't even see it. We were more concerned about what the impact would be of some of the language in it and not the images.[37]

Cleland media consultant Karl Struble, however, took issue with Republican claims that the ad focused on words, not images. As Struble asserted, "Images are more important on television than words. I don't care what the words said."[38]

On another political advertising note, Harmon explained that the series of ten-second spots asking voters "Why would he do that?" in reference to Cleland votes was intended to cause crises for the Democrat's campaign by rotating the ads, each featuring a different message, throughout the state's media markets. The inexpensive ads were central to the Chambliss strategy of constantly hitting the Cleland team. They also reinforced Chambliss's attempts to overtake Cleland in traditionally Democratic parts of the state.[39] Although these ads received some substantial attention during the campaign, they were not the focus of interview comments regarding potential crises.

The Chambliss Team's Perception of the
72-Hour Task Force and the Flag Issue

Republican political professionals rejected Democratic charges that the GOP's 72-Hour Task Force GOTV effort relied on racist appeals. Republicans also refuted Democratic claims that the Chambliss campaign played up an underlying controversy in the gubernatorial campaign surrounding the change to the state flag. When asked to respond to the Democrats' charge that the 72-Hour Task Force implicitly or explicitly rallied white racism surrounding the flag issue, NRSC political director Chris LaCivita said pointedly:

Bullshit. I mean, for the record, that's just bull. That's a typical Democrat. I would expect the Democrats to say that. Democrats can't come to grips with the fact that their message and their candidate's record of higher taxes, crappy support for national defense and voting against the homeland security bill—they can't come to grips with the fact that the people of Georgia rejected that. It wasn't built on racism. The Democrats are always the ones that will scream it. But that's flat out not true.[40]

Another Republican strategist called Democratic claims of connections between alleged racism, the flag issue, and voter-mobilization efforts "revisionist history." The strategist said,

Well, the way I would respond to that is to point out that not a single piece of literature, and not a single phone call or single voter communication undertaken by the Georgia Republican Party in 2002, mentioned the flag. It was not included in any literature. There was not a single radio ad that aired on that issue. There was not a single piece of literature there on that issue.[41]

The strategist also pointed out that two African American Democrats were successfully elected down-ballot to statewide offices, calling into question the impact of race on statewide campaigns. Democrats acknowledged the point but countered that those candidates faced little serious opposition.

Despite widespread anger among Democrats about the flag issue and the 72-Hour Task Force, a few political professionals departed from their colleagues' views. Some Democratic sources affiliated with the Cleland campaign partially agreed with Chambliss team members' claims that even though the flag issue and related GOP turnout helped Chambliss, those issues were not deciding factors in the race.

Context and Missed Strategic Opportunities for the Cleland Campaign

Although context greatly benefited the Chambliss campaign, political professionals said that it limited Cleland's ability to effectively counterattack. For example, after "11 Times" aired, the Cleland side reported in interviews that it was ready to counterattack regarding Chambliss's lack of military service and, by doing so, attempt to create a crisis for the opposition. Political professionals also said they wanted to press the media to investigate Chambliss's allegedly changing accounts of why he had not served. However, according to a Democratic source inside the Cleland campaign, the campaign waited too late—just as some say it did in counterattacking generally—to explain the complicated series of Chambliss deferments: "When we finally decided to do it, it was too late. It was too complicated to start so late."[42]

Republicans dismissed the point, saying that Chambliss had a documented student deferment and a knee injury that always prevented him from military service. Chambliss's Senate chief of staff, Krister Holladay, acknowledged that the deferments were complicated to communicate to voters but explained that the Chambliss campaign did not view the event as a crisis because the Republican team had a clear plan for presenting its own message:

> You normally think of a crisis as an event. I think instead of thinking of it as an event, in terms of a challenge, the issue about Mr. Chambliss' military service or nonmilitary service—his deferment because of a knee injury, student deferment and then medical deferment—communicating that [had to be addressed]. I don't know that I'd call it necessarily a crisis because we believed we had the right answer and the right response. But it was a challenge in terms of communicating that and making sure that the message got out and that it was appropriately delivered. . . . Specifically . . . we had a "Veterans for Chambliss" group . . . who believed that Mr. Chambliss was the right candidate. Mr. Chambliss [also] got the endorsement of the VFW.[43]

Throughout the campaign, the Cleland team was not so fortunate. For example, timing and organization limited its ability to exploit a potential Chambliss crisis shortly after the September 11 terrorist attacks. Chambliss reportedly suggested during a November 2001 meeting of emergency responders in Valdosta, Georgia, that the county sheriff "arrest every Muslim that crosses the state line" (Savage 2001). In addition to the inflammatory nature of the alleged comments, the Chambliss campaign faced a potential crisis because, according to press accounts, the candidate sought to limit media coverage of the comments. The *Washington Post* reported that "Chambliss, according to sources in Valdosta, personally sought to persuade the [*Valdosta Daily Times*] reporter, Bill Roberts, to kill the story using his remarks, and asked the local sheriff to help block publication [but that] an aide to Chambliss said he did not know what the congressman did in connection with the story" (Edsall 2001). Chambliss later complained that media reports took his comments out of context, but he apologized to those offended by the remarks (Edsall 2001; Savage 2001). Press secretary Michelle Hitt argued the event was more a crisis for Chambliss's congressional office than for the campaign. In any case, the episode received little long-term traction.[44]

Political professionals said that context was not on the Cleland campaign's side in turning the alleged Valdosta comments into a full-fledged crisis for the Chambliss campaign. The Valdosta meeting was on Monday,

November 19, 2001. Thanksgiving fell on Thursday, November 22. The fact that the comments occurred during a holiday week, and because the Cleland reelection organization was in its infancy at the time, the Democrat was unable to effectively launch strategic attacks over the comments, as it might have later in the race. Cleland research director Matt McKenna explained:

> I was actually that day on a plane on my way home to Montana for Thanksgiving. [Campaign manager] Tommy [Thompson] was in a car on his way home for Thanksgiving. Everyone was scattered all around everywhere. So this crisis management was being conducted [on] laptops in airports and via bad cell phone connections and leaving messages with people. . . . I think that had [Chambliss] made that comment at a time when we had an actual [campaign] apparatus, a mechanism to move [a] real message, I think we could have made it stick a little bit for him. . . . I think we could've really turned it into an effective hit had we had the structure in place to do that.[45]

The Chambliss Campaign on the Offensive: Crises and Geography

The Chambliss campaign strategy, either intentionally or coincidentally, contributed to what many political professionals said they believed were perpetual crises for the Cleland campaign. According to the interviews, the Chambliss victory strategy revolved around two main issues: portraying Cleland as too liberal for conservative Georgians, especially on homeland security and contentious social issues, and emphasizing Chambliss's strong ties to middle Georgia, an area heavily influenced by Warner Robbins Air Force Base and agriculture—two generally conservative constituencies.[46] Although the area historically voted Democratic, the Chambliss team believed that a hawkish stance on defense and social conservatism could convince swing voters to come to the Republican side. It felt similarly about swing voters in Republican-leaning Atlanta suburbs. The strategy worked.

Chambliss pollster Gene Ulm explained that from the Republican team's perspective, geography represented a totally unexpected crisis for the Cleland side. Ulm speculated that the Cleland team missed the significance of Chambliss's geographic advantage by paying too much attention to Cleland's overall statewide support and not enough to Chambliss's strong showing in Republican-leaning areas that became essential to the 72-Hour Task Force's mobilization efforts.[47] Although these comments are not entirely consistent with Democratic complaints of sampling problems in the Cleland polls, they do reinforce the overall impression (from both sides) that the Cleland campaign or Democrats generally underestimated conservative turnout going into the election.

Geography, and the contrast with conservative Democratic senator Zell Miller, were also central to the Chambliss strategy. Chambliss relied on his natural constituency in middle Georgia and increasingly conservative suburban Atlanta, including outlying areas in north Georgia. As part of its efforts to contrast Cleland and Miller in these and other nominally Democratic areas, the Chambliss campaign aired a unique ad titled "Zell and Max" late in the campaign. Although it was aired by the Chambliss campaign, the ad was devoted almost entirely to two Democrats' voting records. The voiceover told voters that "Zell Miller shares our Georgia values. Max Cleland does not." The ad closed by imploring voters to "replace Max with Sax." Only in the ad's final two frames were there any references to Chambliss.[48]

The Cleland campaign responded with ads of its own featuring Miller. Miller spoke to the camera, telling voters, "My friend Max Cleland and I have voted the same four out of five times in the Senate" and, saying of the Chambliss ads featuring Miller, "Don't let them fool you."[49] However, the effort was not enough to revive Cleland's reputation on national security for many voters. Although Democrats charged that Republicans mischaracterized Cleland's record, Republicans reiterated that Cleland's record was not sufficiently conservative for Georgia's political climate. According to Ulm, "Max Cleland was no Zell Miller. He was out of line with those undecided voters—way out of line. And we had a voting record to prove it."[50]

Indeed, Cleland's alleged liberalism was the most puzzling aspect of the race for many associated with the Chambliss campaign. When invited to pose questions to the Cleland team, Ulm responded, "The thing I can't figure out for the life of me is why the Democrats made him toe the line on so many votes," including taxes, abortion, and homeland security. Why, Ulm asked, did party officials not encourage Cleland to vote like Miller or at least be more moderate?[51]

Former Chambliss House chief of staff and initial Senate campaign manager Rob Leebern agreed, arguing that Cleland created campaign crises for himself with his Senate votes:

I think [the Cleland campaign] had a crisis in their voting record. . . . And I think they made strategic decisions to vote more with the Democratic leadership than they did with the voters in Georgia. And I think that had them dealing with a crisis almost everyday on a litany of issues. It was not that we were having to look for a needle in a haystack. It was the fact that the needles stacked up so high as we tried to figure out which ones would most resonate with voters. And there were a lot of them. So I think his voting record and his actual recorded decisions on the US Senate floor were, in large part, responsible for a lot of his crises that he could not explain.[52]

Democrats offered mixed responses. Some political professionals simply said that Cleland was moderate and supported Bush on some issues but got caught up in a difficult campaign environment exacerbated by Republicans who distorted the incumbent's record. Others said that even though Cleland was moderate by national standards, he was liberal for Georgia. In either case, Democratic political professionals emphasized that Cleland's votes were principled.

Perhaps similarly, some Republicans suggested that the race represented a natural course of events, not necessarily an example of great campaign crises. According to one Republican strategist:

I think if you look at the 2002 US Senate race, I think in the end it is not that much different than the 1996 US Senate race that was also very close but which Cleland won. . . . Georgia [was] trending Republican, and some of that trend caught up with Cleland and, for that matter, with [Governor Roy] Barnes. And there were a lot of people who had moved into Georgia [and] a lot of those people didn't know Cleland. And they'd never voted for him. They had no connection to him. And so he really needed to reintroduce himself to the people of Georgia and make again a case for why he should remain in the Senate. And I just think he failed to do that. I think that the two things that were different between 2002 and 1996, and the reason why we ultimately prevailed, is because Saxby Chambliss was one of the best, if not the best, US Senate candidate we had ever fielded. . . . And I think the second thing that we had in 2002 that we did not have in 1996 was George W. Bush. His job approval rating in Georgia in October of 2002 was 72 percent. And Max Cleland was voting against George W. Bush in Congress, even as the president was enormously popular here.[53]

Concluding Comments on Crises in the Cleland-Chambliss Race

When Max Cleland's campaign began in April 2001, he looked vulnerable but strong. *Atlanta Journal-Constitution* reporter Tom Baxter speculated that Cleland's success or failure would depend largely on political context:

A couple of factors he can do nothing about play heavily into the perception that the Georgia Democrat will indeed face a sharp challenge next year. One is the uncertainty of Georgia's eight Republican U.S. House members, who will have their new districts drawn for them this summer by a Democratic Legislature. That creates a ready-made list of potential statewide candidates. The other is the relative strength of his fellow Democrat, Gov. Roy Barnes, who also will be on the ballot in 2002, and Sen. Zell Miller, who handily won his statewide race last fall. Cleland, on the other hand, won his first Senate race by only 30,000 votes. That makes his race next year as the most likely escape valve for Republican ambition. (Baxter 2001)

The 2002 Georgia Senate race represented an "escape valve" not only for multiple Republican ambitions but also, arguably, for voters. It could be that Max Cleland was simply in the wrong place at the wrong time. To take the Republican view reflected in the interviews, Cleland had long been out of step with conservative Georgia politics. According to this logic, Saxby Chambliss represented an acceptable alternative for those who had long wanted to vote Republican. He represented a candidate closer to conservative Democrat Zell Miller, especially to middle Georgians who, Republicans believed, voted Democratic more out of habit than modern conviction. Under different circumstances, but in a race that many observers said represented a similar Republican strategy, incumbent Democratic senator Mary Landrieu survived a runoff in Louisiana one month after Cleland's defeat; many believed that outcome was affect by lessons learned from the Cleland loss (Baxter 2002).

Many Democratic political professionals conceded that context caught up with Cleland. However, they also said that parts of that context were unnecessary and unethical. What Democrats regarded as inaccurate and unethical attacks on Cleland's record on homeland security were, for Republicans, accurate statements reflecting poor decisions made by Cleland himself. In either case, the context surrounding the 2002 Senate race in Georgia revolved around crises for the Cleland campaign. As Chapter 5 demonstrates, the same was true for Democrat Bob Torricelli in New Jersey.

Notes

1. There is conflicting evidence about the ad's title. "11 Times" is the title listed in National Journal's "Ad Spotlight" feature. David Mark (2006, 133–139), citing interviews with Chambliss campaign manager Tom Perdue, refers to the ad's title as "Courage." The storyboard for the ad, contained in Campaign Media Analysis Group

(CMAG) data made available through the Wisconsin Advertising Project (Goldstein and Rivlin 2005), is titled "GA/Chambliss Cleland Bush" (Creative ID #2669439).

2. The description of the red "misleading" is based on the author's observation of the ad on nationaljournal.com's "Ad Spotlight" feature; http://nationaljournal.com .proxyau.wrlc.org/members/adspotlight/2002/10/1015scga1.htm; accessed December 12, 2006.

3. On Cleland's perspective on his military service, injuries, and VA service, see Cleland (1980).

4. Interview comments and media accounts refer alternatively to endorsement by the VFW and by a VFW political action committee (PAC). Because of legal restrictions on tax-exempt and nonprofit organizations' political activities, the endorsement likely came from a VFW PAC, not the VFW itself.

5. Democratic official, personal interview with author, May 2004, Washington, D.C. Additional information omitted to protect confidentiality.

6. The initial version of the ad was replaced with another without the same opening sequence featuring bin Laden, Saddam, and Cleland.

7. Democratic source inside the Cleland campaign, personal interview with author, May 2004, Washington, D.C. Additional information omitted to protect confidentiality.

8. As noted previously, interview comments and media accounts refer alternatively to endorsement by the VFW and by a VFW PAC.

9. Tommy Thompson, telephone interview with author, May 4, 2004.

10. This information comes from a Democratic source inside the Cleland campaign, personal interview with author, May 2004, Washington, D.C. Additional information omitted to protect confidentiality.

11. Democratic source inside the Cleland campaign, personal interview with author, May 21, 2004, Washington, D.C. Additional information omitted to protect confidentiality.

12. Senator Max Cleland, telephone interview with author, March 25, 2004.

13. Tommy Thompson, telephone interview with author, May 4, 2004.

14. Ray Strother, personal interview with author, May 4, 2004, Washington, D.C.

15. Karl Struble, telephone interview with author, June 8, 2004.

16. Source familiar with Cleland polling, telephone interview with author, May 2004. Additional information omitted to protect confidentiality.

17. Tommy Thompson, telephone interview with author, May 4, 2004.

18. Karl Struble, telephone interview with author, June 8, 2004.

19. On groupthink, see Janis (1982).

20. Cleland insider, telephone interview with author, June 2005. Additional information omitted to protect confidentiality.

21. However, Democratic political professionals refuted reports that the DSCC shifted money from the Cleland campaign to Walter Mondale's upstart bid to defeat Norm Coleman in Minnesota after Paul Wellstone's death.

22. Source familiar with Cleland polling, telephone interview with author, May 2004. Additional information omitted to protect confidentiality.

23. Geoff Garin, telephone interview with author, June 8, 2004.

24. Throughout this chapter, political consultant Tom Perdue's and gubernatorial candidate Sonny Perdue's first and last names are listed to avoid confusion. They are unrelated.

25. Gene Ulm, personal interview with author, April 21, 2004, Alexandria, Virginia.

26. Chris LaCivita, telephone interview with author, June 15, 2004.

27. Gene Ulm, personal interview with author, April 21, 2004, Alexandria, Virginia.

28. Ibid.

29. This is an apparent reference to the 1994 Republican revolution, in which the party took control of both houses of Congress, especially through victories in traditionally Democratic territory, such as in southern states.

30. Chris LaCivita, telephone interview with author, June 15, 2004.

31. Ibid.

32. Krister Holladay, personal interview with author, June 4, 2004, Washington, D.C.

33. As noted previously, Mark refers to the ad's title as "Courage." Research indicates that "Courage" and "11 Times" are the same ad.

34. Tommy Thompson, telephone interview with author, May 4, 2004.

35. Bo Harmon, personal interview with author, April 6, 2004, Washington, D.C., and e-mail correspondence with author, June 8, 2005.

36. Bo Harmon, personal interview with author, April 6, 2004, Washington, D.C.

37. Michelle Hitt, telephone interview with author, June 4, 2004.

38. Karl Struble, telephone interview with author, June 8, 2004.

39. Bo Harmon, personal interview with author, April 6, 2004, Washington, D.C.

40. Chris LaCivita, telephone interview with author, June 15, 2004.

41. Republican strategist, telephone interview with author, May 2004. Additional information omitted to protect confidentiality.

42. Democratic source inside the Cleland campaign, personal interview with author, May 2004, Washington, D.C. Additional information omitted to protect confidentiality.

43. Krister Holladay, personal interview with author, June 4, 2004, Washington, D.C.

44. Michelle Hitt, telephone interview with author, June 4, 2004.

45. Matt McKenna, telephone interview with author, May 16, 2004.

46. For more information on Chambliss's base in middle Georgia, see Barone and Cohen (2003) and Mark (2006, 132).

47. Gene Ulm, personal interview with author, April 21, 2004, Alexandria, Virginia.

48. This information comes from the 2002 Wisconsin Advertising Project storyboards (Goldstein and Rivlin 2005).

49. This information comes from ibid.

50. Gene Ulm, personal interview with author, April 21, 2004, Alexandria, Virginia.

51. Ibid.

52. Rob Leebern, telephone interview with author, July 20, 2004.

53. Republican strategist, telephone interview with author, May 2004. Additional information omitted to protect confidentiality.

5

An Environment of Crisis: The Torricelli-Forrester- Lautenberg Race

Former senator Robert G. Torricelli (D) is one of the most intriguing figures in recent political history. He is also one of the most controversial, engendering tremendous loyalty among his allies and fierce resistance from political opponents (and even a few members of his own party). Although most crises do not unfold until well into the campaign, political professionals said that Torricelli began his 2002 reelection bid in crisis. As the campaign unfolded, other crises developed—not only for Torricelli but also for his Republican opponents, including eventual nominee Douglas Forrester. In an incredible series of events, Torricelli ultimately withdrew from the race, paving the way for what at first appeared to be an easy victory for Forrester. In a matter of weeks, however, Forrester's campaign stalled, unable to capitalize on the void left by Torricelli. In an equally surprising turn of events, former Democratic senator Frank Lautenberg replaced Torricelli on the ballot and eventually won a relatively easy victory. Nonetheless, the quiet end to the race did not diminish the crises that shaped virtually every facet of the rest of the campaigns involved.

One of the most remarkable factors in the New Jersey case study is that it clearly represented both the **expected** and **unexpected** elements of the **internal** dimension of the crisis typology. This was especially true for the Torricelli campaign. Most campaign crises are unexpected, and some political professionals said that crises cannot occur if they are anticipated (see Chapter 2). The events surrounding the Torricelli campaign and, some say, Douglas Forrester's opposing campaign make that proposition tenuous. Even though the Torricelli side knew it faced major external, and probably internal, crises before the campaign began, those crises were nonetheless fatal. Like the Saxby Chambliss campaign's criticisms of the

Max Cleland campaign in Georgia (see Chapter 4), New Jersey Democrats argued that the Forrester team was partly responsible for its own fate. According to many Democratic political professionals, if Republicans had simply exhibited better strategic thinking about the **expected** dimension of their own potential crises, Forrester could have salvaged victory from the jaws of defeat.

Political professionals on both sides focused their interview comments on Torricelli's alleged ethical scandals, which they said represented internal crises for the incumbent's campaign that provided a prime strategic environment for Republicans. However, that environment also eventually proved untenable for both Torricelli and Forrester. In eventually withdrawing from the race, Torricelli cited a media feeding frenzy that made an issue-based campaign impossible. Torricelli also reportedly said that he did not want to be responsible for the Democrats losing control of a closely divided Senate if his seat represented the deciding vote when Congress reconvened in January 2003. In another crisis after Torricelli withdrew from the race, New Jersey Democrats had to replace the senator's name on the ballot, a major unexpected change in the strategic environment. In addition to previous crises, the Forrester campaign suddenly found itself in the midst of a simultaneous **external** and **internal** crisis because the driving mechanism behind their campaign—Torricelli's image problems—was no longer in play.

However, Democratic political professionals cautioned that although the events described above were the most public aspects of the campaign, other events also heavily influenced the outcome of the race. As with the other case studies, Democrats argued that context played a key role in shaping crises for the Torricelli campaign. Democrats were particularly critical of the media, which they said overplayed allegations about Torricelli's conduct and created a campaign environment from which no politician could recover. Many Republicans agreed with Democratic claims that Torricelli's crises were ultimately unmanageable. Many Democratic political professionals also argued that Torricelli faced image problems among New Jersey residents because he had spent much of his Senate tenure outside the retail-politics state traveling for the Democratic Senatorial Campaign Committee. In so doing, they said, Torricelli faced a dilemma that often haunts party leaders, but one that was not a crisis in and of itself.

Crises on the Horizon?

Almost two years before the 2002 general election, the Newark *Star-Ledger* portrayed Bob Torricelli as a politician under siege. According to the newspaper, Torricelli was hiring top lawyers and the Washington crisis management and public relations firm Powell Tate (run by Jody Powell, Jimmy Carter's former press secretary, and Sheila Tate, Nancy Reagan's former press secretary). At the center of the controversy was an ongoing US Justice Department investigation into allegedly questionable fundraising during Torricelli's first Senate campaign in 1996. Nonetheless, Torricelli was successfully raising money and actively campaigning for his upcoming reelection (Sherman and Cohen 2001).

The fact that Torricelli was fighting simultaneous legal and political battles was not surprising. He had always been a fighter, as a campaign commercial would remind voters just before his exit from the race in September 2002. Through dogged determination and fundraising, he had defeated Republican representative Dick Zimmer in the 1996 Senate race. Shortly after being elected to the Senate, Torricelli was tapped to head the DSCC, an arm of the Democratic National Committee responsible for helping Democrats win Senate elections.

Heading into the 2002 reelection campaign, Torricelli also had another advantage: a crowded and expensive Republican primary. At its peak, the Republican field included six candidates who battled each other while Torricelli enjoyed an uncontested nomination. On the Republican side, Essex County executive Jim Treffinger; state senators Diane Allen and John Matheussen; assemblyman Guy Gregg; Forrester, the former West Windsor mayor and former state pension administrator (and millionaire businessperson); and former federal special counsel Robert Ray all vied to unseat Torricelli.

Despite Republican infighting, Torricelli's reelection bid would not be easy. The Justice Department investigation closed, without charges being filed against Torricelli, shortly before the campaign went into full swing. Although this otherwise would have been a political win, the Justice Department referred the matter to the Senate Ethics Committee,[1] which admonished Torricelli in late July 2002. Interviews revealed that political professionals on both sides regarded this highly public episode as a formidable crisis for the Torricelli campaign. Making the situation even more challenging, a major New York television station, WNBC, aired a news special profiling former Torricelli associate and campaign contributor David Chang's allegations that he had provided Torricelli with cash and gifts in exchange for political influence supporting Chang's business interests.[2] Although Torricelli acknowledged poor judgment, he steadfastly denied corruption allegations. (The substance of those allegations, including whether or not they were true, is beyond the scope of this book.) Nonetheless, political professionals regarded the political fallout from the campaign finance allegations surrounding Torricelli as a major **external** campaign crisis, both expected and unexpected.

Although the crowded Republican field spent time and money attacking each other, the GOP candidates were unified in their message that Torricelli's alleged ethical lapses made him unfit for reelection (Kinney 2002a, April 7). Even well before the Republican primary, Forrester attacked Torricelli's ethics and promised voters in radio spots aired around the state that "help is on the way." Forrester also had a special advantage in the Republican field. As chief of the pharmaceutical benefits provider BeneCard Services, Forrester had vast personal wealth. During 2002 first-quarter fundraising, Forrester's campaign raised barely $4,000 in outside contributions, but Forrester loaned his Senate bid more than $3 million (Kinney 2002b, April 16). Forrester also gained an advantage when rival Republican and frontrunner Jim Treffinger's campaign suffered its own crisis when the FBI raided Treffinger's office on April 18, 2002, as part of a separate corruption investigation (Kinney 2002c, April 19). Treffinger withdrew from the race shortly thereafter, leaving a void that the Forrester campaign ultimately filled.

But what Forrester had in money he lacked in name recognition and message. Indeed, the most common interview criticism directed at Forrester was that voters knew little about him or his platform. Political professionals and other observers said that the Forrester campaign created a crisis for itself by repeatedly missing opportunities to publicly give the Republican his own identity. Critics contended throughout the race that Forrester had no message except that he wasn't Bob Torricelli. According to this line of thinking, when Torricelli left the race, the only public justification Forrester had for running—as an acceptable alternative to the allegedly ethically unacceptable Torricelli—no longer held. Shortly after Torricelli's withdrawal, and after a vigorous legal battle, the New Jersey Supreme Court allowed the New Jersey Democratic Party (over Republican objections) to replace Torricelli's name on the ballot with Frank Lautenberg's. Lautenberg was a popular former US senator who had left office only two years earlier. When he entered the 2002 campaign, observers believed that Democrats would easily hold the seat, which they did.

Many political professionals on both sides said they believed that the Forrester team spent too much time complaining about whether it was fair for Torricelli to leave the race so late in the campaign and concentrating on legal battles designed to keep Torricelli's name on the ballot. Instead, they said the Forrester campaign should have redirected its energies toward reintroducing Forrester to voters, particularly before Lautenberg joined the race.

However, members of the Forrester team countered that they deliberately focused most of the campaign's messages on Torricelli's alleged misdeeds before his withdrawal and that doing so represented the best avenue toward winning the election. Although it eventually lost the race, the Forrester team argued that the plan to defeat Torricelli on ethical grounds was the right strategy at the time and would have been a winning one had the rules of the game remained consistent. From the GOP perspective, the fact that Torricelli was allowed to withdraw from the race and to be replaced by another Democrat represented an illegitimate last-minute change in the election that denied the Forrester campaign a fair contest.

As this overview suggests, the 2002 Torricelli-Forrester-Lautenberg saga was complex. Mountains of data surround the case: well more than 1,000 newspaper articles, not to mention numerous broadcast news and specialized media reports. Although New Jersey contains no major media markets of its own, several state newspapers and the New York and Philadelphia broadcast markets ensured volumes of coverage on the race. In terms of campaign crises, however, the 2002 Senate race in New Jersey was fairly straightforward. The crises that occurred marked major focal points for the political professionals working in each campaign, and the interview data established that political professionals believed, more so than in any other case, that campaign crises overwhelmingly affected the outcome of the race.

The Torricelli Decisionmaking Team and Organization

Although Torricelli's political influence was widespread, his strategic decisionmaking team was relatively small. Democratic operative Ken Snyder served as campaign manager. David Plouffe, Torricelli's 1996 campaign manager, former Democratic Congressional Campaign Committee executive director, and, by 2002, a consultant at Axelrod Associates, handled the senator's political advertising along with David Axelrod. Political consultant Joel Benenson served as pollster. Monica Lesmerises, who served as research director for both the Torricelli and Lautenberg campaigns, was often mentioned during interviews as being involved in strategy sessions. Political professionals also said that Torricelli's Senate communications director, Debra DeShong, was active in dealing with the media throughout the Justice Department investigation and during the campaign, although she was not part of the campaign staff. Danny O'Brien, Torricelli's former Senate chief of staff and 2001–2002 New Jersey Coordinated Campaign manager, was also frequently mentioned as part of the strategic decisionmaking team.

Despite the small strategic group inside the campaign, political professionals said that Torricelli drew on a wide political network for legal and personal advice. That included Torricelli's former wife, Susan Holloway Torricelli, who served as a longtime fundraiser to the senator and reportedly maintained a close friendship with him even after their divorce. Political professionals emphasized that Bob Torricelli, an experienced and tireless politician by all accounts, participated actively in strategic decisionmaking. Torricelli's extensive party connections also came into play in campaign decisionmaking. The Torricelli campaign relied on the DSCC to run all but one television advertisement in the race.[3] Some political professionals associated with the Torricelli campaign said the large number of players as crises grew more intense sometimes made decisionmaking unwieldy, suggesting a separate **internal** *organizational* crisis.

Campaign Crises: The Torricelli Team's View

During interviews, political professionals associated with the Torricelli campaign agreed that the campaign finance investigation and scandal it created represented crises for the Torricelli team. However, political professionals differed in their reasoning for classifying these events as crises. Torricelli team members said the investigation and appearance of wrongdoing caused a substantial *strategic disruption* for the campaign, making the **external** dimension of the typology untenable. Others inside the campaign said that Torricelli could have waged a substantive issues-based campaign if the media had allowed him to do so.

Nonetheless, the Torricelli team also knew that crises were coming (representing the **expected** dimension of the typology). As Torricelli campaign manager Ken Snyder explained, the incumbent team not only faced external crises from media investigations and attacks from the Forrester team but also began from the premise that the race would be an ongoing exercise in crisis management. That situation quickly grew worse as other crises unfolded. According to Snyder:

> The Torricelli campaign was situated in the context of a crisis. . . . He had just come off a four-year federal investigation and was beginning [an] extensive and lengthy ethics investigation . . . that sort of overlapped almost exactly with the campaign. So, you go in understanding that it's going to be an exercise in crisis management. Then all of the other things that naturally come up in a campaign are additional crises that built to a crescendo when the [Senate] Ethics Committee severely admonished him and a judge ruled that the case wouldn't be sealed [a decision that provided public access to various allegations in the case]. Those are a

couple tough blows to take. And then, what I consider one of the most damaging and unprecedented blows Torricelli took, was when WNBC aired a forty-*minute*, uninterrupted documentary that was like one big negative commercial.[4]

The following section explores these events in more detail.

Torricelli Crises Surrounding the Justice Department and Ethics Investigations

Political professionals reported that simultaneous **internal** and **external** crises developed from the Justice Department investigation and the Senate Ethics Committee admonition of Torricelli on July 30, 2002.[5] (As noted above, after the Justice Department decided not to file criminal charges against Torricelli, it referred the matter to the Senate Ethics Committee, which considered whether Torricelli had violated Senate rules.) Externally, these events created a severe *strategic disruption* for the Torricelli campaign by again putting it on defense in a very public way, even though the general circumstances were expected. Although they knew the race would be challenging, political professionals working for the Torricelli campaign said they did not expect the severity of the admonition or the timing of its release. The result was that, at a time when the Torricelli team had hoped that they could finally be out from under the cloud of the Justice Department investigation and concentrate on substantive campaigning against Forrester, the Ethics Committee's admonition instead renewed focus on Torricelli's alleged behavior. The admonition letter and a subsequent Torricelli floor statement received substantial negative media attention and further opened the door to attacks from Republicans.

Among other points, the Ethics Committee "severely admonished" Torricelli and concluded that he acted with "poor judgment [and] displayed a lack of due respect for Senate Rules" and "created at least the appearance of impropriety" in accepting gifts from Chang (Inouye et al. 2002). That afternoon, Torricelli spoke on the Senate floor, accepting the committee's findings and apologizing to his constituents. He also declared that he "never stopped fighting for the things in which I believe. I never compromised in the struggle to make the lives of the people I love better" (Congressional Record 2002, S7565). The speech's emphasis on constituent service foreshadowed a crisis-management theme that would soon be used in a prominent Torricelli television advertisement.

Some political professionals inside the Torricelli campaign complained that the organizational structure required to fight competing campaign and legal battles made a bad situation even worse. In addition to the campaign team, an expansive group of legal advisers was assembled to shepherd Torricelli through the Justice Department and Senate Ethics Committee investigations. Political professionals said that vital information about the investigations, to protect Torricelli's legal interests, could not be shared with campaign staff. Yet the information became central to the campaign because of extensive media attention.

The following excerpt is from a senior source inside the Torricelli campaign and is consistent with comments offered in other interviews.

> You have to understand for a long period of time, [the legal team's] goal was to prevent charges against [Torricelli] and that was the central focus of the legal effort. The political concerns [that] arose after that were secondary, and I can't argue that at all. But once the US attorney decided not to file charges and referred it to the Ethics Committee, then [the issue was] on political ground. . . . I don't think we had until the eleventh hour a real great sense that the Ethics Committee report was going to be as negative as it was. I mean, we were all led to believe it was going to be the old "slap-on-the-wrist and move on." . . . But it turned out to be a big boulder on the road and I think the political side of the operation came to realize that much later than we should have because of the lack of knowledge and information about what was going on in the legal side of things.[6]

However, one professional who worked closely with the Torricelli campaign noted that Torricelli was closer to his official staff than to the campaign staff and feared that sharing legal details with some members of the campaign team could result in leaks to the media. The individual also argued that "90 percent" of information known to the legal staff did not affect the campaign.[7]

To make matters worse, the media also targeted Torricelli through legal channels; a group of news organizations, including WNBC and *The New York Times*, asked a federal court to release "the entire contents of a Justice Department letter that describes the evidence prosecutors gathered in their five-year investigation of [Torricelli's] campaign and personal finances," including details about his alleged relationship with David Chang (Kocieniewski 2002). Torricelli had pursued legal action to keep the so-called Chang letter out of the public eye. A federal appeals court granted the media's request to make the document public on September 20, 2002, just weeks before the November election. This episode, too, received substantial media attention. More important, Torricelli insiders said, the senator's efforts to keep the letter secret contributed to the appearance of wrongdoing regardless of his actual innocence or guilt. This set of circumstances, political professionals said, not only created a *strategic disruption* crisis for Torricelli in making it virtually impossible for him to wage an effective campaign but also confirmed in many voters' minds the appearance of a *candidate scandal.*

Crisis Management and the Apology Ad

The Torricelli team tried to mitigate the potential ethics crisis with its one and only television spot, titled "Fighter," which began airing on August 1, 2002.[8] The dimly lit ad featured Torricelli sitting at a desk and speaking directly to the camera. Continuing his constituent service theme from the Senate floor statement, Torricelli recalled his service to the state and declared, "I'm a fighter, and frankly, the hardest thing for a fighter to do is admit mistakes. . . . Although I broke no laws, it's clear to me that I did exercise poor judgment and actions, which I deeply regret."[9]

Some political professionals inside the campaign complained that the sixty-second ad was too long, drew too much attention to Torricelli's problems, and was aired too often without other positive information from the campaign. In addition, Democratic political professionals said, even as the apology ad aired, Torricelli continued to be combative with the media, which sent mixed messages to the public. According to Torricelli campaign manager Ken Snyder, who refers below to the ad:

> The problem is there was a disconnect between what people are seeing on TV and hearing Bob [Torricelli] say in the media because he wasn't contrite in any way, shape or form in the media. . . . He never really actually said he was sorry for anything. . . . But we ran it too much. And the thing that I didn't take into account was that it's a sixty-second ad running at a time when no other ads were really running and was a highly unusual kind of ad. And we didn't need to run it as much as we did.[10]

In the first-round interviews, in particular, political professionals argued that when faced with crises, especially ethical scandals, politicians can usually win a reprieve with a straightforward apology.[11] Why, then, did Torricelli's Senate speech and the "Fighter" ad not work as anticipated? Many political professionals associated with his campaign said that Torricelli's apology was not quick and did not appear genuine. In fact, political professionals said that Torricelli believed that he had done nothing wrong, as he maintained throughout the campaign. Most important, however, interviewees said, the apology was ineffective because the media created an environment in which no apology would kill the story.

Forrester campaign officials also questioned why the ad struck such a somber tone, both in presentation and content. Forrester media consultant John Brabender, commenting on Torricelli's dark suit and dim lighting, compared the ad to "a scene from *The Godfather*."[12] Others asked why Torricelli was not filmed in crowds of constituents instead of sitting alone at a desk.

Torricelli media consultant David Plouffe disagreed, saying the mood was appropriate for the occasion, reflected Torricelli's wishes, and was heartfelt:

> I think it was a very genuine apology. I think for someone who suggests that Torricelli should then be with people—that would have made it very political. This was a conversation between he and his constituents, and I think that it had to be a fairly somber setting, a serious setting. . . . So I [disagree with what] other people say, "Well, you know, he should have been with the crowd, or this or that." To me that would have been completely inauthentic.[13]

External Crises and the WNBC Special

Just weeks after the Senate Ethics Committee admonished Torricelli, and just as efforts to reframe his race began, the Torricelli campaign experienced what many political professionals said was by far its greatest crisis. On September 26 during its 5:00 P.M. newscast, New York television station WNBC aired a forty-minute special, without commercial interruption, featuring a prison interview with Torricelli accuser David Chang. The program, entitled "The Prisoner and the Politician," featured a lengthy interview with Chang, who detailed his allegedly corrupt relationship with Torricelli.

Torricelli officials said they regarded the program as overzealous and biased.[14] More than one political professional recalled crying as the piece aired because they regarded it as the final blow to the incumbent. A source who worked closely with the Torricelli campaign called the report "one of the most traumatic [events] of my career" and complained that "it was stunning in its length. It was stunning in its depth and reporting. It was stunning in what I thought was irresponsible reporting."[15]

WNBC's Jonathan Dienst, who reported the story, defended the piece. According to Dienst, the project began as a general investigation into Chang's allegations and relied on meticulous research:

> The public had a right to know whether these allegations were true or false. We then entered into a significant search for either proving or disproving the allegations and asking the senator, who continued to deny any and all charges. . . . And we proceeded and nagged sources in gov-

ernment, in the Torricelli campaign, along with Mr. Chang, merchants in New Jersey. We obtained documents, receipts, materials, and other information that raised serious questions about the denials the senator was offering. And it was only until we were able to substantiate or confirm some of the allegations that Mr. Chang [was] making that we were comfortable to go on the air. And what we uncovered was an extraordinary amount of apparent corroboration for Chang's story, which we felt the voters needed and had a right to know.[16]

Dienst added that he and others repeatedly requested in-depth interviews from Torricelli for the program and that long investigative pieces were not unusual for the station's reporters.

A Rapidly Declining Campaign Environment

Regardless of Democratic political professionals' feelings toward "The Prisoner and the Politician," they reported that the negative publicity surrounding the program exacerbated an already rapidly declining campaign environment for Torricelli. However, Torricelli pollster Joel Benenson suggested that the impact from the WNBC special was not as traumatic as popular wisdom suggests. According to Benenson, polling data did not indicate a major loss of support after the program aired.

Instead, Benenson argued that the judicial order to unseal the Justice Department's "Chang memo" outlining the alleged relationship between Torricelli and Chang was a more significant crisis point for the campaign. Although Benenson is a former journalist, his comments echoed his colleagues' disappointment in media coverage of the race.

[The memo] didn't include anything that was really substantively damaging. But it was on the front page of every newspaper . . . so that within twenty-four hours the whole issue of the scandal and the Ethics [Committee] report was back in the news again. What became apparent with that story . . . was that this was a subject that would never go away, that the press would recycle old news in a way that they typically don't, and write it in as negative [a] way as they possibly could. . . . It no longer mattered what the facts were. . . . Allegations were being treated as fact by the press. So even someone sitting in a federal prison, who had been largely discredited and largely considered not trustworthy as a witness, gets forty minutes of airtime on NBC television. Well, that was a pattern that we weren't going to escape.[17]

The final straw for the Torricelli campaign came as September 30, 2002, approached, when polling by the Newark *Star-Ledger* (the state's most influential newspaper) revealed a notable drop in public support for the senator. With some advance warning about what the newspaper would publish on Monday, Democratic political professionals said they attempted to get the *Star-Ledger* to rerun its poll or to briefly delay publishing the results until the Torricelli team could conduct its own polling over the weekend to verify those results. However, the campaign's polling eventually confirmed the bad news. Interviews revealed that Torricelli decided to withdraw from the race largely on his own. Even some of his closest advisers reportedly did not know about the decision until his September 30 press conference announcing his exit from the race.

In the end, political professionals associated with the Torricelli campaign agreed that campaign crises defined the 2002 New Jersey Senate race. However, some also believed that New Jersey returned to its political roots despite the dramatic impact of Torricelli's campaign crises. As Torricelli media consultant David Plouffe noted, even under extraordinary crisis circumstances, Democrats were still victorious in the state:

> Obviously, the fundamental crisis in that race, which was the whole ethics investigation running on Torricelli, had monumental impact in terms of the two major personalities involved, him and Lautenberg. But it wasn't like the crisis could have been dealt with any different way. These were unusual circumstances you're dealing with in a political race, you know, unsealed memos in the Justice Department and the biggest [television] station in America essentially running an hour of exposé on Torricelli. These were unusual circumstances that you couldn't put the genie back in the bottle after that.[18]

Democratic political professionals also emphasized that Torricelli's message would have been a winning one if only it could have been heard. The greatest evidence of that belief, they said, is that Frank Lautenberg essentially ran the campaign the Torricelli team had tried to run for the previous eighteen months.

The Torricelli Campaign on the Offensive

In interviews, members of the Torricelli campaign maintained that they tried to change the subject—a crisis-management technique often mentioned throughout the first-round interviews—regarding the ethics crisis by attacking Forrester on policy issues. DSCC issue advertising hammered Forrester's stance on the environment and gun control. The DSCC ads also attacked Forrester's record as chief executive of BeneCard, charging that Forrester was responsible for denying his own employees coverage for HIV medications, despite the fact that BeneCard was a pharmaceutical

benefits provider. The Forrester campaign flatly denied Democratic assertions at the time in media accounts and again during interviews for this
book.

Political professionals inside the Torricelli campaign said that they
faced a dual challenge in airing some of their best material against Forrester. First, they contended that the media emphasis on the Torricelli investigations made waging a policy-oriented campaign impossible. Second,
as with the Cleland campaign's difficulties in attacking the intricacies of
Saxby Chambliss's military deferments, Torricelli insiders said that attacking Forrester's alleged role in overseeing BeneCard's prescription benefits
plans was too complicated to sell to voters and the media. Torricelli and
Lautenberg research director Monica Lesmerises said she believed that the
media simply would not engage on substantive issues long enough for the
Torricelli campaign to make a detailed case of their allegations concerning
BeneCard. According to Lesmerises:

> We just felt like we had something so great and we just couldn't get it writ-
> ten. . . . It was banging your head against the wall because nobody would
> talk about anything else. . . . I really felt we were treated unfairly by the
> press considering it is a natural instinct [of] political reporters to do "he
> said–she said" stories. But half of the Torricelli story was always the inves-
> tigation. It was never . . . "The Torricelli campaign said Forrester did this
> but Forrester says actually he gave people a good deal." It wasn't stories
> like that. It was, "Torricelli did this but Forrester said he's a criminal."[19]

Indeed, Democratic political professionals said that the Torricelli campaign's poor relationship with the media could have been classified as a
crisis in and of itself. Torricelli staff expressed uniform agreement that the
media acted overzealously in covering the Justice and Senate ethics investigations. However, some also said that Torricelli was unnecessarily antag-
onistic toward the media throughout his political career. One journalist
who covered the race said that although Torricelli's "Fighter" ad "pre-
tended" to answer reporters' questions, the senator would never talk with
reporters in detail about the allegations against him.[20]

Other Democrats, however, suggested that Torricelli was brought
down by an entirely different kind of crisis. According to one Democratic
official, although Torricelli's alleged ethical crises were significant, Torricelli's service to the DSCC also represented a crisis by preventing him
from focusing on New Jersey's retail politics.

> [Torricelli] got sunk by his own colleagues. . . . [The DSCC leadership po-
> sitions] created a crisis for him, and then when he got labeled as corrupt by

the federal government, that's all the voters knew about him. They didn't know anything else about him. In fact, he was a hugely effective senator [but] . . . Bob goes [into the race] largely undefined to the electorate and the only thing they know about him is that he's [allegedly] corrupt. They didn't know about the fact that he was one of the great senators of his short-lived career.[21]

The Forrester Decisionmaking Team and Organization

Although Bill Pascoe held the title of campaign manager, he fulfilled the duties of a general consultant throughout the campaign. Gene Ulm at Public Opinion Strategies served as pollster, and John Brabender of BrabenderCox was the media consultant. Deputy campaign manager Matthew Barnes, communications director Mark Pfeifle, and press secretary Tom Rubino were also frequently mentioned during interviews, although there was some disagreement about the extent to which Pfeifle and Rubino were strategists as opposed to implementers (concepts discussed in Chapter 3).

Forrester insiders also reported that, at times, National Republican Senatorial Committee political director Chris LaCivita and executive director Mitch Bainwol were closely involved in the campaign. Despite Forrester's tenure as West Windsor mayor and his previous run for governor, political professionals said the Republican candidate was not a major player in strategic campaign decisions. Many political professionals described Forrester as a "good government" Republican who simply believed he could do a better job as US senator than Torricelli and was deeply committed to the campaign but left most strategic details to his campaign consultants and staff.

Campaign Crises: The Forrester Team's View

The Forrester team concentrated its interview comments on Torricelli's campaign crises, especially the ethics investigations. However, political professionals inside the Forrester campaign also discussed a few events that they said represented crises for the Republican side. First and foremost, they argued that Torricelli's unexpected withdrawal from the race represented a major **external** crisis (given the sudden change in opponents, a *strategic disruption* to say the least). Second, after Torricelli's withdrawal, the Forrester team regarded the ballot change allowing Lautenberg to replace Torricelli as a crisis for Forrester. In fact, the Forrester team argued that Lautenberg's presence on the ballot made winning the election virtually impossible. Third, there was some evidence of **internal** *organizational* crises for the Forrester campaign.

The Forrester team spent most of its crisis-management efforts reacting to unexpected withdrawals from Treffinger in the primary, Torricelli in the general, and the unexpected addition of Lautenberg late in the general election. Interviews also revealed that political professionals believed that the Forrester team faced distinct **internal, unexpected** crises. For example, members of both the Republican and Democratic teams (including both the Lautenberg and Torricelli organizations) regarded the Forrester team's failure to do proper self-research on the Republican candidate's potential weaknesses as an organizational failure that led to an **internal** crisis for Forrester's campaign. One of the most prominent examples occurred when Newark *Star-Ledger* reporter David Kinney learned during an interview that Forrester had previously written a regular column for a community newspaper. Although the Forrester campaign knew about the columns, campaign manager Bill Pascoe acknowledged that he took at face value Forrester's assertions that there was nothing politically sensitive in the writings and decided not to investigate further, due to the high cost of professional political research. That approach worked until a few days after an interview with Kinney, during which Andrea Forrester reportedly made an offhand remark about her husband's sense of humor, as displayed in the columns. A few days later, Kinney published excerpts from the columns, highlighting Forrester's opinions on issues ranging from taxes to sex education. In one column, Forrester reportedly argued that an assault weapons ban should "'remain beyond public debate'" and that "'it isn't any of my business whether my neighbor likes to shoot semi-automatic weapons or not'" (Forrester, quoted in Kinney 2002d, October 13).

The gun-control comments later became fodder for Democratic ads against Forrester and for attacks during debates. Forrester press secretary Tom Rubino complained that the media focused only on sensational excerpts from the columns while ignoring the broader context. Nonetheless, the fallout from Forrester's writings created an **external** crisis for his team. The late-breaking story in the *Star-Ledger* revealing the columns appeared on October 13, just weeks before the general election (Kinney 2002d, October 13).

In fact, there were two areas in which political professionals said better research could have benefited Forrester: first, on the issue of his newspaper columns; and second, on a minor crisis early in the campaign in which Forrester was portrayed in a newspaper article as being responsible for raising property taxes while West Windsor mayor. As with the Torricelli campaign, political professionals again complained about the media allegedly exploiting the facts. The latter incident came to light during the primary campaign when a reporter called Pascoe asking why Forrester was presenting himself as an antitax candidate but had raised taxes as mayor.

The campaign responded by explaining that Forrester and the West Windsor Township Council had acted responsibly in raising taxes to pay for a better sewer system, which residents had demanded. However, the issue devolved into a *strategic disruption* when Forrester began using the episode to reshape his image as being a "builder" who could responsibly spend tax money, instead of his previous message of being a "fighter" who wanted to cut taxes and appeal to Republican primary voters. Consequently, as Forrester tried to appeal to good-government Republicans as well as fiscal conservatives, his already low profile became confused by mixed messages.

As Pascoe explained:

> Now we had a candidate [who] was not really the guy who wanted to cut everybody's taxes all the time. He really was a good-government—a "goo-goo" Republican, who did things that . . . were sometimes [necessary] when you needed to raise taxes, and just wanted to make sure that we spent tax money responsibly. And he saw this as an opportunity kind of to reshape his own image . . . and he was talking about being "the builder." [I said to the consulting team that] "Doug is no longer on message. He's no longer talking about the need to cut taxes." . . . [W]e decided that we needed to go into the field with a survey, for no other purpose than to demonstrate to our own candidate, that what he was saying was politically damaging.[22]

In the end, political professionals said the survey data accomplished its objective by reining in Forrester's divergent messages. However, it also cost the campaign thousands of dollars in polling fees and required substantial time away from planned business for the candidate, campaign manager, pollster, and media consultant (all of whom convened for a daylong meeting less than a month before the primary)—all for the sake of convincing the candidate of what his advisers were already saying. Nonetheless, even though Pascoe characterized the episode as a crisis, he noted that it provides an example of a positive outcome from crises in forcing campaigns to reassess strategies.[23]

Strategy and the Forrester Campaign's Focus on the Ballot Switch

Republican political professionals said they regarded Torricelli's withdrawal from, and Lautenberg's unexpected entry into, the race as the defining event—and certainly the major campaign crises—for the Forrester campaign. From the typology perspective, the candidate switch was the essence of a *strategic disruption* because the event was so unexpected for Republicans. Throughout the interviews, Republicans reported that running against Torricelli was the entire strategic premise for their campaign. Republicans also rejected Democratic charges that they failed to define Forrester. As Republican pollster Gene Ulm noted, the Forrester campaign regularly released substantive policy information about its candidate.

Nonetheless, Ulm and other Republicans said that there was no way to make the race about anything other than Torricelli, especially considering the intense media scrutiny surrounding the race. According to Ulm, "To say that you could make the race about something else is, I think, flawed in that kind of environment." In addition, Ulm argued that the Forrester focus on Torricelli made strategic sense: "The whole entire Forrester campaign was built on [the] strategic premise that Torricelli was damaged goods. . . . All the money on earth would not have rehabilitated Bob Torricelli. It can't be done. The public recognition of how he functioned as a senator was so corrupt and so well-known."[24]

Despite their messages highlighting Torricelli's alleged weaknesses, Republicans said they fully expected the incumbent to remain in the race, as did Democrats. Republicans were nonetheless conscious of a state deadline for Torricelli's name to be replaced on the ballot under conventional procedures in case he did unexpectedly withdraw. New Jersey law precluded political parties from replacing candidates on the ballot less than fifty-one days prior to the general election (Kocieniewski and Peterson 2002). Forrester press secretary Tom Rubino said that the Republican campaign backed off in its rhetoric attacking Torricelli as the deadline approached:

> We started to worry when we saw our polling numbers just going [up]—Doug was so strong that we checked the deadline and held back a little bit when we were getting into that period near the end. We held back on what we were putting out [in press releases]. . . . And so there was that thought that, "Just in case [Torricelli was considering leaving the race], let's hold off a little bit. Just take it easy a little on him, but not pull back totally."[25]

Once the deadline passed, Republican political professionals said, they believed Forrester would head to a close but certain victory.

When Torricelli did withdraw, Republicans concentrated on publicly condemning Democratic efforts to replace him on the ballot as illegal; the GOP also launched extensive legal challenges to oppose the change. Employing surrogates such as the NRSC and national Republican leaders was essential to the campaign's efforts to spread the message through the media that Democratic so-called party bosses were allegedly conspiring to orchestrate an unfair and illegal election. The Forrester campaign and the NRSC took to the air with that message in the media and in renewed political advertising. In one prominent ad, titled "The Lesson," sponsored by the New Jersey Republican Party, parents were asked what message the ballot switch sent children. As nationaljournal.com reporter Mark H. Rodeffer summarized at the time:

> A schoolboy exasperated by a test says: "Aw man, I can't do this. I quit!" He asks his teacher, "If I fail this test, can I have Frank Lautenberg take it for me?" After his opponent in a one-on-one basketball game makes a basket, another boy announces he's quitting the game and says, "Let Frank Lautenberg play for me." Walking away from the game, he adds: "Torricelli can quit, I can quit. I'm not gonna lose." (Rodeffer 2002a)

Meanwhile, Democrats argued that the Forrester team created a crisis for itself by wasting valuable opportunities to present the Republican's policy platform during the time between Torricelli's exit and the New Jersey Supreme Court's decision to allow Democrats to replace Torricelli with Lautenberg on the ballot. Indeed, Democrats alleged that the Forrester team never defined Forrester as a candidate and missed a second opportunity to do so after Torricelli withdrew from the race. From the Democratic perspective, the Forrester team spent the entire campaign attacking Torricelli, leaving Forrester woefully undefined once voters looked to him for answers after Torricelli withdrew from the race. Torricelli media consultant David Plouffe explained:

> Forrester was out there . . . basically saying, "The voters should not have a choice and let's keep them from being involved . . . or let's not allow another Democrat to replace Torricelli." And, you know, to me there was a legal strategy they should pursue, but that could have been done quietly. I mean, Forrester should have been out there saying, "Listen, I'm glad Torricelli is gone . . . but the fact of the matter is I'm running for positive reasons, and here they are and whatever the courts decide, I'm ready to roll." Instead, he was basically whining and complaining, and within a position [of] trying to keep a choice away from the voters. And the voters overwhelmingly thought that Torricelli should be replaced. So I think that was their crisis and they handled it very poorly.[26] .

Torricelli pollster Joel Benenson offered a similar assessment:

> They should have [used Torricelli's exit] to get on the high road and say, "[We're] running for senator because we believe we have a better vision for

how New Jersey needs to be represented in the [Senate]. And Bob Torricelli and Frank Lautenberg may not have been kissing cousins, but they come from the same political spectrum, and it's not a spectrum that's working for New Jersey." . . . To be whiny about the process doesn't help you. Anytime your candidate is talking about the political process, you're losing.[27]

However, Forrester campaign manager Bill Pascoe maintained that from a strategic perspective the Forrester team did not need to better define their candidate given the environment for most of the campaign—and for Republicans, the environment they believed was unfairly changed. Other Republican sources supported that position during interviews. According to Pascoe:

> The biggest crisis we faced in that campaign was the night that Bob Torricelli withdrew from the race [because] we had to deal with a radically new political environment. . . . All of [a] sudden, we're presented with a new strategic environment. We've got a new candidate that we're running against, and by definition, that meant that the campaign that we had been running was at that point inoperable. We couldn't continue running that campaign because guess what: the other guy can also say, "Well, so what? I'm not Bob Torricelli either." . . . What you're trying to do in a campaign essentially is to examine the environment, the field of battle, and you want to draw distinctions with your opponent, and not just any distinction. . . . A well-run campaign *is* an exercise in division, by definition.[28]

With Torricelli out of the race, drawing contrasts for Forrester became more difficult.

The interviews also suggested that when choosing which campaign crises to fight, the NRSC decided that given the altered context in New Jersey, the Forrester race could not realistically be saved. Some Republican sources said that the NRSC threatened to cut off Forrester's party funding unless his campaign concentrated on litigation opposing the ballot switch. As LaCivita explained:

> We proceeded with a legal strategy, frankly, because at the time it was the only option open and available to us. It's not the NRSC's job . . . to reshape the campaign. . . . You're talking the New York media market and the Philadelphia media market in a race that demographically just did not favor us. So, it was a matter of spending resources to define a campaign in a state where all the odds were stacked against us. We were going with states where we had a better opportunity. We had to make a resource decision, a tactical-resource decision based on reality. So, we peaked too soon. . . . The worst thing that could have happened was for [Torricelli] to drop out of the race. And he did.[29]

Another senior Republican official agreed. As the official noted, the fact that Lautenberg was so well-known and that he had no ethical crises in his political past made the task doubly difficult for Republicans:

> New Jersey is a hugely expensive place to engage in any kind of paid [media] because you're vying, obviously, to New York and Philadelphia. And once Torricelli was not the nominee, the probability of success went [down substantially] in a very, very expensive context in which the opportunity cost of that dollar was better spent in Georgia and Minnesota and some other states. . . . That race was not winnable once Torricelli was off the ballot.[30]

Organizational Crises for Forrester After the Ballot Switch

Republicans said that low morale and lost momentum accompanied the ballot switch, potentially leading to *organizational* crises for the Forrester campaign. Media consultant John Brabender said that the Forrester campaign was one of the best-functioning organizations he had seen in his long career—until Torricelli's exit. After the switch, however, the campaign reportedly became sidetracked. As Brabender explained, not only did the campaign begin focusing on the emotional "unfairness" they felt during this period; the legal unfairness they perceived was also being imposed beyond their control.

> We felt like we were being cheated. . . . It was a very tough feeling after working very hard for that many months, and having things go as well as they were for that to happen. Plus it seemed like it was unfair and put us in an unbalanced position [particularly in terms of campaign finance]. . . . Think about this: Bob Torricelli could accept a $5,000 PAC contribution from somebody and use that $5,000 to run an ad against Doug Forrester. . . . Lautenberg the next day can take another $5,000 from that same organization, and run another $5,000 against Doug Forrester. So now they have double the PAC limit that they can collectively get to run against Doug Forrester than Doug Forrester has a right to get. So there [were] all these things that, with this change, that just felt terribly, terribly unfair. So, I think what happens, and rightfully so to some extent, but logically the campaign starts focusing more on how unfair this is . . . rather than . . . doing what you should be doing campaign-related.[31]

Press secretary Tom Rubino pointed out an additional **internal** *organizational* crisis for the Forrester team in the aftermath of the ballot switch. In addition to the sudden change in the strategic premise of running against

Torricelli (which prevented planned counterattacks to cause crises for Torricelli), the Forrester campaign lost significant investments in materials and resources. According to Rubino:

> The main part of our campaign was to highlight [Torricelli's] negatives, obviously because that was the easy way to hurt his campaign and keep him from any . . . positive message. And we did that very effectively. So, now when you get a candidate that's taken out after the deadline and they're putting somebody new, well, you've already spent a significant amount of money implementing your strategy. [We] had ads that were being produced, mail pieces—all that stuff has to be scrapped. That's money that you can't get back. And you need an extraordinary amount of money now to re-vamp your whole message.[32]

The Forrester Campaign on the Offensive

Political professionals inside the Forrester campaign said they had a good working relationship with the media and actively solicited coverage of Torricelli's campaign crises and Forrester's attacks on Torricelli. However, the media circus became a double-edged sword even for Republicans. Republican political professionals said that they suffered from the same media environment surrounding Torricelli's ethical scandals as did Democrats, making Republicans' attempts to have a policy-oriented debate just as impossible as it was for the Torricelli team. In addition, a source close to the Forrester campaign defended the campaign's strategic balance of attacking Torricelli and touting Forrester: "We were interested in having voters know who Doug Forrester was, but there's more [incentive] to highlight Torricelli's weaknesses because, at the end of the day, this is about winning and losing. And we determined that the best way to win was the strategy we [adopted]—and we just beat them 30 days too soon."[33]

Democrats, by contrast, said Forrester was a weak candidate whose lack of substance shone through when he was unable to wage a policy-oriented campaign against Lautenberg. Some Republicans also reported that they believed that not making the case for Forrester more forcefully was a strategic error, although there is little evidence that they believed doing so would have changed the outcome of the race.

A Snapshot of the Lautenberg Campaign

Although a few Torricelli campaign officials transitioned to the Lautenberg campaign, most did not. According to one Democratic political professional, a long rivalry between Torricelli and Lautenberg decreased the

Torricelli staff's chances of being absorbed into the Lautenberg campaign. However, Torricelli staff said they did turn over research to the Lautenberg campaign and argued that Lautenberg's campaign was the issue-based effort that the Torricelli team had planned to run all along.

This chapter devotes little analysis to the Lautenberg campaign because there was such widespread agreement during interviews—on all sides—that although Lautenberg benefited from Forrester's message crises, the Democrat's campaign was free from its own campaign crises. Also, political professionals on all sides said Lautenberg's victory was virtually guaranteed once Torricelli was removed from the landscape. Lautenberg offered New Jersey voters an opportunity to return to their Democratic roots, which Torricelli's crises had overshadowed until that point. During the brief campaign that ensued, Lautenberg kept a low profile—a point Republicans tried to attack by implying that Lautenberg was too old for the job. Lautenberg remained above the fray, running a campaign based on his long Senate experience.

Lautenberg campaign officials echoed other Democrats' comments that the Forrester team exacerbated its crises by not reintroducing Forrester to voters after Torricelli's withdrawal. According to a senior adviser to the Lautenberg campaign,

> Forrester was still little-known because most of his campaign had been a negative campaign on Torricelli, and therefore he himself had built no equity of his own with the voters. And so we were in a situation where Senator Lautenberg's equity immediately trumped Forrester's lack of name recognition. And that's why it was a crisis for the Forrester campaign and why they worked so assiduously to deny the Democrats the ability to place him on the ballot.[34]

In addition, Lautenberg campaign manager Tom Shea noted that the legal focus on the ballot switch was not as great in the Lautenberg campaign as in the Forrester campaign, which allowed the Lautenberg team to concentrate on making a positive case for the former senator's election. Finally, Lautenberg officials rejected Republicans' last-ditch efforts in political advertising to connect Torricelli to Lautenberg. According to Shea,

> It wasn't as if there needed to be any distinction whatsoever [between Torricelli and Lautenberg] because [Lautenberg] had been here for eighteen years, [number] one. And the echo chamber of politics, media, the Trenton crowd, it was not even close to a secret that they couldn't stand each other. So, just the idea, especially with the press, that the Forrester

campaign was trying to link Bob Torricelli to Frank Lautenberg was just laughable to anybody who knew anything.[35]

After the US Supreme Court refused to intervene in the case and remove Torricelli's name from the ballot, Republicans said they basically resigned themselves to defeat. According to Forrester media consultant John Brabender,

> It almost seems like we never even ran against Lautenberg. I don't know how else to explain it. The campaign became surreal at that point. Lautenberg's people did everything they were supposed to. They kept their candidate and hid him, basically, realizing that this was a Democratic state, and that they were going to be the Democrat. And there's nothing that they did that surprised me even in the least.[36]

Concluding Comments on Crises in the Torricelli-Forrester-Lautenberg Race

The Torricelli campaign faced a remarkable political obstacle from the outset: a recently concluded Justice Department investigation into Torricelli's previous campaign finance practices. That investigation also had ethics overtones. Although Torricelli was never charged in the case, a Senate Ethics Committee investigation loomed on the horizon and became a major liability at a critical moment. Political professionals reported that they expected these challenges and knew the campaign would be an exercise in crisis management. They did not expect the overwhelming external environment, especially what they believed was hostile treatment from broadcast media outlets.

The Forrester campaign faced its own set of crises as well. The Forrester team engaged Torricelli even before Forrester won the Republican nomination. In an unusual set of circumstances, Republican frontrunner Jim Treffinger withdrew from the race after an FBI raid on his office. The Forrester team regarded the event as a major *strategic disruption* but nonetheless an opportunity that allowed Forrester to surge to the forefront. Conversely, the Forrester team suffered a major crisis when Torricelli unexpectedly withdrew from the race. Political professionals said that the event marked a premier *strategic disruption* because the entire campaign had been based on the premise that Forrester represented an alternative to Torricelli. Many Democrats, and some Republicans, said they believed that the Forrester team wasted a valuable opportunity to reintroduce Forrester to voters in the period between Torricelli's exit and the New Jersey Supreme Court decision allowing Frank Lautenberg to run in Torricelli's stead. The Lautenberg campaign sailed to victory once the crisis-filled environment of the Forrester-Torricelli contest subsided. Political professionals from both sides reported that the Lautenberg campaign provided New Jersey's Democratic-leaning voters a safe haven from Forrester, who had previously been the only major alternative to Torricelli in the race. There is no substantial evidence of crises for the brief Lautenberg campaign.

Beyond crises, however, the 2002 New Jersey Senate race reinforces important and constant truisms in US electoral politics. Even during extraordinary and unique crises such as those in the 2002 campaign, fundamental forces related to party identity, the importance of local politics, and the influence of the media all played a major role in the outcome of the race and shaped the environment in which the race occurred. The New Jersey case study is therefore an important reminder that even though crises can be highly individualized events, they do not necessarily overcome other environmental factors that would be present in the state or district at any time. Crises undoubtedly dominated the 2002 New Jersey Senate race. They apparently did not, however, overcome the state's Democratic legacy once those crises had subsided.

Notes

1. The committee is formally known as the Select Committee on Ethics.
2. For an early profile of the alleged relationship between Torricelli and Chang, see Schmidt and Grimaldi (2001).
3. However, this does not necessarily imply coordination between the campaign and the DSCC in the campaign finance sense.
4. Ken Snyder, telephone interview with author, March 23, 2004. Emphasis in original.
5. Mary Jo White, the US attorney investigating the case, reportedly concluded that the government could not win a criminal conviction against Torricelli. The government also reportedly determined that Chang was a questionable witness. However, the matter was referred to the Senate Ethics Committee to investigate possible violation of Senate rules. See Kocieniewski with Golden (2002) and Inouye et al. (2002) for more details.
6. Senior source inside the Torricelli campaign, telephone interview, April 2004. Additional information omitted to protect confidentiality.
7. Source who worked closely with the Torricelli campaign, telephone interview with author, March 2004. Additional information omitted to protect confidentiality.
8. Although the ad is officially titled "Fighter," political professionals on both sides called it "the apology ad." Interviews and the Wisconsin Advertising Project data (Goldstein and Rivlin 2005) suggested that the Torricelli campaign was reserving funds to run advertising in October. The DSCC aired several ads prior to Torricelli's withdrawal.

9. This information comes from CMAG storyboards, made available by the Wisconsin Advertising Project (Goldstein and Rivlin 2005).

10. Ken Snyder, telephone interview with author, March 24, 2004.

11. For a discussion of this tradition within African American politics, see Taylor (2004).

12. John Brabender, telephone interview with author, April 7, 2004.

13. David Plouffe, telephone interview with author, April 19, 2004.

14. Indeed, many Democrats' comments about the report echoed the same degree of bitterness that some Max Cleland campaign staffers conveyed when discussing the "11 Times" ad.

15. Source who worked closely with the Torricelli campaign, telephone interview with author, March 2004. Additional information omitted to protect confidentiality.

16. Jonathan Dienst, telephone interview with author, July 23, 2004.

17. Joel Benenson, telephone interview with author, April 6, 2004.

18. David Plouffe, telephone interview with author, April 19, 2004.

19. Monica Lesmerises, personal interview with author, July 2, 2004, Washington, D.C.

20. Journalist who covered the 2002 New Jersey Senate race, telephone interview with author, March 26, 2004.

21. Democratic official, personal interview with author, May 2004, Washington, D.C. Additional information omitted to protect confidentiality.

22. Bill Pascoe, telephone interview with author, February 2, 2004.

23. The Forrester campaign's struggles with the candidate's writings and off-message comments illustrate the link between **internal** *organizational* crises (failure to complete sufficient background research) and **external** crises in making Forrester vulnerable to attacks and media inquiries. The episode also borders on a *candidate political error* crisis due to Forrester's changing messages without adequate attention to campaign strategy as determined by the consulting team.

24. Gene Ulm, personal interview with author, April 21, 2004, Alexandria, Virginia.

25. Tom Rubino, telephone interview with author, May 6, 2004.

26. David Plouffe, telephone interview with author, April 19, 2004.

27. Joel Benenson, telephone interview with author, April 6, 2004.

28. Bill Pascoe, telephone interview with author, February 2, 2004. Emphasis in original.

29. Chris LaCivita, telephone interview with author, June 15, 2004.

30. Senior Republican official, personal interview with author, May 2004, Washington, D.C. Additional information omitted to protect confidentiality.

31. John Brabender, telephone interview with author, April 7, 2004.

32. Tom Rubino, telephone interview with author, May 6, 2004.

33. Source close to the Forrester campaign, telephone interview with author, May 2004. Additional information omitted to protect confidentiality.

34. Senior adviser to the Lautenberg campaign, telephone interview with author, March 2004. Additional information omitted to protect confidentiality.

35. Tom Shea, personal interview with author, April 29, 2004, Washington, D.C.

36. John Brabender, telephone interview with author, April 7, 2004.

6

A Crisis of Epic Proportions: The Wellstone-Coleman- Mondale Race

Even all-encompassing electoral crises rarely involve genuine life-and-death matters. Some crises, however, encompass both electoral turmoil and human tragedy. Such was the case in the 2002 Senate contest in Minnesota—a race that initially featured incumbent senator Paul Wellstone (DFL) and Republican challenger Norm Coleman. Minneapolis *Star Tribune* reporter Eric Black offers one of the most thorough accounts of early crisis-management efforts; the date is October 25, 2002, thirteen days before the general election:

> Norm Coleman is at a loggers' rally. Walter Mondale is at a political fundraiser. Paul Wellstone is airborne. Everything is about to change. [A] colleague tells Minneapolis attorney David Lillehaug of reports that a plane chartered by the Wellstone campaign has crashed. Lillehaug, who has close political ties to the senator, borrows a phone from the maitre d' at [a] restaurant and reaches Wellstone headquarters. . . . The look on Lillehaug's face is so frightening that the maitre d' makes the sign of the cross. . . . Not only Wellstone, but his wife, Sheila, and daughter, Marcia, are dead, along with five others. . . . Coleman immediately suspends his campaign, hops on his plane and heads for St. Paul. On the flight home, he reads aloud from a book of daily prayers that he carries. Back in the Twin Cities, Coleman's friend and confidant, Erich Mische, organizes a crisis meeting.[1] (Black 2002)

Crises on the Horizon?

The deaths of Paul Wellstone and the other passengers and crew aboard his plane make most of the crises examined in this book seem trivial. In human terms, those other crises *were* trivial. In terms of campaign crises and the theory developed in the previous chapters, however, the Minnesota case is comparatively simple. Although the events were tragic, the case-study interviews established that the plane crash that killed Wellstone and seven others was *the* defining campaign event—and a political crisis—for all three campaigns. There was also widespread agreement that the tone of a nationally televised memorial service for Wellstone, his family, and colleagues represented a crisis for Walter Mondale's campaign; it was also a strategic windfall for Coleman and other Republicans. (Mondale, an elder statesman and Jimmy Carter's vice president, replaced Wellstone on the ballot after the crash.) In fact, political professionals in all three campaigns described the memorial service as perhaps the most significant event (other than the crash) shaping the campaign context. There was also some evidence of an averted *organizational* crisis within the Coleman campaign before Wellstone's death.

"That campaign actually defines the word 'crisis,'" Chris LaCivita, political director for the NRSC during the 2002 cycle, said when asked about the Coleman campaign. "I guess . . . the most defining crisis, obviously, was the day Wellstone's plane went down. No one is trained and no matter how many campaigns you're in . . . there's just no training mechanism. And it's really relying on instinct."[2] Clearly, Wellstone's death was the ultimate **unexpected, external** campaign crisis. Although political professionals emphasize the importance of calm, strategic thinking during crises, no amount of strategic thinking could prepare either side for the political and emotional reality of what the plane crash meant.

Wellstone's death created a situation for the Coleman campaign that could have easily become politically overwhelming, particularly given widespread media attention to the crash. In her analysis of the case, Amy Jasperson (2004) finds that, after the plane crash, Wellstone received significantly more favorable media coverage than Coleman did at a time when audience share rose significantly. In addition to strategic questions of how to appropriately respond, Republicans therefore faced an electoral threat resulting from an already close race and public grief surrounding Wellstone's death.[3]

The Wellstone Decisionmaking Team and Organization

Longtime aide Jeff Blodgett served as Wellstone's campaign manager. Diane Feldman of The Feldman Group did the campaign's polling. Mandy Grunwald of Grunwald Communications served as media consultant. Jim Andrews served as general consultant to the campaign. Former Wellstone aides Robert Richman and Dan Cramer, by 2002 working as consultants at the political-consulting firm Grassroots Solutions, were also involved in campaign strategy. Cramer was the firm's lead connection to the Wellstone campaign, while Richman worked primarily with the state Democrat-Farmer-Labor (DFL) Party. In late September, Cramer joined the Wellstone campaign as a staff member, supervising field operations.

Interviews offered conflicting reports about whether Paul Wellstone was actively involved in making strategic decisions or whether he largely left strategic direction to others. Like Norm Coleman and Walter Mondale, Wellstone's political network extended outward for specialized advice. This included several former aides and longtime friends. A former US attorney for Minnesota, David Lillehaug, provided legal advice to the campaign and assisted with debate preparations. Longtime Wellstone state director Connie Lewis was designated to do political work and monitored information about Wellstone's record during the campaign but concentrated mostly on running Wellstone's Senate office in the state. Wellstone's Senate chief of staff, Colin McGinnis, was also mentioned during interviews, but he reportedly concentrated on official business. Several other members of Wellstone's kitchen cabinet, including the senator's wife, Sheila Wellstone, were regularly mentioned during interviews.

Minor Wellstone Crises Before the Crash

Prior to Wellstone's death, political professionals associated with his campaign reported only minor crises, if any. However, Democrats did describe Wellstone's opposition to a 2002 Iraq War resolution as a potential crisis for the campaign. In theoretical terms, the vote could be described as a *candidate political error*.[4] However, as with many candidate political errors, Wellstone's vote reportedly revolved around personal conviction, even though it meant potential political crisis for the campaign. As *Washington Post* reporter Helen Dewar wrote shortly before Wellstone's death:

> [Wellstone] had built a political career on standing by his convictions, which included a decided preference for international cooperation and diplomacy over war. . . . So far Wellstone is alone among the handful of endangered incumbents in coming out against the resolution. None of them has more at stake on the Iraq vote than Wellstone, according to political observers in Washington and Minnesota. That's partly because of the closeness of his race against Republican Norm Coleman and partly because of the senator's history of marching to his own drumbeat. (Dewar 2002)

Commenting on the Iraq vote, Wellstone campaign manager Jeff Blodgett explained,

We announced our position on October 3rd. Literally one month before the election, here we were voting on these highly charged, huge issues of war and peace and life and death, all shoved into the final stages of election. . . . And the amount of time spent on that and the discussion and the worry about what his principled stand was going to do politically was definitely a crisis. It turned out it wasn't. It turned out it helped him.[5]

Indeed, during interviews, other Wellstone staff, including Connie Lewis and Diane Feldman, played down the idea that the vote was a crisis because Wellstone's stance was in keeping with his previous positions. The campaign team believed it would ultimately be popular with constituents.

Blodgett added that Wellstone's decision to break his initial pledge of only serving two terms, and the senator's announcement well before the election that he had multiple sclerosis, represented potential crises for the campaign but never really developed. Finally, Blodgett reported that the Wellstone campaign attempted to create "mini crises" for Coleman by attacking the challenger on some of his statements toward Wellstone's defense positions and Coleman's positions on Social Security and the Boundary Waters of Minnesota.[6] However, these issues did not surface in interviews with the Coleman team. The Wellstone team was also quick to point out that these potential crises were overshadowed by the plane crash.

An Overwhelming Crisis: Wellstone's Death

It goes without saying that the plane crash that killed Paul Wellstone, Sheila Wellstone, Marcia Wellstone Markuson, campaign staff Tom Lapic, Mary McEvoy, and Will McLaughlin, and pilots Richard Conry and Michael Guess represented a crisis for the Wellstone campaign and others involved in the race.[7] In addition to the emotional turmoil for campaign staff, the campaign organization was in turmoil. In this ultimate *strategic disruption* the campaign could not continue, as it no longer had a candidate. In addition to coming to terms with Wellstone's death, the campaign team was immediately faced with an array of organizational and strategic challenges. These ranged from notifying victims' families before the media reported the crash to navigating the legal requirements of ending one campaign and beginning another.

Most immediately, the campaign faced simultaneous *media* and *organizational* crises of confirming and reacting to Wellstone's death, both emotionally and officially. Wellstone campaign manager Jeff Blodgett explained:

At that point, the decisionmaking team became myself and [state director] Connie Lewis . . . which started with doing nothing before we contacted all the families so that they wouldn't hear about it on the news. . . . The second thing was to inform the staff, which by this time was a very large staff. It was over 100 people in field offices all over the state. . . . And so we had to assemble everyone in the office and in the conference room with a speakerphone, and that took time . . . I'll never forget the gasps of horror and the sobbing by everyone in that room and on the phone when I told them what had happened. And then I had to list off the [names of] staffers after talking about Paul, Sheila, and Marcia because people weren't even tracking that. [Then we] . . . needed to talk to the media . . . mostly just so we could be the ones to announce it.[8]

Beyond those immediate emotional and organizational concerns, several other major questions emerged. Wellstone pollster Diane Feldman explained the grim array of political and practical questions that had to be considered:

First it was the decision of who the candidate was going to be and when [that person was] going to become a candidate and how [that person was] going to become a candidate. What happens to the Wellstone campaign money and how does somebody raise the money to mount a two-week campaign in the short period of time? And what was the role of the party in that? What, frankly, was the process for selecting a candidate and what was the timetable associated with that? And . . . for Jeff [Blodgett] and for Connie Lewis, there are all of the organizational tasks that surrounded that: the recovery of the bodies, the planning of the funeral and the memorial service.[9]

As Wellstone attorney David Lillehaug explained, the campaign also faced an array of unexpected legal questions:

There were myriad legal issues that came up immediately. . . . The Wellstone [campaign] committee needed to wind down in a legal manner so that it would not taint whoever the party's nominee was. And there were a host of legal issues and then a host of employment issues as well. How do you deal with these people who have put their heart and soul in the campaign and then don't have jobs anymore? And how do you do that without making an illegal [campaign finance] contribution to what turned out to be the Mondale committee? So I was working on that and I was also working that afternoon on what the law was with respect to ballot succession.[10]

That afternoon, Lillehaug also consulted with attorneys for the state and national Democratic parties concerning campaign finance. In a strategic sense, however, the Wellstone campaign was finished.

The Coleman Decisionmaking Team and Organization

Interviews established that Norm Coleman assembled an experienced and fairly large campaign team. Ben Whitney served as campaign manager. Gene Ulm at Public Opinion Strategies headed polling efforts. Tom Mason worked on Coleman's communication strategy. Republican voter-contact specialist Jeff Larson was also reportedly involved in strategic decision-making for the Coleman campaign. The campaign employed two media firms at different points in the race, a distinction that some political professionals said in interviews reflected an **internal** *organizational* crisis for the Coleman campaign. For most of the campaign, Dresner, Wickers and Associates provided paid media advice. Late in the campaign, political professionals inside the campaign said that the firm's strategic input was limited, as Scott Howell of Scott Howell and Company took the lead role on paid media. The NRSC also took keen interest in the race, with regular involvement from Chris LaCivita, Mitch Bainwol, and Terry Nelson. Republican operative Heath Thompson also joined the campaign late in the race to provide strategic advice at the White House's urging, Coleman insiders said. Political professionals also said that Coleman, an experienced politician and former St. Paul mayor, was an active strategic player. Longtime Coleman associates Erich Mische and Vin Weber, a former Republican congressman from Minnesota, also reportedly took active strategic roles in the campaign.

Internal Crisis and the Change in Media Consultants for the Coleman Campaign

Even in this most dramatic of cases, there was often evidence of more mundane, "routine" campaign crises. For example, political professionals said that the Coleman campaign realized during the summer of 2002 that they faced a potential crisis when polling numbers were unexpectedly low and paid media efforts were not having the anticipated effect. At that time, Dresner, Wickers was conducting Coleman's paid media work. Coleman campaign manager Ben Whitney explained, "[The change in media consultants] was a crisis because I personally believe . . . we would [not] have won the election had we not changed our media consultant to Scott Howell." Calling the event a "structural crisis" for the Coleman organization, Whitney continued:

> I think that, yes, there was confluence in August that the consultants had made a bet about early advertising. We did not have the resources to

compete in August, which is ordinarily a down time. The Democrats continued to heavily invest both by the campaign and the Democratic Senatorial [Campaign] Committee, continued to put money up, and they outspent us, and our poll numbers really reflected that when we did our pre–Labor Day poll.[11]

Similarly, according to a Republican source close to the Coleman campaign, there was anecdotal evidence of message problems for the Coleman campaign over the summer, but "it was just sort of validated when the bottom fell out of some of the polling. That's what led that crisis to a head. That's when we made the change in media firms. . . . I just think that that was critical for the Coleman campaign because I just think that if they hadn't made the change, Coleman probably wouldn't [have been elected]."[12] Another Republican source close to the Coleman campaign disagreed that the change in media firms represented a crisis, but the individual volunteered that the new ads were effective.[13] Political professionals said that Dresner, Wickers retained an advisory role after the switch, although a diminished one. (In fairness, however, Dresner, Wickers staff were not solicited for interviews for this book because they were not identified by Coleman political professionals as part of the strategic decision-making team during campaign crises.) Around this time, Heath Thompson and Erich Mische also took a more active role in campaign strategy.

The Coleman Campaign and the Crisis of How to Respond to Wellstone's Death

In political terms, the main crisis for the Coleman campaign was how to respond to Wellstone's death while appearing appropriately sensitive but also not losing strategic ground. In interviews and media accounts (e.g., Black 2002), political professionals inside the Coleman campaign said they were keenly aware of John Ashcroft's (R) loss to Mel Carnahan (D) two years earlier in a Missouri US Senate race. In that case, Carnahan, son Randy, and aide Chris Sifford were also killed in a plane crash shortly before the general election, which prompted Ashcroft to suspend his campaign. Ashcroft's silence after Carnahan's death, although apparently intended to be respectful, was later widely regarded as a strategic error.[14]

The magnitude of the situation was so great, and the nature of the event so unusual, that Wellstone's death seemed "beyond crisis," as Coleman confidant and future chief of staff Erich Mische noted during an interview.[15] Nonetheless, Coleman campaign manager Ben Whitney explained that even during extraordinary situations crisis management can and did occur:

> Sure, I think there were a lot of things out of our control, there is no question about that, because we couldn't choose who our opponent was going to be. We couldn't necessarily impact directly how the people of Minnesota would respond to the death of their senator. . . . But there were things in our control. . . . For example . . . you do decide to pull down your campaign right away and you have to make sure that your ads come off and you've got to make sure if you had any negative literature that it doesn't get out there, that you stop your mail, you pull your campaign to a complete and screeching halt. And you could say that's not [crisis] management, but it is. But I wouldn't say that is the major management [issue]. I would say the major management [issue] was to figure out how to relaunch the campaign.[16]

Interviews suggested that Wellstone's death represented at least three distinct crises for the Coleman campaign: (1) the decision to halt the campaign; (2) the decision to relaunch the campaign; and (3) preparing to relaunch the campaign against an initially undefined candidate (until it was clear that Mondale would run). All took root in the *strategic disruption* of Wellstone's death and its **unexpected, external** character. However, the events also represented significant **internal** *organizational* crises for the Coleman campaign because they required unexpected retooling of the campaign and literally stopping and restarting the campaign team.

In restarting the campaign, political professionals reported that many questions concerned how to publicly reintroduce Coleman to voters. This was especially true for discussions of political advertising. The campaign's major debut began by airing a Coleman ad titled "Looking Forward." The ad ran statewide the Wednesday before the election. In the ad, Coleman stood, wearing a dark jacket, with a windblown field in the background. Looking directly into the camera, Coleman struck a somber tone by extending sympathies to the affected families. After a quick fade to black, Coleman reappeared and told voters, "And now I have to ask you to look with me into the future." He went on to cite his two-year campaign and its platform, declaring that the election was about the future.[17]

Political professionals associated with the Coleman campaign praised their candidate's leadership during the tragedy. A few Democratic political professionals rejected that claim, saying they believed that Coleman's reaction was staged for political advantage and that the accident distracted voters from Coleman's allegedly shifting policy positions. Republicans flatly rejected those views. Indeed, they argued that Coleman's ability to strike a genuine and appropriate tone was a key asset in restarting the campaign through the "Looking Forward" ad. According to Heath Thompson:

We decided, "Here's the reality. The reality is we have a candidate who is truly, just completely grief-stricken, and basically in shock because of the magnitude of what's happened. That's the way most people feel. If we try to artificially give him some statement or have a formal conference or do something in the campaign, we're going to come across looking like a bunch of insensitive jerks. Let's just let him go home and if he's up to it, and he feels up to it—and he indicated he did—just step outside the door and tell folks what he was thinking and what he felt, that his prayers were with the family and everything and just let Norm react like Norm was really reacting." That's very difficult for campaigns to do because there's no control [over the candidate], but we made a concerted decision that that was the best way for us to handle it.[18]

When asked to respond to political professionals' comments about the importance of limiting candidates' strategic influence and controlling messages tightly during crises (see Chapter 3), Thompson continued,

It was hard. There were a lot of folks in that room who were like, "No, we can't do that; it's insane, we've got to script every word. If he says the wrong thing we're going to blow it." [But] this is much bigger than having the right sound byte. He needs to show his heart because his heart was hurting just like everyone else's. They've competed against each other; they were big rivals in a very intense campaign.[19]

That process, Thompson said, resulted in the "Looking Forward" ad. During "really, really big crises" such as Wellstone's death, Thompson said, much of the campaign's survival depends on the candidate's innate political skills. Consultants, he and some other political professionals emphasized, can only do so much.

Other political advertising represented potential—but ultimately averted—crises for the Coleman campaign. Some Republican political professionals were particularly concerned about an NRSC ad critical of Walter Mondale's policy positions that was scheduled to air in the campaign's final days. In fact, the ad never ran but the concept was controversial. The Coleman campaign learned of the ad, political professionals said, through the media, and Coleman publicly condemned such attacks. Coleman insiders described the episode as a crisis because some believed it could have cost Coleman the election if the ad ran and generated public backlash against the popular elder statesman. In contrast, NRSC officials wanted to run the ad, and according to Chris LaCivita some NRSC officials believed the ad could make the difference between victory and defeat for Coleman. With the ad already at stations and ready to air, LaCivita made the last-minute decision to pull the commercial. Even so, various media outlets reported on the controversy.

Mondale campaign manager Tina Smith suggested that coverage of the episode inflicted damage on her candidate's campaign, even though the ad never aired. According to Smith:

> I thought the way that they handled that outside ad was brilliant because they got the coverage for the content without getting blamed for the negative attack. . . . It opened the door to an opportunity for people to link Mr. Mondale in 2002 with old policies from the seventies [when Mondale served in the Senate and as Jimmy Carter's vice president]. . . . If they had aired the ad . . . then it would have been seen as a nasty thing. . . . But because [the ad never ran], they didn't get any of the blame, but they got that word out.[20]

Despite these crises—whether potential or realized—Republicans also implemented successful field efforts in the final days of the campaign. The NRSC also contributed substantial resources to the campaign in the final week. As in Georgia, prominent visits to the state from top Republican officials, including President George W. Bush, buoyed the Coleman campaign.

Crises for the Mondale Campaign

Political professionals cited three events, beyond Wellstone's death, as crises for the Mondale campaign. First, political professionals from all three campaigns said they believed that the Wellstone memorial service represented an **unexpected, external** crisis for the Mondale campaign because of the hostile environment it created among many voters who thought the event had been overly politicized (see below). Media coverage that constantly replayed portions of the service for several days afterward also suggested an **external** *media* crisis for Democrats. Second, Republicans pointed to the television debate between Mondale and Coleman just before the election as a crisis for Mondale because the former vice president reportedly performed worse than expected, whereas Coleman performed better than many Democrats had expected. However, Democrats played down the impact of the debate. Third, and perhaps most important, Democrats argued that the Mondale campaign was in perpetual crisis— from organizational problems in merging Mondale's twenty-year-old campaign team with Wellstone's political professionals, to external crises of many voters not remembering Mondale, and to the campaign not having enough time and money to wage an effective contest. Indeed, time was the central factor in the brief Republican campaign against Mondale.

Constant Crises for the Mondale Campaign?

Most of the Wellstone campaign organization transitioned (after being officially terminated from the Wellstone campaign) to the Mondale campaign.[21] Wellstone campaign manager Jeff Blodgett, attorney David Lillehaug, and Mondale campaign manager Tina Smith served as links between the Wellstone and Mondale organizations, as all knew, or were, senior officials in one or both campaigns. Wellstone field director Dan Cramer also moved to the Mondale campaign, taking on additional duties supporting Tina Smith. Mandy Grunwald served as media consultant. Despite some consistency between the two organizations, political professionals said that most of Mondale's strategic decisionmaking team changed compared with Wellstone's. Mondale reportedly relied on several old political contacts for strategic advice, including former speechwriter Marty Kaplan, press aide Maxine Issacs, political consultant Chuck Campion, and pollster Al Quinlan of Greenberg Quinlan Rosner Research. Mondale's son, Ted, also provided strategic advice and was heavily involved in Mondale's fundraising. Ted Mondale also served as a surrogate for his father at public appearances.

Despite his experienced campaign team, political professionals said during interviews, Mondale faced virtually insurmountable logistical problems. In addition, the enthusiasm among Wellstone's campaign team did not carry over to the Mondale effort. According to Dan Cramer, "It wasn't that [the campaign staff] didn't like [Mondale]; they just didn't know him."[22] Republicans, and some Democrats, said the same was true for Minnesota voters. Cramer also pointed out that ongoing grief and attending "five funerals in four days" made maintaining organizational momentum extremely difficult.

Moreover, some political professionals said that the enormity of Wellstone's death made Mondale's victory virtually impossible, regardless of individual difficulties. Wellstone state director Connie Lewis explained,

> The whole thing was a crisis, I think. I don't even think it ever got out of crisis. The crisis was there was no time. . . . The memorial service was a crisis. The whole thing, the whole ten days was a crisis. It was sort—I guess the [Wellstone] memorial service was probably the biggest problem that they had. . . . [Mondale] had such a very short time to reintroduce himself. And then that became so much a focus of attention and got the Republicans ginned up and all that.[23]

Tina Smith confirmed the *constant crisis* perception of the Mondale campaign and illustrated the link between the emotional fallout from

Wellstone's death and logistical problems (and arguably *organizational* crises) for the Mondale campaign:

> I mean, really, the whole experience was sort of a series of minor-to-middling crises that were precipitated by both external and internal factors and everything, to use your typology. I mean, a few things you could expect, but most everything was unexpected. . . . You expect things that you are able to plan for, and there was no time to plan. Therefore, nothing was truly expected. There [were] . . . literally hundreds of small crises all the way through.[24]

Smith continued:

> [The following episode] sort of was actually another small crisis. The people on the Wellstone campaign, and in particular the scheduler . . . were grappling with intense feelings of personal guilt, particularly around the decision [to put] Paul and Sheila and everyone else on the plane. And so the idea that they would then turn around and put somebody else on a small plane . . . they literally couldn't even go there. . . . The Mondale people, on the other hand . . . didn't have any feelings of personal guilt. It never would occur to us that it was the fault of anybody that this terrible thing had happened, and so we were able to be much more practical about thinking about the pros and cons of flying versus not flying. And it caused a bit of a crisis because . . . the Wellstone people basically said at one point, at a crisis moment, "If you want to get on an airplane and fly, you're going to have to schedule it yourself because I refuse to do it. I will not do it." So we decided that it was best to drive— to use this big bus, which we did, and we did fly back. We did fly back from Moorhead just because we just honestly ran out of time.[25]

Although the episode perhaps seems minor in retrospect, as Ted Mondale explained, the inability to fly had serious strategic implications given Minnesota's geography: "In the last four or five days of any race you're [typically] hopping your candidate around from media market to media market via a pretty fast airplane, generally. So, definitely, our ability to move [Walter Mondale] as a candidate was limited. There are some pretty [big] distances in this state between population centers."[26]

Ted Mondale also pointed out that his father's campaign started with very little money (a *fundraising* crisis). In addition, the Wellstone ad buys could not legally transfer to the Mondale campaign. According to Ted Mondale, "We basically had one day of television as opposed to [the Coleman campaign's] five or six days of television."[27] He added that lack of funding had major ramifications for the campaign's ability to respond to the memorial service using paid media.

The Wellstone Memorial as Crisis for Mondale and Opportunity for Coleman

On October 29, 20,000 mourners gathered at the University of Minnesota to honor Wellstone and the other victims of the crash. Political professionals from all three campaigns said that what unfolded represented a heartfelt attempt to provide solace, but also became an enormous political spectacle. What had been expected to be a tribute gradually appeared to many to be a political rally combining Wellstone's legacy with the ongoing Senate race. Consequently, political professionals agreed that the episode became a crisis for the Mondale campaign.

As the three-hour service continued, overt political appeals increased, reaching their apex with an emotional speech by a close Wellstone friend, Rick Kahn. The following day, Minneapolis *Star Tribune* reporters summarized some of the most dramatic moments of the Kahn speech:

> [Kahn said], "We are begging you to win this Senate election for Paul Wellstone." In a move that brought gasps of delight from some and stony silence from a few, Kahn then began urging select Republicans to drop their partisanship and work for Wellstone's replacement. He singled out some by name. To US Rep. Jim Ramstad (R-Minn.), Kahn said, "You know that Paul loved you. He needs you now. . . . Help us win this race." (Kumar, Smith, and Lopez 2002)

Crowds also cheered when video screens inside the arena featured prominent Democrats at the service, including former president Bill Clinton and Senators Hillary Rodham Clinton (NY) and Ted Kennedy (MA), yet "jeered when U.S. Senate Minority Leader Trent Lott, R-Miss., and former GOP Sen. Rod Grams of Minnesota were on the screens" (Kumar, Smith, and Lopez 2002). "It was during Kahn's speech that [Minnesota] Gov. Jesse Ventura and First Lady Terry Ventura got up shaking their heads and walked out. Lott also walked out during the service" (Kumar, Smith, and Lopez 2002). Ventura later appointed Independent Dean Barkley to fill the remainder of Wellstone's term.

Some Republicans criticized that statewide media coverage of the service had been tantamount to free political advertising for Democrats, and they demanded equal time. Republicans also charged that the service violated an agreement between the two parties to suspend campaigning until the day after the service. In interviews, most Democrats agreed that the memorial was mishandled. However, they also said that it was intended to reflect Wellstone's legacy.[28]

Political fallout from the memorial continued during the final days of the race. The Minneapolis *Star Tribune* implored voters in an October 31 editorial to focus on the Coleman-Mondale race instead of the "political rally" the memorial service allegedly became. The paper also took issue with the tone of the service, particularly Kahn's comments:

> In the second half of his speech, Kahn strayed from memorializing Wellstone. For 10 to 15 minutes he turned the gathering into a political rally for the Wellstone legacy. It was inappropriate, but more to the point, it was irrational. Kahn appeared so caught up in grief, loss and anger that he lost his way. . . . However they were intended, Kahn's words were an affront to the Republican candidate, Norm Coleman, and those who support him. We can understand Kahn's state of mind, but we must repudiate his message. There can be no capitulation in this race. Coleman and Mondale owe Minnesotans a vigorous contest of ideas. (Minneapolis *Star Tribune* 2002)

Reflecting the *Star Tribune*'s sentiments, many media outlets reportedly felt that Democrats had taken advantage of three hours of live statewide coverage of the service (Jasperson 2004). Coleman confidant and future chief of staff Erich Mische explained:

> I think the press is watching [the service] and for the first hour, hour and a half, everybody is kind of going, "OK." And then all of a sudden, the total tone of it changed and it becomes hate and it becomes accusatory. It becomes partisan. . . . And I think that, probably more than anything else, took the wind out of most people in Minnesota. . . . I'm at the campaign office with folks and we're sitting and we're talking . . . and the TV is on in the other room and all of a sudden you hear the phones picking up and ringing, ringing, ringing, and all of a sudden it's like, "What the hell's going on?" . . . It was so completely foreign to what most people expected it to be that I think there were a lot of people that were angry. But I think a lot more people were just simply stunned. It was just kind of like, "Huh? What just went on here?"[29]

Even so, Mische added, "I think people need to cut [Rick Kahn] and people involved with that event some slack. I think it was bad judgment—I think judgment clouded by extreme grief and despair. Put me in the same circumstance and would I make the same decision that they made? I probably would, only because I think you would just be so overcome with that grief and emotion."[30]

From the typology perspective, the Wellstone memorial was **external** and **unexpected**, especially in terms of the tone it struck and the consternation it apparently caused among much of the electorate. Republicans— and some Democrats—viewed the memorial service as a major *strategic disruption* for Democrats because it represented a profound loss of control. Calling the memorial service a "crisis of epic proportions," NRSC political director Chris LaCivita explained:

> Any time a campaign loses control of an event, it becomes an epic crisis. . . . No political operative in his right mind would have allowed [the memorial service] to happen. And I just can't imagine that their folks allowed that to happen. . . . The campaign did not take care in ensuring how the whole thing was to be portrayed. And it completely, I think quite frankly, did the memory of Paul Wellstone a great disservice. . . . I think [the memorial service] was just poorly executed.[31]

Indeed, Democrats centrally involved in the memorial service freely admitted that they were not thinking clearly and that they made decisions based on emotion and exhaustion, not as strategic-minded political professionals. Wellstone campaign manager Jeff Blodgett explained:

> It was deep grief that affected all of our judgments about what was the right thing to do. And not just that, but how you do something like this in the white-hot political environment that the Minnesota Senate election had become? How do you do all that [and] at the same time, just want to do something for someone who is a friend and your leader to say good-bye to him? . . . Now, I say that also defending much of what went on there. . . . The very successful right-wing advocacy spin and then spin by Republican operatives about it in the days after, that was really where the big impact came. And it distorted what happened there and left out all but a small part of what happened there. . . . Looking back on it, the last thing a political professional wants is to have one event change the outcome of an election. And you can argue that that's what happened at the memorial service. So that's something that I, for the longest time, spent a lot of time analyzing. And I just came to the conclusion that it was just extraordinary circumstances that came together that caused a lot of bad decisions to be made.[32]

Democratic political professionals also suggested that the tone of the memorial to those in attendance did not necessarily match the impression presented on television. Some Democratic political professionals said that the distinction between those viewing the memorial inside the arena versus those viewing it on television clouded Democrats' strategic judgment. According to field operative Dan Cramer:

> I think part of the delayed reaction [in recognizing the political significance of the memorial service] was [that] we were in our grief. Part of it was the difference between being in the memorial service—that rally atmosphere that that became—and watching it on television. . . . Again, it was so outside what we had thought about for that [the memorial]. We had viewed it as a eulogy for Paul, and hadn't contemplated the political ramifications. I think it took us a day or two to begin realizing this was a major political event. . . . That was a mistake of devastating proportions.[33]

Ted Mondale also suggested that context, timing, and lack of resources made it difficult for the Mondale campaign to distance itself from the overly political portions of the service:

> There was nothing we could do about it. We had no money. We couldn't put any ads up. You couldn't buy any ad time. . . . You had to go through the mourning process. . . . And you had a message that was sent out [through the memorial service] six days or so or whatever before an election where a huge amount of people felt that the Democrats, "those people," cared more about politics than the death of [Wellstone and the others on the plane]. And [voters] took it internally [as if it were] someone in their family: their mom, their sister, their brother.[34]

Several Democrats reported that they felt the service changed the outcome of the race. Others said they believed that the memorial service was a key factor in the outcome, but they also emphasized other obstacles, especially the limited time to reintroduce Mondale to Minnesota voters. Democrats also criticized what they regarded as an unethical national Republican effort to overemphasize the tone of parts of the memorial.

Despite their objections to the service, Republicans said they viewed the public backlash against the memorial not only as a *strategic disruption* for the Mondale campaign but also as an opportunity for the Coleman campaign. Ben Whitney explained:

> That was one of the most extraordinary things that I'll probably ever see in politics, is what happened after the memorial service. The next day, literally hundreds of people just showed up in our office. They were writing checks leaning against each other's backs. . . . We gave out 12,000 lawn signs in three days. There were just dozens and dozens of full-time volunteers who came [saying], "I want to help." But what happened is we got

all this energy and that we could manage the structure to put that energy to good use on behalf of the campaign. I think that was probably one of the most important parts of the crisis-management things that happened.[35]

Indeed, there was strong evidence of a shift in public sentiment after the memorial. For example, Amy Jasperson (2004) not only finds that media coverage toward Democrats become more negative after the memorial; she also notes that in tracking polls Mondale's previous 6 percent lead over Coleman fell to just 2 percent—well within the margin of error.

Nonetheless, Republicans said they did not believe that even the extraordinary events surrounding the memorial service accounted for Coleman's victory. Not surprisingly, they argued that Coleman was on track to win the election even before Wellstone's death. Equally unsurprisingly, Democrats argued that Wellstone was clearly on track to beat Coleman prior to the senator's death. Overall, Republicans described a series of events that all came together to affect the outcome of the race. In short, individual crises combined to create a multifaceted, crisis-filled environment. According to Coleman pollster Glen Bolger:

> [The memorial service] was obviously an unexpected, unplanned event. But it was also something that took an unexpected turn and there was a backlash against it that nobody could have anticipated. . . . I think that several things formulated [Coleman's victory]. I think that going into the day of the crash, I believe that Norm was going to beat Senator Wellstone. We had pulled ahead and our message was sticking very well, and we had very good ads. Then after Wellstone died and they picked Mondale, Mondale had a slight lead but it was not overwhelming. Then I think the [memorial] helped a lot, but I'm not sure it was just the [memorial]. There were certainly other aspects as well; there was the debate. I think Norm solidified the campaign there.[36]

Other members of the Coleman campaign agreed that Mondale's allegedly aggressive debate performance, when combined with the negative reaction many voters had to the memorial service, sealed his electoral fate. According to Heath Thompson:

> To me, after the accident and then the death of the senator, the whole— once you get past the tragedy of it all, and folks on the [plane], the whole politics and race of it was all about tone on both sides. What kind of tone you struck, not just about what happened to [Wellstone] and how everyone felt about it, but how you viewed things and how you were going to go forward. I think it was a very dissonant note that [Mondale] sounded in that debate by just being so ornery. I think it probably backfired.[37]

Most Democrats disagreed with respect to the debate, saying that an aggressive stance was essential, especially given Mondale's limited opportunities to make his case to voters. Dan Cramer explained:

> I don't think the debate rose to the level of crisis. I think there was a strategy going in and there is some, probably, disagreement whether that strategy worked or not. I happen to think he did what he had to do and any backlash from that pales in comparison to what would have happened if he hadn't looked aggressive and senatorial, unable to take charge. I don't think it comes close to rising to the level of crisis.[38]

Mondale officials also said the debate was not regarded as a crisis within the campaign.

Concluding Comments on Crises and the Wellstone-Coleman-Mondale Race

Perhaps more so than any of the other case studies, the Minnesota race reminds us that even the most spectacular crises might not account for all turning points in congressional campaigns. **External** crises were the most obvious events in this race, especially the political fallout from Wellstone's death and memorial service. Even in this most dramatic of cases, however, evidence of mundane crises also appeared. When considering crises from a multifaceted perspective there was evidence of **internal** *organizational* crises for the Coleman campaign surrounding the change in media consultants. The same was true for Walter Mondale's upstart campaign. These are but a few examples of the various events that political professionals identified as crises, even as there was widespread agreement that the plane crash was clearly the defining element of the race. The point here is not to undercut the importance of the crash or the deaths that accompanied it but to note that even in this case various other factors also influenced the outcome. The same is true for all campaigns, even as scholars, the media, and the public often focus on a single event.

The race also provides a powerful example of the importance of strategic thinking during campaign crises. Political professionals connected to the Wellstone campaign said they did not think strategically enough in the aftermath of Wellstone's death, albeit in an environment clouded by intense grief. As with all other campaign crises, context also played a major role in the case. Political professionals on both sides of the aisle, and from all three campaigns, suggested that the political context created by the memorial service severely limited Mondale's chances of success while strengthening Coleman's. As with some of the other cases, the Minnesota race suggests that even during the most dramatic cases decisions about campaign organizations, finances, strategy, and personnel can affect elections and public perceptions of campaigns. Just as the New Jersey case suggests that crises might not fundamentally alter a state's political culture, the Minnesota case suggests that crises do not excuse campaigns from keeping their organizations running smoothly even during tough times. Indeed, effective campaigning is often most important during crises.

Notes

1. Original paragraph breaks have been removed from the cited text.

2. Chris LaCivita, telephone interview with author, June 15, 2004.

3. For an analysis of media coverage of the Minnesota case after Wellstone's death, see also Rackaway, Smith, and Anderson (2004). That paper also compares coverage after the Wellstone and Mel Carnahan (D-MO) deaths.

4. See P.L. 107-243 (2002).

5. Jeff Blodgett, telephone interview with author, May 28, 2004.

6. Ibid.

7. The National Transportation Safety Board determined in 2003 that the crash probably resulted from crew "failure to maintain adequate airspeed" while attempting a landing, which resulted in a stall. See National Transportation Safety Board (2003, ix).

8. Jeff Blodgett, telephone interview with author, May 28, 2004.

9. Diane Feldman, telephone interview with author, June 30, 2004.

10. David Lillehaug, telephone interview with author, August 12, 2004.

11. Ben Whitney, telephone interview with author, June 3, 2004.

12. Source familiar with the Coleman campaign, telephone interview with author, June 2004. Additional information omitted to protect confidentiality.

13. Source close to the Coleman campaign, telephone interview with author, June 2004. Additional information omitted to protect confidentiality.

14. On evidence of a "eulogy effect" in sympathetic media coverage after Carnahan's death, see Smith, Rackaway, and Anderson (2002) and Rackaway, Smith, and Anderson (2004).

15. Erich Mische, personal interview with author, June 2, 2004, Washington, D.C.

16. Ben Whitney, telephone interview with author, June 3, 2004.

17. This information is based on the author's viewing and is adapted from Rodeffer's (2002b) nationaljournal.com "Ad Spotlight" summary.

18. Heath Thompson, telephone interview with author, June 23, 2004.

19. Ibid.

20. Tina Smith, telephone interview with author, June 15, 2004.

21. The Federal Election Campaign Act prohibits campaigns from sharing certain assets, such as personnel and certain strategic information, if the value of that item would exceed limits for campaign contributions. See, e.g., 2 U.S.C. sec. 441a(f). In this

case, because the Wellstone campaign continued as a legal entity even after Wellstone's death, transferring staff or assets to the Mondale campaign, without proper safeguards, could have been viewed as an excessive contribution from the former to the latter.

22. Dan Cramer, telephone interview with author, June 24, 2004.

23. Connie Lewis, telephone interview with author, July 14, 2004.

24. Tina Smith, telephone interview with author, June 15, 2004.

25. Ibid. The timing of this example is unclear in the interview data, as the Mondale campaign did not actively begin campaigning until after the October 29, 2002, memorial service. Apparently the scheduler referred to in the text is a former Wellstone staffer who had transitioned to the Mondale organization.

26. Ted Mondale, telephone interview with author, June 30, 2004.

27. Ibid.

28. Background information on the memorial service comes from interviews, Kumar, Smith, and Lopez (2002), and viewing by the author.

29. Erich Mische, personal interview with author, June 2, 2004, Washington, D.C.

30. Ibid.

31. Chris LaCivita, telephone interview with author, June 15, 2004.

32. Jeff Blodgett, telephone interview with author, May 28, 2004.

33. Dan Cramer, telephone interview with author, June 24, 2004.

34. Ted Mondale, telephone interview with author, June 30, 2004.

35. Ben Whitney, telephone interview with author, June 3, 2004.

36. Glen Bolger, telephone interview with author, June 21, 2004.

37. Heath Thompson, telephone interview with author, June 23, 2004.

38. Dan Cramer, telephone interview with author, June 24, 2004.

7

Subtle Crises and Fair Fights: The Cantwell-Gorton Race

Democratic hopes for regaining control of the Senate in 2000 looked dim.[1] Heading into the November elections, Democrats faced a sizable deficit if they were going to take back the chamber for the first time since 1995. The Republican majority had slipped to 54–46 in July 2000 when Georgia governor Roy Barnes appointed Zell Miller (D) to fill the late Paul Coverdell's (R) seat (*Cook Political Report* 2000, 4–5). However, even the Democrats' best hope—a presidential win by Al Gore, which would have made vice presidential nominee Joe Lieberman the deciding vote in the Senate—still required the party to pick up enough seats to split the chamber 50–50. The stakes, therefore, were high for Democrats nationally and especially in Washington State, where they hoped former congresswoman Maria Cantwell could defeat longtime Republican senator Slade Gorton.

As the election approached, Gorton appeared a likely winner, even if by a slim margin. Gorton was used to tough contests; he had even lost his Senate seat for two years in the 1980s but was reelected. In 1994, a Republican landslide nationally, Gorton secured a comparatively slim 56 percent of the vote, but he remained popular. In addition to overcoming Gorton's legacy in 2000, Cantwell faced a tough Democratic primary against Deborah Senn, who was initially viewed as the frontrunner. Gorton had no primary opposition.

But by the week before Election Day, *The Rothenberg Political Report* (2000) labeled the Cantwell-Gorton race a "toss-up." Cantwell's messages emphasizing protecting Social Security, the environment, and online privacy had appealed to increasingly liberal western Washington, especially Seattle-area voters. Cantwell also capitalized on her youth—she was barely forty-two when elected to the Senate—and portrayed Gorton as an out-of-touch politician whose time had passed. Interest groups invested heavily in the race, as did the national and state parties.

Cantwell eventually won, but only after a three-week automatic recount that resulted in the closest victory of all Senate races that year: 2,229 votes out of 2.4 million cast. In addition to being extremely close, the race was enormously expensive, especially for the time. Cantwell spent more than $11 million, contributing more than $10 million of her own fortune, which she had earned as an executive at RealNetworks, an online media company. Gorton only spent about half what Cantwell did ($6.4 million). Cantwell's win tied the Senate at 50–50, but Republicans maintained control of the chamber via George W. Bush's election as president and Dick Cheney's position as vice president and tiebreaker in the Senate.

The stakes in this case were certainly high and the election was close—far closer than any of the other three races profiled in the previous chapters. Nonetheless, many political professionals on both sides said during interviews that the race was free from campaign crises. Others strongly disagreed. Specifically, political professionals on the ground (as opposed to outside strategists) from each campaign said that although there were no scandals or other spectacular events in the race, a central part of the Cantwell team's strategy was to create crises through attacks on Gorton. Some Republicans agreed, saying the Gorton campaign was hurt by Cantwell's messages, resulting in a substantial *strategic disruption* at a key moment late in the race, when Cantwell criticized Gorton's support for a controversial mining provision. In addition, although both sides boasted strong campaign organizations, some Republicans said that they suspected Cantwell suffered a *fundraising* crisis when the value of her RealNetworks stock—reportedly a major source of campaign resources—plummeted. Democrats offered mixed responses but played down the event's significance.

This case is different from the Georgia, New Jersey, and Minnesota cases presented previously. In some ways, it represents a race in which major crises were not obvious. Indeed, political professionals agreed that the race's most dramatic moment—the long recount—was not a crisis in a strategic sense. However, despite disagreement among political professionals in both campaigns about which events represented crises, this case has important theoretical ramifications. First, it is fitting to end the case studies here, as the very disagreement about whether or not crises occurred harkens back to the working definition of campaign crises (see Chapter 2): *Campaign crises are interactive events that the campaign team believes represent a significant disruption to the campaign strategy or plan. Campaign crises may be **internal** or **external** and are usually **unexpected**. The full complexity of campaign crises is rarely explained by a single event.*

More than any other case, the Cantwell-Gorton contest illustrates the importance of the "belief" component of the working definition of crises. The case also reinforces some of this book's most important findings about relationships among political professionals during crises, in some instances confirming the data reviewed in Chapter 3 and, in others, offering new insights. This case also reinforces how the typology of campaign crises can be useful in understanding the competing perspectives on crises—and whether they existed—in this race.

Finally, the 2000 Washington State race provides an alternative to the political context that exacerbated campaign crises in the other three cases. The Cantwell-Gorton case demonstrates that although political context can worsen campaign crises, as the importance of environmental policy perhaps did for Slade Gorton, context can also help limit campaign crises. Even when facing a protracted recount, the fact that both sides felt the campaign environment was fair and legitimate went a long way toward minimizing the potential for crises.

Crises on the Horizon?

Political professionals from both campaigns were quick to point out during interviews that the 2000 Senate race in Washington State was a civil affair. Members of each campaign team knew and respected each other. Political professionals in both campaigns noted that the race was free from political scandals, even if crises did exist. They said that although the race was hard-fought, both candidates had strong reputations and were regarded highly. Therefore, potential crises revolved around policy issues, especially, many political professionals said, Slade Gorton's record on the environment. Democrats criticized that record. The Gorton team worked to highlight favorable portions and attacked Cantwell, portraying her as a "tax-and-spend" Democrat and criticizing her positions on Social Security and health care.

During interviews, most discussion of campaign crises centered around Gorton's support for a controversial mining process. Some political professionals believed that Cantwell's attack on Gorton's efforts represented a significant *strategic disruption* for Gorton's campaign. Under a Gorton amendment (sometimes called a "rider") to a 1999 appropriations bill, a stalled mining project in eastern Washington was allowed to proceed, despite previous Clinton administration rulings to the contrary.[2]

According to political professionals, Texas company Battle Mountain Gold planned to essentially explode the top of a mountain, known as the

Crown Jewel site, and filter the exposed gold using cyanide. The Gorton amendment was controversial not only because of the possible environmental effects of the mining process but also because of Gorton's reported personal involvement in the case. An accomplished lawyer and former Washington attorney general, Gorton personally wrote the amendment, according to his former chief of staff, Tony J. Williams. Gorton's staff knew the amendment would be controversial to environmentally sensitive Washingtonians, especially in increasingly liberal western Washington.

Gorton, however, supported the mining project. He faced economic concerns from the eastern part of the state, where unemployment was high, especially in the county where the mine would be located. Gorton also reportedly viewed the denial of operating permits for the mine as a product of overzealous federal bureaucracy. Nonetheless, as Gorton faced reelection, his campaign team expected that the Cantwell team would attack Gorton's involvement in the episode, which they did. The case therefore illustrates the **expected** dimension of the crisis typology.

What the Gorton team did not expect, however, was the timing of the attack on the mining provision. According to Williams, the Gorton team expected that the criticism would come weeks before it did. In fact, the timing evolved differently, providing a major *strategic disruption* to Gorton's plan of debating the mining issue to a draw or even a slight victory. When the criticism came later than expected, that plan could not be executed.

Other members of the Gorton team disagreed that the episode represented a crisis. For the most part, these political professionals said that Slade Gorton just plain lost and that he was a victim of changing political context, especially around Seattle. From this perspective, there were no notable crises in the campaign. Rather, the case was simply a hard-fought race in which one candidate had to lose. Political professionals also pointed out that in a race so close, any number of factors could have decided the outcome. Different political professionals' perspectives on whether crises occurred—opinions that appeared to be affected by their work locations and job functions—suggest that consultant influence in campaigns might not be as great as some of the other findings in this book suggest.

The Cantwell Decisionmaking Team and Organization

Cantwell reportedly relied on a fairly small decisionmaking team. Political professionals said that Cantwell, a former US House member and experienced politician, was particularly involved in campaign strategy. Ron Dotzauer, a former Cantwell business partner, political consultant, and elected official, served as campaign manager. Liz Luce served as deputy campaign manager and was heavily involved in the campaign but was reportedly not a major strategic decisionmaker. However, Luce had extensive campaign experience and had served as an elected official in the state. Along with Cantwell's family, Luce provided important moral and logistical support to Cantwell. Mark Mellman, who served as pollster, was reportedly an especially trusted Cantwell adviser. Karl Struble and David Eichenbaum served as media consultants. State and national Democratic Party officials were also involved in the race, particularly during the recount. Former Washington State Democratic Party political director Christian Sinderman served as a strategic adviser to Cantwell and as communications director during the campaign. Sinderman was particularly active before a large campaign organization was assembled. Jed Lewison was also involved in the campaign's communication strategy. Joe Hansen represented the Democratic Senatorial Campaign Committee in the race and headed the committee's recount efforts.

Campaign Crises: The Cantwell Team's View

Political professionals associated with the Cantwell campaign said that they approached campaign crises mostly offensively. Interviews revealed little evidence of crises for the Cantwell campaign, although minor points arose. One such area concerned fundraising. Despite the fact that Maria Cantwell spent millions of dollars of her own money on the race, political professionals associated with her campaign said they faced major opposition spending when the outside group Americans for Job Security attacked Cantwell late in the primary and throughout the general election campaign. The conservative organization aired substantial television ads criticizing Cantwell's record on Social Security, taxes, and the environment. Political professionals said the timing of those attacks made it difficult for Cantwell to define herself coming out of the August primary and going into the sprint to the November election.

Political professionals also mentioned two other potential crises for the Cantwell campaign (albeit with less frequency than other issues). First, some interviews suggested *organizational* crises due to Cantwell's alleged desire to micromanage the campaign. However, even as some Cantwell insiders complained about micromanagement, they also emphasized that Cantwell's intelligence and experience greatly helped the campaign. Second, there was also discussion of the protracted recount as a campaign crisis, even though neither side could do much to manage the outcome. Overall, the recount proceeded smoothly.

Cantwell on the Offensive: The Crown Jewel Mine

Political professionals disagreed during interviews about whether Cantwell's attacks on Gorton's record rose to the level of crisis for either campaign. The Cantwell team and groups such as the League of Conservation Voters and the Sierra Club focused much of their offense on Gorton's environmental record, but the attacks were not a guaranteed win for Democrats. As *Seattle Post-Intelligencer* reporter Joel Connelly (2000a) noted in a preelection profile, Gorton's position as chairman of the Senate Appropriations Committee's subcommittee on interior issues put environmental groups that opposed the incumbent in a tough position; Gorton had regularly supported individual conservation projects, despite some groups' objections to his overall record. Nonetheless, the Cantwell team believed it had a major wedge issue with Gorton's support for the Crown Jewel Mine, which Battle Mountain Gold had long sought to develop and operate in Okanogan County near the Canadian border. By early 1999, Battle Mountain had reportedly spent more than $80 million on the project but was denied operating permits by the US Interior and Agriculture Departments (Connelly 2000b). Shortly afterward, Gorton reportedly "attached a legislative rider to a spending bill for U.S. operations in Kosovo that basically ordered the government to approve the mine" (Connelly 2000b). The Cantwell team dubbed the amendment a "rider of the night," saying Gorton had sold out to special interests (Connelly 2000b). The episode became central to the Cantwell team's attempts to keep the Gorton campaign playing defense (a *strategic disruption* from the typology perspective).

Political professionals associated with the Cantwell campaign reported that Crown Jewel was important for representing Cantwell's contention that Gorton had a poor environmental record motivated by poor decisions. Specifically, the Cantwell team said they believed Gorton's support for Crown Jewel represented his alleged failure to connect to increasingly liberal Washington voters, particularly on environmental issues. They also viewed Crown Jewel as the final straw in Gorton's allegedly having "gone Washington" (D.C.), a criticism meant to imply that Gorton had traded the values of Washington State for power and special interests found in the nation's capital. By contrast, the Cantwell team used prominent television ads to frame its wealthy candidate as one who would not be prisoner to interest groups.

In fact, using Crown Jewel offensively was central to Cantwell's strategy even before she officially became a candidate. Communications director Christian Sinderman reported that during an October 1999 meeting with Cantwell the candidate identified Crown Jewel as a way to define her campaign and to provide a metaphor for Gorton's tenure. Although Sinderman said that he was uncertain whether Cantwell's attacks over Crown Jewel were necessarily intended to create a crisis for Gorton, he believed the negative impact on Gorton's public image was substantial:

> It reinforced what people already [thought]. I mean, the goal of a good contrast message is to reinforce already-held negative beliefs about your opponent. And this reinforced that he had been in Washington, D.C., for an awful long time, that he was too cozy with special interests and that he was hostile to the environment. And those were all messages that worked against him and they were all illustrated easily by one example. Because, again, the way it happened was with a legislative rider, right? And nobody knows what a legislative rider is other than it sounds really sneaky.[3]

Political professionals associated with the Cantwell campaign said that the Democrat staked out her opposition to the mine at her first campaign event to develop what is typically called "issue ownership" throughout the race. Cantwell campaign manager Ron Dotzauer explained:

> We set the stage for the gold mine issue almost at the outset of Cantwell's entry into the campaign. Our first major earned-media strategy was around the gold mine. And the reason being, we wanted to own that issue, not [primary opponent] Deborah Senn. We did a media event at the [mountain] before the bus tour [announcing Cantwell's candidacy]. We flew over there and one of the TV stations went with us and we did an event. They got print and TV coverage. . . . Then once we made that claim and we had credibility on that issue, we knew we could always come back to that issue again . . . because we owned it. And, so, the plan was always to come back to that issue . . . [because] in some ways it symbolized a lot of what the campaign was all about.[4]

Calling the issue "our best shot" at defeating Gorton, Luce agreed that Crown Jewel highlighted Gorton's ties to so-called special interests and represented a contrast between the old and new politics of Washington State.[5]

The Cantwell team reserved its sharpest criticisms on the issue until late October 2000. Shortly before the election, the Cantwell team aired an ad titled "Buckhorn Mountain" (the location of the mine) beginning with a shot of the mine site and a voiceover calling the location "natural and unspoiled, but not if Slade Gorton gets his way." The next frame featured a dramatic explosion and prominent newspaper headlines noting Gorton's stewardship of the amendment allowing mining at the site. The ad also featured a young girl filling a glass with water, providing a dramatic connection between concerns about potential environmental impact and Washington's most vulnerable citizens. The ad closed by citing financial contributions to Gorton from the mining industry.[6] *Post-Intelligencer* reporter Joel Connelly (2000b) published a front-page article on October 23 outlining connections between mining interests, including Battle Mountain Gold and its employees, to Gorton and the Washington State Republican Party around the time that Gorton introduced the amendment, which increased potential traction on the issue for the Cantwell team.

Gorton, however, staunchly defended his support of the project. To Gorton, denying the mining permits was a bureaucratic abuse of power, which hurt Okanogan County, where unemployment was near 10 percent (Connelly 2000b). According to 1999 census data, more than 20 percent of the population lived in poverty.[7] Particularly in eastern Washington, mining, timber, and related industries had been major sources of employment even though they were unpopular with more politically liberal and technology-oriented western Washington.

The Gorton campaign responded to Cantwell's advertising with a set of spots titled "Cantwell Is Losing," which began by telling voters that Cantwell was "saying desperate things" in an effort to win. The second ad in the series directly confronted the Crown Jewel issue, telling voters that Cantwell's claims "that Slade Gorton wants to blow up mountains and poison little children" were "outrageous and ridiculous."[8]

The Gorton Decisionmaking Team and Organization

Gorton Senate chief of staff and campaign director Tony J. Williams was central to Gorton's decisionmaking team. As chief of staff (within Senate rules permitting certain amounts of campaign duties), Williams reported that doing strategic advance work to prepare for Gorton's reelection was a major part of his job, even years before the election. Gorton also relied on J. Vander Stoep, a close adviser and former chief of staff and campaign manager. Eddie Mahe served as general consultant to the campaign, while Paul Curcio of Stevens Reed Curcio and Potholm served as media consultant. Bob Moore and Hans Kaiser of Moore Information served as pollsters. Political professionals inside the campaign said that Gorton concentrated on being a candidate and largely left strategy to others after the brief loss of his Senate seat in the 1980s.

Campaign Crises: The Gorton Team's View

Like the Cantwell campaign, political professionals associated with the Gorton campaign disagreed about which events, if any, represented crises.

However, also like the Cantwell campaign, political professionals on the ground in Washington State reported a strong belief that Gorton's support for the Crown Jewel Mine represented a crisis for the campaign. Gorton's closest advisers were adamant that the event spelled serious trouble, even though they expected some kind of attack on the issue. In addition to Crown Jewel representing a crisis on its own, these political professionals said, the unexpected timing of Cantwell's advertising on the issue represented a major *strategic disruption*. Members of the consulting team generally disagreed, however, as did the Cantwell team's consultants.

Some Gorton interview comments also described voter turnout as a crisis for the Republican. Specifically, some members of the Gorton team regarded the media's early (and, ultimately, erroneous as mediated by the US Supreme Court) prediction that Al Gore had carried Florida in the presidential race as a crisis or at least a major contributing factor to Gorton's loss. The erroneous Florida prediction, political professionals said, had discouraged Republicans who planned to vote late in the day from going to the polls. Democrats said that Al Gore's turnout efforts helped Cantwell, but they disagreed that the early call by media outlets suppressed turnout for Gorton.

Some members of the Gorton team also said they believed that Cantwell's substantial spending advantage represented a crisis for Gorton. Williams, Gorton's campaign director, stated matter-of-factly that the Republican, unlike his opponent, was unwilling to invest his own money in the race. However, political professionals associated with the Gorton campaign also said that they suspected a financial crisis for the Cantwell campaign late in the race after the value of her RealNetworks stock—whose earnings reportedly funded much of her investment in the campaign—fell sharply. (Cantwell later obtained a loan secured by the DSCC.[9])

Disagreement About Crises and the Crown Jewel Mine

The preceding discussion suggests that most of the debate over crises in the 2000 Washington State Senate race focused on the Crown Jewel issue. Political professionals acknowledged trying to attack each campaign regularly to get the opponent off message. But whether this represented a crisis of the same magnitude as in the other case studies is open to debate. Some strategists associated with each campaign suggested that although Crown Jewel contributed to a context that did not favor Gorton, the overall campaign environment, not crises per se, largely determined the outcome of the race. Nonetheless, political professionals also said that there was disagreement within the campaigns about how big a factor Crown Jewel was likely to be before the issue unfolded. The interviews suggested that at least some of this disagreement depended on one's professional position. In particular, there was evidence of differences of opinion between consultants and nonconsultants, as well as those based in Washington State and those who worked elsewhere (e.g., in Washington, D.C.). The next section explores those findings in more detail.

Those on the ground in Washington State in both campaigns, particularly those in the Gorton campaign, said that they believed even before the race began that Gorton's support for the Crown Jewel amendment (the so-called rider) would represent a crisis for the campaign (reflecting the **expected** dimension of the crisis typology). According to J. Vander Stoep:

> The environmentalists who are extremely sophisticated and active hate those kind of riders just on general principles, but this one particularly. And the project apparently was planning to use [cyanide to filter the gold] and I, of course, hear about all this after it's in the [news]paper. But there we know there's going to be the killer attack. . . . So you have a perfect torpedo now, created by Slade himself, for the other side to shoot: "He kowtows to the mining interests and promotes the use of cyanide in the water." . . . So there was a crisis that we knew that was going to come in the campaign.[10]

In crisis terms, Gorton's support for the amendment arguably represented a *candidate political error*, although Williams reported that Gorton stood by his decision at the time and after, providing an important reminder that even campaign crises do not necessarily reflect poor judgment or disingenuous policy decisions.

For those who believed that Crown Jewel represented a crisis, timing was essential. While the Gorton campaign had planned to publicly debate the issue earlier in the campaign, they were unable to do so when Cantwell's "Buckhorn Mountain" ad attacking Gorton aired. According to Williams:

> I remember it distinctly. We were all sitting there and we had a week to go and we're closing out the campaign and we're sitting in our office with the evening news on, because, of course, that's when all the political ads run. And all of a sudden there's the gold mine blowing up and, at that point, [there was a] conference call in fifteen minutes with the campaign team deciding what to do. And by the next day, we had a spot—a new ad up—that responded to that. So, if that ad had appeared a month earlier when we anticipated, we actually already had an ad ready to respond to it and we were willing to spend four or five days arguing the issue out. So, it would have been part of the campaign plan. It would not have been a crisis. With a week to go and 10 percent of the voters still left to decide their choice, that made it a crisis.[11]

Members of the Gorton consulting team had a different view. They confirmed that how to handle Gorton's support for the mine was central to campaign strategy from the beginning, but they disagreed that the event represented a crisis—precisely because it was expected and because the campaign had a plan to deal with the issue. As Gorton general consultant Eddie Mahe asked, "We knew about that damn gold mine for months. How does something [anticipated] that long become a crisis?"[12] Nonetheless, Mahe added:

> I probably never, ever thought of it as being even as big a political challenge as was thought of by others inside the campaign, most notably Tony [Williams]. . . . And in Washington State, the Evergreen State, if somehow you're seen as being impure on the environment issue, it can, in fact, have a direct impact on both behavior and particularly that squishy middle [of voters]. So there was a political challenge there to work our way around it because there is a certain vulnerability on that issue.[13]

Gorton media consultant Paul Curcio agreed that some political professionals viewed Crown Jewel as a crisis but also argued that Cantwell's claims about Gorton's environmental record were suspect:

> When I came into the campaign, I kept hearing about the gold mine issue, the gold mine issue, the gold mine issue. . . . I did not have the historical reference on this [but] it always seemed . . . that in order to make this thing work, you had to say outrageous things about a man about whom there's never been a whiff of any kind of controversy or anything like that. And the charge would have to basically be that he put people's lives in danger . . . he's going to poison children. And it seemed to me . . . for it to have any power, you had to say outrageous things, which in turn would make it, I thought, ridiculous and not work.[14]

Crown Jewel, Context, and Crisis

As noted previously, Williams argued that even though the campaign had a plan to confront the Crown Jewel issue, that plan could not be implemented as intended. Because the Gorton team recognized Crown Jewel as a major liability, Williams and Vander Stoep said that they expected Cantwell to attack on the issue several weeks before the election. Although the Gorton team did not expect to win the issue with voters, it thought that it could at least bring Cantwell to a draw by publicly debating the merits of the mine's contribution to economic development versus its negative impact on conservation. But when Cantwell's television advertisement finally came, it was too late for the Gorton campaign to put its plan into action. According to Williams:

> [Crown Jewel was] just such a toxic issue. And by "toxic," I mean we couldn't explain it away in thirty seconds, [but Cantwell] could, in thirty seconds, make us have to spend an hour trying to explain it away. . . . Secondly, by doing it when they did it, I think it limited some of their effectiveness because there was so much other clutter out there. But it also meant our only response could be, "It's a desperate act in a last-minute campaign." And the problem with that is that doesn't really leave the voter with anything.[15]

Williams's description fits political professionals' definitions of a *strategic disruption* because of the interruption to the campaign plan. However, Williams and Vander Stoep both said that even though they believed Crown Jewel clearly represented a campaign crisis it did not decide the election.

Some members of the Cantwell team shared the view that Crown Jewel was not the deciding factor in the campaign and perhaps not a crisis for Gorton. According to one Cantwell insider,

> I think [the "Buckhorn Mountain" ad] helped confirm the fact that Slade had lost touch and "gone a little Washington, D.C." But . . . the campaign didn't turn on that ad. It really didn't. At that point, the race was very, very close. . . . I don't think that [the ad] turned the race upside down. . . . Did it make a difference? Maybe. Everything made a difference. When you win an election that close, everything matters.[16]

Another Cantwell strategist echoed that sentiment and suggested that language and proximity to the campaign account for the disagreement over whether or not Crown Jewel represented a campaign crisis:

> Part of this may be a semantic difference in terms of what people [believe] constitutes a crisis. . . . I just think it's in a different category than . . . investigating Torricelli, whether it's twenty minutes on [WNBC] in New York devoted to essentially an investigatory attack on Bob Torricelli—that's just a different quality of crisis it seems to me, or some others are [a] major revelation that really dominates the headlines. [The Crown Jewel issue] dominated the race to a certain extent, but it didn't dominate the sort of culture of the state in the same way. . . . I get a lot of calls from campaigns all the time, from the campaign manager saying, "We've got a crisis," that sounds to me more like the normal course of

campaign events. But from their perspective, it's a crisis because it's in their lap, not mine.[17]

Gorton adviser J. Vander Stoep also suggested that the on-the-ground perspective of the campaign staff based in Washington State provided a unique understanding of why Crown Jewel represented a crisis for Gorton:

[Washingtonians] have a very high commitment to this beautiful place, Washington State, and they don't want to see it messed up. . . . They're beating the drum each day that he is "brown."[18] And . . . the [Gorton] campaign is busy saying, "He's not brown, he's just not a radical environmentalist." And now along comes the [Crown Jewel issue], what we view as the trump card, which is, "Now, wait a minute, he says [he] cares about the environment, but he's willing to put cyanide in the water on behalf of a Texas mining company." Well, we consider that to be—and we tested surveys—a very lethal attack on Gorton, hitting his credibility where he says he cares about the environment.[19]

Gorton pollster Hans Kaiser agreed that one's role (and physical location) in the campaign affected views of campaign crises. And although Kaiser acknowledged that Crown Jewel was a major issue in the campaign, he said he believed that several other factors were more important in determining the outcome. According to Kaiser:

Well, I think if you were there on the ground, that's how you would perceive [Crown Jewel, as a crisis] because it seems pretty bad. But if you saw the ads that the Cantwell campaign ran, they were a little over the top. . . . I suppose it could have been a crisis. But I think the Gorton campaign responded as best as they possibly could with the ads that they came up with. And I think they neutralized that "Battle Mountain" spot. . . . [Based on preelection polling] it looked like we were going to bring it home. And then in the last five days, things just fell apart. And I don't think it was because of the mine issue. . . . I think there was a whole confluence of events. But if you were in the campaign and you were making decisions and what were you supposed to do, that would be obviously the thing that was preying most on your mind would be the gold mine because that was the only thing you could really control.[20]

The DSCC's Joe Hansen held a similar view, saying that Gorton lost mainly due to changing political context:

The fact is that I think that this was a natural realignment that's happened in the Pacific Northwest, specifically as it related to [an economic transition]. And the gold mine issue is an issue as it relates to the overall trend in the Pacific Northwest of going from a natural-resource economy to an information-technology economy . . . and others of the region who have long campaigned on a Pacific Northwest economy of timber and fishing all of a sudden find themselves with a bunch of dot-comers that they don't understand, don't communicate with and did not deal with.[21]

The Crisis That Wasn't: The Recount and Psychological Crises

Both campaigns expected a close race, but they were in for a long wait. Counting provisional ballots, absentee ballots, and a mandatory recount took three weeks *after* Election Day. As lawyers and some staff from each campaign, as well as state and national party organizations, monitored the recount, the Cantwell and Gorton operations were largely suspended. Both candidates went into seclusion with their families, as did each campaign's top staffer. Ron Dotzauer went to his ranch and dug postholes. Tony Williams went on vacation to Mexico with his wife. Everyone waited.

Political professionals from both sides said they trusted Washington State's recount system. Both campaigns and state and national parties dispatched observers to all of Washington's thirty-nine counties to monitor the counting of provisional ballots and the recount, although both sides also said that the process went smoothly and required little crisis management. Neither side chose to pursue legal action, unlike in the New Jersey case (or the presidential battle between George W. Bush and Al Gore, which eventually went to the US Supreme Court). As Williams explained of the absentee and recount periods, "There was no campaign; there was [a] very intense intelligence gathering operation to be sure we didn't get screwed. And I am 99.6 percent certain that there was an entirely clean election."[22]

Despite the order associated with the recount, political professionals on both sides said the period represented a kind of psychological crisis, even though there was little for either campaign to do in a strategic sense. Dotzauer explained:

> Well, for the first several days, we're all sitting there crunching numbers.
> . . . Every day there was another [statistical] modeling done with every new count and every recount. And so that's the thing that started driving us all nuts, OK? And that was every day. "Are we going to win or are we not?" . . . And we finally decided, "Look, we just needed to shut this down until it was over with and wait to comment."[23]

A Cantwell strategist agreed, saying that despite mental anguish, the campaigns trusted the recount process:

We had the recounting, but we didn't have situations where some court, some external force that had not yet acted, was going to render some decision. The ballots are already there; [people have] already voted. There was not really a controversy about how they were being counted and so on and so forth. . . . A result was going to happen eventually, but for many days it . . . felt very crisis-like and uncomfortable.[24]

Finally, on December 1, 2000, the recount confirmed Cantwell's narrow victory. The end was remarkably simple and befitting of the civil relationship between the two campaigns. The Cantwell team learned of its victory by following recount results on the Washington secretary of state's website. Slade Gorton conceded the election with a simple note to Cantwell congratulating her and complimenting her campaign strategy.

Concluding Comments on Crises and the Cantwell-Gorton Race

As in the other case studies, context played a major role in crises surrounding the Cantwell-Gorton race. Unlike other case studies, context also played a major role in the debate over whether crises occurred at all. There is evidence of minor crises for each campaign. The Crown Jewel Mine issue provided the clearest example of a *strategic disruption* crisis for Gorton (and a *candidate political error* given his support for the amendment authorizing the project) and an opportunity for Cantwell. Most political professionals, in each campaign, based in Washington State contended that the Cantwell campaign used Crown Jewel as a key element in their strategy to create crises for Slade Gorton. Other political professionals believed that Crown Jewel was part of a campaign environment slightly favoring Cantwell. This debate is reminiscent of one in the Georgia case study surrounding the role that homeland security played in Saxby Chambliss's victory over Max Cleland.

But the Washington State case is different. The campaign context was more orderly than in the other races, providing for a hard-fought, but not particularly bitter, campaign. As one Democrat said of the race, "Everybody really trie[d] to be nice." Washington State's smooth election administration system helped that atmosphere, as did the focus on policy issues in the race and the absence of major *candidate scandals*. Despite the extraordinarily close outcome, the race had an air of mutually accepted legitimacy not seen in the other cases.

In addition, professionals' positions affected the likelihood of viewing Crown Jewel as a crisis. For many involved in the race, political context simply did not support the idea of major campaign crises. In their view, someone had to lose, and that happened to be Slade Gorton. Others disagreed, saying that Crown Jewel clearly represented a crisis for the Gorton campaign, even if it was expected. These political professionals viewed the context surrounding the Cantwell-Gorton case differently. They said they believed that Washington State's political culture, emphasizing a progressive commitment to the environment, as well as changing demographics in western Washington supporting those ideals, made Crown Jewel a major reason for Gorton's loss and was, in fact, a campaign crisis.

Notes

1. In addition to the material cited from the *Cook Political Report*, background information from this section comes from the 1998 and 2002 editions of the *Almanac of American Politics*, archived online and accessed via American University's subscription service at http://nationaljournal.com.proxyau.wrlc.org/pubs/almanac/1998/ and http://nationaljournal.com.proxyau.wrlc.org/pubs/almanac/2002/; accessed May 29, 2005.

2. The appropriations bill was P.L. 106-31 (1999); 113 Stat. 57. The relevant language appears to be at 113 Stat. 90.

3. Christian Sinderman, telephone interview with author, June 28, 2004.

4. Ron Dotzauer, telephone interview with author, June 16, 2004.

5. Liz Luce, telephone interview with author, May 25, 2004.

6. Unless otherwise noted, political advertising information for this chapter comes from Goldstein, Franz, and Ridout (2002).

7. Poverty data appear in the U.S. Census Bureau's online profile of Okanogan County, http://quickfacts.census.gov/qfd/states/53/53047.html; accessed June 4, 2005.

8. At least two political professionals inside the Cantwell campaign said that Cantwell had to be persuaded by the consulting team to run the ad because she feared it was too negative.

9. On the loan being secured by the DSCC, see the 2002 edition of the *Almanac of American Politics*, available at http://nationaljournal.com.proxyau.wrlc.org/pubs/almanac/2002/; accessed May 29, 2005.

10. J. Vander Stoep, telephone interview with author, July 15, 2004.

11. Tony J. Williams, personal interview with author, October 21, 2003, Washington, D.C.

12. Eddie Mahe, telephone interview with author, May 14, 2004.

13. Ibid.

14. Paul Curcio, telephone interview with author, May 14, 2004.

15. Tony J. Williams, personal interview with author, April 13, 2004.

16. Cantwell insider, telephone interview with author, June 2005. Additional information omitted to protect confidentiality.

17. Cantwell strategist, personal interview with author, July 2004. Additional information omitted to protect confidentiality.

18. "Brown" refers to those believed to be hostile to conservation, unlike environmentally friendly "greens."

19. J. Vander Stoep, telephone interview with author, July 15, 2004.

20. Hans Kaiser, telephone interview with author, May 5, 2004.

21. Joe Hansen, telephone interview with author, May 17, 2004.

22. Tony J. Williams, personal interview with author, April 13, 2004.

23. Ron Dotzauer, telephone interview with author, May 20, 2004.

24. Cantwell strategist, personal interview with author, July 2004. Additional information omitted to protect confidentiality.

8

Conclusion

It is a long journey from an isolated discussion of scandals to uncovering the rich diversity of campaign crises—a topic that has received far too little attention in the existing literature, but which clearly affects campaigns on a daily basis. Many crises have nothing to do with scandal and they can be even more politically damaging than scandals. Crises clearly occupy political professionals' thinking. Importantly, crises are at the forefront for political professionals not only when the chips are down. Rather, political professionals said during interviews that constantly being on guard for crises—and on the lookout for ways to exploit crises for opponents—is a major part of modern campaign strategy. Crises, then, are important facets of campaigning itself.

Defining Crises

As noted previously, existing scholarship explores the numerical loss of votes, effects on fundraising, or likelihood of quality challengers emerging from candidates' ethical transgressions (scandal). That work provides a solid understanding of the *impact* of *one kind* of campaign crisis. By contrast, the preceding case studies displayed aspects of all nine definitions of campaign crises described by political professionals. Some definitions are more common than others. To take just a few examples, *candidate political errors* are surprisingly rare. Slade Gorton's support for a controversial mining project in Washington State is one of the most prominent examples of this kind of crisis cited in the case studies. However, as with many events falling into the *candidate political error* category, the Gorton campaign argued that the candidate's position reflected principled beliefs rather than an unplanned crisis. Despite popular notions to the contrary, candidates can and do make decisions based on substance, even when those decisions can hurt their chances at the ballot box.

Conversely, candidates can and do make decisions that ruin their reputations and careers—but not all that often. Political professionals say that *candidate scandals* are spectacular but rare. The allegations surrounding the investigations of Bob Torricelli in New Jersey are the best examples of the *candidate scandal* frame presented in this book. Even in the 2002 New Jersey Senate race, however, some political professionals described a setting in which the scandal perhaps had less to do with Torricelli's alleged actions than with a media-fueled environment that made conventional campaigning untenable. Others were quicker to blame Torricelli for his own downfall.

Most crises are comparatively mundane but far more common. *Attack* crises are present in every case, especially the Chambliss campaign's criticisms of Max Cleland's record on homeland security. *Media* crises are also prevalent, especially the public spectacle surrounding the New Jersey case study. *Organizational* crises, too, are common and provide the best illustration of the **internal** dimension of the typology. *Organizational* crises certainly existed for Paul Wellstone's campaign after the senator's death, for the Coleman team in stopping and restarting its campaign, and for the Mondale campaign in having to come into being and wage a competitive fight in just ten days. In the case studies, political professionals did not emphasize *polling* crises, which represent unexpectedly poor public perceptions of the campaign or its candidate. However, some political professionals said that poor polling results, which they believe signaled a crisis, fostered the Coleman campaign's change in media firms late in the race. Polling results also helped foster Bob Torricelli's withdrawal from his race. *Fundraising* crises were relatively uncommon—or were not classified as crises—which is consistent with their sparse treatment by political professionals during the first-round interviews. Nonetheless, fundraising crises are probably common occurrences, as are lots of other crises, in underdog campaigns. The sparse mention of *fundraising* crises during the interviews provides an important reminder that this book focuses on competitive campaigns, in which resources and professionalism probably helped reduce the potential for some crises. The Mondale campaign provided the best example of a *fundraising* crisis as discussed here.

Existing works on political scandals miss many of the crises discussed above. And even though crises are often less visible than scandals, political professionals warned that even quiet crises can be dangerous because they receive little attention until it is too late to make corrections. Although scandals can often be managed through good communications, even the best consulting team cannot manage a dysfunctional campaign organization or resurrect a candidate's poor public image late in the game. When the full impacts of an attack from an opponent, poor polling results, or a small bank account are realized, political professionals said that the damage is often too grave to repair. *Strategic disruptions*, which interact with many other types of challenges, represent the most common and dramatic crises. The data presented throughout the book suggest that there is, indeed, something different about *strategic disruptions*. The key difference about this type of crisis compared to others is the magnitude of its consequences—and the unexpected ways in which those consequences occur. Wellstone's death and Torricelli's withdrawal are two examples. Both created overwhelming environmental changes that superseded the previous campaign context.

Understanding this broad definition of campaign crises also enhances our understanding of congressional elections. Existing works on scandal (Banducci and Karp 1994; Born 1990; Bridgmon 2002; Brown 2001; Dimock and Jacobson 1995; Goidel and Gross 1994; Jacobson and Dimock 1994; Lough 1998; Peters and Welch 1980; Roberds 1997) focus only on outcomes. Furthermore, the traditional 5 percent threshold for identifying marginal seats (Ansolabehere, Brady, and Fiorina 1992; Fiorina 1997; Jacobson 1987) also takes an after-the-fact approach, relying on past election returns to determine competitiveness and suggesting that most seats are extremely safe. As we have seen, competition, like crises, is about more than outcomes. Crises are an overlooked ingredient in what makes seats marginal. More important, when understanding how widely political professionals define crises, it is clear that crises are common in races that fall outside traditional measures of competitiveness.

To summarize, the richness that political professionals use to define campaign crises suggests that, even though the universe of *scandals* is relatively small, campaign *crises* are a constant threat. Even if campaigns are not defending against or fostering crises at a particular time, political professionals are always on the lookout for crises. The variations in political professionals' crisis definitions support the idea that context is king. Most of what determines a campaign crisis is whether or not the campaign team thinks the event is a crisis.[1] Political professionals similarly rejected rigid decision rules and uniform strategy. Consistent with Michael John Burton and Daniel Shea's work on campaign strategy (2003; see also Shea and Burton 2006), when it comes to defining and managing campaign crises, politics is a craft, more art than science.

Implications for Campaign Organizations

The 2008 election cycle gave no indication that interest in consultants and their role in campaigns is fading anytime soon. Top consultants to both major party presidential nominees were not only prominent spokespersons for the campaigns; they were the subject of substantial media attention in their own right (see, e.g., Bailey 2008; CBS News 2008; Joshi 2008; Lizza 2008). These developments, and others below the public radar, suggest that consultants will continue to be the major strategic voices in House, Senate, and other campaigns at all levels.

It is no surprise that political consultants take the lead during crises. However, unlike the current works that establish consultants' leadership roles during campaigns in general, Chapter 3 allows political professionals to describe, in their own words, why consultants have become such important strategists in congressional campaigns. Chapter 3 also examines how political professionals feel about the division of labor inside campaigns, particularly the transition away from powerful campaign managers and toward consultants. Detailed discussions of these developments are virtually untouched in the current literature, particularly from political professionals' firsthand perspectives.

Throughout this book, the findings support the work establishing political consultants' preeminence in campaign strategy, theme, and message (Dulio 2004; Dulio and Nelson 2005; Johnson 2000; Johnson 2001; Johnson 2007; Medvic 2001; Shea and Burton 2006; Thurber, Nelson, and Dulio 2000; Thurber and Nelson 2000; Thurber 2001). Crisis management, as with campaigns in general, depends heavily on the services of general consultants, media consultants, and pollsters. These are the main strategic leaders that Dennis Johnson (2000) identifies. However, the book also uncovers evidence that individual job functions are less important than Johnson (2000) suggests. This is especially clear in case studies involving experienced campaign teams, such as those in the Gorton, Torricelli, and Wellstone campaigns.

Demographic profiles of the modern consulting industry (Dulio 2004; Johnson 2000; Johnson 2001; Johnson 2007; Medvic 2001; Thurber and Nelson 2000) portray consultants as a fairly segmented group. If we focus solely on which people are most likely to do particular jobs during campaigns, general consultants would be expected to assume overall strategic responsibility, with media consultants and pollsters providing targeted strategic advice and products according to their comparatively technical expertise. Campaign managers are left to implement the core strategic decisionmakers' campaign plan.

The case studies suggest a more nuanced division of labor. Indeed, no other transition in professional politics highlights the division between strategy and implementation—and the emergence of political consultants' tremendous power—more than the shifting relationships between consultants and campaign managers.[2] Media consultants and pollsters are increasingly hired as overall strategists, not simply technical experts—thereby arguably taking the place of traditional campaign managers. Ironically, what began as a professional transition away from generalist managers in favor of specialized consultants appears to be headed back toward broad professional expertise among political consultants. In the end, modern political consultants are all strategists, regardless of individual title. Nonetheless, the interviews also revealed that some political professionals fear that the increasing emphasis on campaign strategy endangers effective implementation—suggesting that an important role for managers remains.

As during campaigns in general, parties and consultants never experience completely allied or adversarial relationships—a topic of great debate in the existing literature. Winning campaigns—and surviving crises—is about getting results. If parties can help, such as by providing research or crisis teams, then consultants view parties favorably. This finding is consistent with the literature establishing that campaigns appreciate specific services provided by parties but not when those services come with strategic strings attached (Abbe and Herrnson n.d.; Dulio and Nelson 2005; Herrnson 1988; Herrnson 2000a; Herrnson 2000b; Hrebenar, Burbank, and Benedict 1999). Overall, however, especially when the slightest strategic mistake can exacerbate a crisis, candidate-centered campaigns—and especially their consultants—want to be left alone.

Although *consultant*-centered campaigns are becoming the norm (Shea and Burton 2006), the *candidate*-centered campaign remains alive and well. Indeed, as campaigns circle the wagons to prevent leaks and to preserve effective decisionmaking during crises, they can become more candidate-centered than normal, especially by limiting strategic input from outsiders. Those concerned about consultant power and democratic accountability can take heart in the finding that political professionals consistently cited candidates as strategic leaders during crises. This is good news for representative democracy. At the same time, being part of the decisionmaking team does not necessarily mean that candidates are independent leaders. In fact, political professionals often described candidates' strategic leadership only in passing while emphasizing consultants' preeminence.

Strategy, Tactics, and Crises

A deeper understanding of campaign strategy and tactics must include crises because the political professionals charged with managing campaigns report that crises are a constant threat. Accordingly, unlike the works on scandal, which tend to assume a defensive posture, political professionals remind us that through the right strategy and tactics, crises (and even scandals) can be both offensive and defensive. Furthermore, crisis management is built into good campaigns from the beginning.

Overall, the findings advance the literature on campaign strategy and tactics and confirm some previous research. In particular, this book examines how political professionals make strategic decisions. The data extend the strategic politicians thesis (Jacobson and Kernell 1983)—the classic rational-choice framework for analyzing *candidate* behavior—to political professionals (if not entire campaign organizations). However, unlike in the typical rational-choice works, political professionals are hesitant to set predetermined decision rules and tactics when battling crises. Gut instincts and professional experience, they say, still play a major role.

Political professionals reported that planning is essential before and during campaign crises because it limits uncertainty (the **unexpected** dimension of the crisis typology). In their efforts to maximize their own expected events, political professionals are eager to create crises through unexpected attacks on opponents designed to disrupt those opponents' campaign plans. Of course, good planning is essential to every campaign, but it becomes especially important when outcomes matter most. Planning also helps campaigns understand not only how to respond to crises but also how to identify strategic opportunities. These findings are consistent with Michael John Burton and Daniel Shea's (2003) "forward mapping" theory and Joel Bradshaw's (2004) warnings about reactionary campaigns suffering constant organizational crises.

Aggressive offensive strategy limits opponents' opportunities to counterattack and sends an important message of strength to voters and the media. These attempts to offensively frame the debate reflect Stephen Medvic's (2001; 2003) theory of "deliberate priming," which relies on consultants to mold campaign images for strategic advantage. As Medvic (2003, 20) notes in analyzing his own extensive interviews with political consultants, "Ultimately, a number of consultants said a campaign's strategy amounts to influencing the question that voters ask themselves in the voting booth. If they are asking a question that only one candidate can answer 'correctly,' that candidate is most likely to win their votes. The key here is that the 'correct' answer to any given question is pre-determined [via deliberate priming]." When it comes to campaign crises, deliberate priming depends not only on imparting the right message about one's candidate but also on limiting possibilities for the opponent to do the same.

Chapter 3's attention to families also reveals an essential—but often ignored—element of political campaigns and strategic decisionmaking. Joel

Bradshaw (2004, 51) argues that "the essence of strategy is that it defines choices that the campaign has made about how and where it will use its resources. Much of the value of this strategic decisionmaking is that you know what you are *not* going to do."[3] In their understandable zeal to protect candidates and their feelings, political professionals said that families—and sometimes candidates themselves—are especially vulnerable to impulsive nonstrategic thinking. Limiting the influence of candidates and families is an effort to control the **internal** dimension of the crisis typology. When it comes to campaign ethics, however, political professionals emphasized that, especially during public crises, the wishes of candidates and families must be respected. Political professionals conceded that the pressure of campaign crises can sometimes make ethical misconduct tempting, but they also stressed that campaign staffs must be extra vigilant to guard against ethical lapses, for both moral and strategic reasons.

Comparing Case Studies and Considering the Typology

Max Cleland's loss to Saxby Chambliss in Georgia (Chapter 4) has clear connections to the theory about campaign crises developed in Chapters 2 and 3, but crises were not a foregone conclusion in the race. After all, there is a difference between simply being in the wrong place at the wrong time and translating that circumstance into a crisis. Cleland faced uncertain prospects heading into the election, but it wasn't clear that crises would emerge. Yet, what has been described as a "perfect storm" of unexpected vulnerabilities, especially on homeland security, high Republican turnout due to the 72-Hour Task Force, and shifting political geography favoring Republicans, created a difficult—some said impossible—situation for Cleland. Over and over again during the first-round interviews, political professionals emphasized the importance of context when defining campaign crises. The key element in making these particular circumstances a perpetual crisis for the Cleland campaign appears to be that the Democratic side either did not anticipate the campaign environment that developed or was unable to overcome that environment once the team realized the campaign was in trouble. In any case, the **external** dimension of the typology was clearly not in the Cleland campaign's favor. The point is not to draw normative conclusions or to establish definitive statements about why Saxby Chambliss won and Max Cleland lost. What is clear is that the outcome of the race represents the **unexpected** and **external** dimensions of the typology. Unfortunately for the Cleland campaign, crises that fell into **unexpected**, **external** territory for Democrats were largely part of the Chambliss campaign plan, from social issues to the 72-Hour Task Force.

The New Jersey case study also has rich connections to the typology of campaign crises and the theory developed in the first-round interviews. First, the Forrester and Torricelli campaigns provide the best examples of connections between the **internal** and **external** dimensions of the typology. The Torricelli campaign began with substantial **external** crises resulting from the Justice Department investigation. The external environment only grew worse for the Torricelli campaign as the Senate Ethics Committee admonished the senator, the Justice Department letter detailing the alleged relationship between Torricelli and David Chang was released, the WNBC special aired, and external and internal polling numbers reportedly began to plummet.

Political professionals associated with the Torricelli campaign said that when each of these events occurred, the campaign's internal stability suffered. Political professionals reported that they were never able to effectively present Torricelli's campaign themes to voters because the campaign team was preoccupied with "putting out fires," a crisis-management description that emerged throughout the interviews. This scenario is the hallmark of *strategic disruption* crises that so often consume campaigns. Political professionals also reported that the Torricelli campaign suffered from internal *organizational* crises resulting from competing campaign and legal efforts on the senator's behalf. Forrester campaign officials reported a similar evolution of crises as Torricelli's withdrawal from the race created significant *organizational* crises, especially in terms of morale, inside the GOP campaign. Internally and externally, Republican political professionals said they believed that the Torricelli-Lautenberg ballot switch represented a *strategic disruption* that doomed Forrester's candidacy.

Especially for the Torricelli campaign, the New Jersey race also provides a powerful example of how expected events can foster crises. These findings contradict the *constant crisis* view established in Chapter 2. Political professionals espousing the *constant crisis* view argued that modern campaigns are inherent crises, and that effective strategic planning and opposition research can prevent or minimize virtually any event. However, Torricelli's campaign team fully expected crises to occur. The Torricelli campaign also contended that it had a plan to respond but that executing that plan became impossible because of what Democrats regarded as an unexpectedly harsh media environment. To cite a different example, no amount of planning could have prepared any of the affected campaigns in the 2002 Minnesota Senate contest, although the Coleman and Mondale campaigns were faced with a wealth of strategic questions about how to proceed after Wellstone's death. The view that modern campaigns are always crises therefore remains debatable, but it seems unlikely that even the most experienced political professionals could prepare for and succeed in every situation.

There was certainly the potential for crisis in the Washington State race, ranging from the Crown Jewel issue to the recount, but political context helped limit those factors. The race was free of notable scandal for either candidate. Both campaigns, and both candidates, respected one another. Both sides regarded Washington State's election administration system as fair and transparent. Differences on policy issues also defined the race. Political professionals said that all these factors helped instill both sides with a sense of legitimacy surrounding the campaign.

Mutually accepted legitimacy was not present in at least some parts of the other races. In Georgia, for example, Democrats regarded the Chambliss campaign's attacks against Max Cleland's positions on homeland security as out of bounds, reaching an allegedly new and unacceptable level of campaign conduct. Political professionals in both Georgia and Washington said that changing political winds hurt the incumbent senators in each state. But Democrats associated with the Cleland campaign also suggested that the Chambliss campaign exploited the political environment to cause crises for Cleland. (As noted, the Chambliss campaign responded that the Cleland team should have anticipated that the incumbent's views would become unattractive to voters.) In New Jersey, some Republicans argued that Democrats stole Doug Forrester's rightful victory at the last minute. Even in Minnesota, Democrats said that tragedy unfairly turned the tide of the election, even as many also argued that some of their colleagues mishandled the Wellstone memorial. This was not really the case in Washington State, where both sides acknowledged that context helped Cantwell but neither side criticized the other's tactics per se.

Crises and the Test of Time

Three election cycles (2004, 2006, and 2008) have occurred since the research for this book began in 2003, providing an opportunity to consider how political events and scholarship evolved in the interim and to consider how various aspects of the findings have stood up to the test of time. Given the breadth of expertise and experience reflected in the interview pool, it seems unlikely that the main findings would differ substantially from those presented here if similar research occurred in the near future. Campaigns have also not fundamentally changed during the intervening elections. This suggests consistency in the findings, particularly about what political professionals believe constitutes campaign crises, how strategic decisions are made, and how campaigns are organized. Given the results of recent elections, however, at least two areas suggest potential avenues for additional research. (Other possibilities for future research appear in the next section.)

First, political professionals typically described crises as specific events that shape the campaign context and vice versa. By contrast, the *constant crisis* school of thought suggests that events that some define as crises are really just the routine ups and downs of competitive campaigns. Many of the interviewees rejected that argument, saying that crises are, indeed, distinct events that are unique to particular campaigns. What is less clear is whether campaign crises would be defined or managed differently when large groups of candidates face the same campaign context, such as during the Republican congressional sweep of 1994 or the Democratic ones of 2006 and 2008.

Second, the Bipartisan Campaign Reform Act (BCRA) was enacted in 2002. The BCRA first affected the 2004 election cycle. Because the interviews were conducted between 2003 and 2005, the interviewees were certainly aware of the BCRA; in many cases they had observed the law in action during the 2004 cycle. There was little evidence from the interviews that political professionals believed that the BCRA would affect their understanding of campaign crises. This is unsurprising, because the interviews addressed broader questions of campaign strategy rather than the comparatively technical disclosure, fundraising, and political advertising requirements associated with the BCRA. Indeed, the BCRA does not appear to have changed the fundamental nature of campaigns, although additional research examining fundraisers or election lawyers might certainly reveal other dimensions of campaign crises affected by the BCRA that were not uncovered here.[4] In addition, political parties' resilience even after passage of the BCRA (see, e.g., Corrado, Magleby, and Patterson 2006; Green and Coffey 2007; La Raja 2008) could temper some of the pessimism surrounding parties discussed in Chapter 3. Nonetheless, even though parties have remained financially strong following enactment of the BCRA, this does not appear to have changed their general lack of strategic leadership with respect to individual campaigns, as political professionals described in Chapter 3.

Crises, how campaigns respond to them, and who inside the campaign makes decisions about crisis management determine which candidates voters choose at the ballot box. Although some things about crises are unique—such as the pace of decisionmaking or divisions of labor that occur inside campaigns during crises—much about campaign crises presents broader themes. Lessons about leadership among political professionals, candidates, and their families; strategic attacks on opponents; negative advertising; and the roles of political parties and outside organizations can all be explored through understanding campaign crises.

The theory and typology developed in this book can be useful tools for scholars, and for political professionals. But regardless of how one chooses to define a crisis or to organize his or her thinking on the subject, the interviewees' comments suggest that pivotal campaign moments—whether those professionals choose to call them crises, challenges, or a routine day at the office—occupy a great deal of time and energy. Crises are not isolated events, and they are not necessarily sensational. Of course, major scandals often determine election or defeat, but so do seemingly mundane events, such as being off message, seeing the electoral environment change beyond the campaign's control, or simply not raising enough money. Some political professionals would be hesitant to define the latter category of events as crises, but most of their colleagues did just that throughout the interviews. According to at least some political professionals, crises are the fabric of modern campaigns.

Does this mean that campaigns are hopelessly negative or that all politics is ruthless? No. In fact, political professionals said that their own ethics and the candidates' ethics matter even more when the chips are down than when the campaign is running smoothly. Similarly, just as so-called attack advertising can involve legitimate policy contrasts (Jamieson, Waldman, and Sherr 2000; Lau and Pomper 2004), political professionals said that pointing out an opponent's weaknesses can play an important role in weeding out candidates who are unsuitable for public office. Nonetheless, some political professionals cautioned that there is a difference between ensuring a spirited contest and engaging in unethical campaigning. It is unclear, however, exactly what "unethical" campaigning means (see, e.g., Lau and Pomper 2004 and Maisel and West 2004). To complicate matters, political professionals, candidates, and voters can have different opinions about what campaign tactics are ethically acceptable (Garrett, Herrnson, and Thurber 2006). Regardless, the interviews make clear that many political professionals believe that their jobs depend on avoiding or creating crises—or both. Especially during an era in which opponents, the media, bloggers, and outside groups all have immediate access to information about candidates and any potential missteps, political professionals' views are understandable. All these lessons—which were ever present in the research—suggest that crises will continue to be a factor in US campaigns for the foreseeable future.

Foundations for Future Research

This book is a beginning, not an end. The renewed study of political consultants began in the late 1990s as a new subfield developed (Thurber

1998). That subfield has provided a thorough accounting of who consultants are and what they do. This book has attempted to provide greater clarity about the world in which political consultants and other political professionals work and live. It has explored how those professionals make strategic campaign decisions and why. In doing so, it has moved the consulting subfield forward and contributed to moving beyond demographic (but nonetheless valuable) descriptions of the consulting profession. The study of campaign crises remains in its infancy, but we now have a foundation on which to begin. On both topics, much remains to be learned.

Given the differences in defining crises versus scandals, an important next step would be exploring whether crises have the same quantitative effects as scandals. As one political professional suggested during an interview, using polling data to track specific strategies and tactics employed during crises would be invaluable for researchers as well as practitioners. As the case studies demonstrate, campaigns do use polling to approximate their effectiveness. However, a large-scale inquiry could uncover generalizable patterns that individual campaigns do not have the time or inclination to address. Nonetheless, this task presents substantial practical difficulties in gaining access to polling data and privileged, real-time information about strategies and tactics surrounding events that might not yet be recognized as crises.

Other questions concern campaign organizations. Despite political professionals' prominence, recent elections have provided reminders that the role of candidates should not be underestimated. Candidates best know their experiences and beliefs. Ultimately, candidates must personally connect with voters, even if they do so through political professionals. Some candidates continue to be primary strategists in their campaigns. In 2006, for example, Nancy Boyda (D) won a congressional seat in Kansas after reportedly taking control of her campaign and installing her husband as campaign manager, following a 2004 loss overseen by Washington-based consultants (Layton 2008).[5] An in-depth examination of candidate roles is beyond the scope of this book, but it is nonetheless a worthy topic for future study.

As Chapter 2 discusses, there is some evidence that Democrats and Republicans, and media consultants and pollsters, define crises differently. This is particularly true when discussing attacks. The findings presented here are based on the views of experienced political professionals, primarily consultants. It is possible that nonconsultants, or those with less experience, would define crises differently. Given the distinction between strategists and implementers, it is also possible that those on the front lines of campaigns would more quickly classify events as crises than would consultants. In fact, consultants reported that some of the tension that exists between them and other members of the campaign team has to do with what consultants perceive as a lack of experience. When it comes to defining crises and understanding how campaigns respond to them, much remains to be learned about the interactions among different types of political professionals.

In addition, the small but steady stream of consultants pursuing elective office or high-level political appointments represents a virtually untouched research area. Although most consultants remain largely behind the scenes, some have chosen to run for office themselves. For example, former consultant Tom Cole (R-OK) was elected to Congress in 2002 and chaired the National Republican Congressional Committee during the 2008 election cycle. On the Democratic side, former Bill Clinton fundraiser and Democratic National Committee chair Terry McAuliffe ran for the Virginia governorship in 2009.[6] Many political appointees have had some campaign involvement, but appointment of professional consultants to policy positions is a relatively recent phenomenon (even though consultants have long been used in communications positions).[7] The case of David Axelrod provides one of the most prominent and recent examples of high-profile consultants transitioning to policymaking roles after their candidates were elected. Axelrod served as a Torricelli media consultant in 2002 and as Barack Obama's chief consultant in 2008. Axelrod later worked in Obama's presidential transition team and as a senior adviser at the White House (Vogel 2008; Romano 2009). Similarly, GOP consultant Karl Rove served as deputy chief of staff in the George W. Bush administration after guiding Bush to victory in 2000 and 2004.

It is natural that those who have dedicated their professional lives to electing others might want to take the plunge themselves. It is also unsurprising that successful candidates would choose to rely on members of the campaign team after taking office. From a research standpoint, these developments suggest that political professionals today may be more than the historically camera-shy tacticians who move from campaign to campaign. Rather, some consultants appear to be increasingly active spokespersons for their campaigns and might more frequently now be considered for official positions of one form or another.

With these developments in mind, attention to political professionals' career paths and official influence could expand the existing literature, which is largely limited to describing the consulting profession in the context of their campaign roles. Future researchers may also wish to explore political professionals' influence in government from a so-called revolving-door or ethical perspective, as has been applied to the related profession of lobbying (see, e.g., Cohen 1998; Salisbury et al. 1989). A consulting perspective could also extend the research on political appointees' motivations and qualifications (see, e.g., Heclo 1977; Garrett et al. 2006).

Consultants and Candidates: A Brief Afterword

Just as the themes discussed in the book extend across elections and over time, many of the political professionals mentioned in this book went on to shape campaigns during the 2004, 2006, and 2008 election cycles. In doing so, they continued the tradition of being largely independent actors, moving from job to job and campaign to campaign. In most cases, as is typical for political professionals, their work was behind the scenes.

A few political professionals became prominent themselves or were attached to high-profile campaigns. On the Democratic side, 2002 Torricelli media consultants David Plouffe and David Axelrod occupied key roles in the Obama presidential campaign in 2008. Plouffe was Obama's campaign manager. As noted above, Axelrod served as a senior strategist.[8] Joel Benenson, who served as Torricelli's pollster, also did polling for the Obama campaign. On the Republican side, Ralph Reed, who chaired the Georgia GOP in 2002, became a candidate himself during the 2006 cycle. Reed lost a primary bid for Georgia lieutenant governor. Other political professionals on both sides of the aisle went on to prominent roles in various candidate, party, or issue campaigns after participating in interviews for this book. Some also served as media commentators.

Whether they won or lost, the candidates profiled in the case studies remained active and pursued a variety of public and private causes (most of which are not discussed here). Despite her razor-thin victory over Slade Gorton in 2000, Maria Cantwell was reelected comfortably in 2006. Gorton also continued to be active in public service. In 2003–2004, he was a member of the 9/11 Commission, which investigated the federal government's response to the September 11 terrorist attacks.[9] New Jersey voters returned Frank Lautenberg to the Senate in 2008. Doug Forrester, his 2002 Republican opponent, was GOP nominee for governor in 2005; he lost the race to Democrat Jon S. Corzine. Robert Torricelli maintained a relatively low profile after 2002 and reportedly has worked as a lobbyist (Hernandez and Chen 2007).

Two candidates profiled in the case studies faced particularly tough elections in 2008. Norm Coleman's reelection race against comedian and actor Al Franken (DFL) was so close that the outcome triggered a mandatory recount. (Dean Barkley, appointed by Governor Jesse Ventura to fill the remainder of Paul Wellstone's term in 2002, was an independent candidate in the 2008 race.) Legal wrangling over the election lasted for almost eight months. Coleman finally conceded the race on June 30, 2009, after a Minnesota Supreme Court ruling effectively ended the contest.[10] Until the final weeks of the 2008 campaign, it appeared that Saxby Chambliss would enjoy easy reelection in Georgia. On Election Day, however, neither Chambliss nor his Democratic opponent obtained more than 50 percent of the popular vote. Under Georgia law, that triggered a December 2008 runoff election, which Chambliss won handily (Bacon 2008). Max Cleland's 2002 loss continues to be a rallying cry for Democrats. Cleland campaigned prominently on behalf of Democratic nominee John Kerry during the 2004 presidential campaign. After leaving the Senate, Cleland served on the board of directors for the US Export-Import Bank. In May 2009, President Obama announced his intention to appoint Cleland as secretary of the American Battle Monuments Commission (White House 2009).

Concluding Comments

Just as the careers of these consultants and candidates have often extended beyond the cases detailed here, campaign crises and the book's broader findings about modern professional politics extend beyond the early 2000s period on which the cases focus. Indeed, crises appear to be alive and well. Recent election cycles have provided numerous examples of events that resemble many of the concepts that political professionals discussed during interviews. A few of the most prominent examples surfaced during the 2004 and 2008 presidential races, suggesting that research on campaign crises can and should be extended to executive contests. The evaporation of Howard Dean's status as presumptive Democratic presidential nominee in 2004, John Kerry's difficulties staying on message following criticisms from the 527 organization Swift Boat Veterans for Truth in 2004, the collapse of Democrat Hillary Clinton's frontrunner status in 2008, and Republican John McCain's widely reported campaign disarray the same year are but a few examples of likely crises and crisis management at work in recent presidential contests. From the typology perspective, the Obama campaign reportedly stuck to its campaign plan relentlessly, avoiding any major *strategic disruptions. Fundraising* crises were present in the McCain campaign, and perhaps the Hillary Clinton campaign, as each faced better-funded opponents. Organizational conflict was reportedly a prominent challenge during the McCain campaign (see, e.g., PBS 2008).

Recent congressional campaigns also included potential crises. Turmoil in the financial markets and controversial bailout proposals forced many congressional candidates to take unpopular policy positions just weeks before the 2008 elections (Thompson 2008; Eilperin 2008). Also in 2008, in the North Carolina race for Senate, Democratic challenger Kay Hagan won a tight contest against Senator Elizabeth Dole (R) after a Dole ad, which was widely perceived as suggesting that Hagan was an atheist, generated negative publicity and Hagan mounted a counterattack (see, e.g., Schouten 2008). In one of the most dramatic Senate races of the 2008 cycle, after weeks of ballot-counting, Alaska senator Ted Stevens (R) conceded defeat to Anchorage mayor and Democratic challenger Mark Begich (Kane 2008; Rosen 2008). Days before the election, Stevens had been convicted of filing false financial statements, but the senator maintained his innocence. A federal judge later granted a Justice Department request to dismiss the case; he also ordered an investigation of federal prosecutors, whose conduct had been widely criticized during the case (see, e.g., Doyle 2008). These are but a few examples of apparent crises continuing to shape US politics.

Media accounts alone do not mean that crises occurred in the races discussed above (or others). Firsthand accounts from those who were there are essential to understanding whether the relevant campaign teams believed crises occurred and whether those events represented a significant disruption to the campaign plan. In fact, even knowing what the campaign plan really is would be virtually impossible without talking with those who wrote and implemented the plan. This book has reinforced the importance of doing so.

Those looking for universal truths about which events are crises might be disappointed by the variations in defining or identifying crises, but then they have missed the point of the book. The purpose of the book is not to diagnose campaign crises from afar. Instead, the goal has been to more fully understand how political professionals think about their world. Crises are an important and largely unexplored part of that world, but their importance does not begin and end with crises per se. Whether one classifies particular events as crises, or as particular kinds of crises, matters less than what those events reveal about how political professionals think about their jobs and about how they believe voters think about campaigns.

Overall, the key themes and findings have remained consistent since the research for this book was first conducted. Crises may include scandals, but political professionals believe that crises often have nothing to do with scandals. Campaign crises are complex interactive events. That complexity means that political professionals sometimes disagree about whether particular events are crises. Nonetheless, these professionals remain constantly on guard. Offensive attacks can be unrealized crises—but crises nonetheless. Many political professionals said that this scenario contributed to Max Cleland's loss in Georgia. Similarly, in Washington State many political professionals said they believed that no crises occurred. Others strongly disagreed. For those who believed that crises occurred, the reality of their impact was no less damaging simply because some of their colleagues did not share similar viewpoints. Those seeking universal lessons might be disappointed by this outcome, but they should not be. This book is devoted to understanding campaign reality as political professionals see it. Reality is complicated.

Exploring the reality of campaign crises contributes to a better understanding of campaigning itself, such as how political professionals define campaign crises, which political professionals assume leadership roles during crises, and how campaigns respond strategically when crises occur. This includes contributions to the literature on campaign scandals, political professionals, campaign strategies and tactics, and congressional elections. The typology of campaign crises presented here provides a framework for considering campaign crises within an academic framework. Many questions remain unanswered. Future researchers can take heart in knowing that a generous community of political professionals and talented scholars are eager to continue the search.

Notes

1. Gaining access to political professionals' worlds through elite interviewing, participant observation, and case studies ensures that campaign context—the unifying theme running throughout this project—is fully appreciated. The complex environment surrounding campaign crises, therefore, presents a challenge to scholars interested in studying crises (or other multifaceted campaign interactions) with game theory or similar approaches. However, an interesting set of work (see, e.g., Carson 2005; Larocca 2004; Scheufele 2001; Shah 2001) has pushed the boundaries of strategic political communications and campaigning. Nonetheless, political professionals' emphasis on context and suspicion of rational-choice structures presented here and elsewhere (see, e.g., Bradshaw 2004; Burton and Shea 2003; Faucheux 2002) should remind scholars that external validity is essential when modeling campaign behavior.

2. The discussion of the division between strategists and implementers also suggests that political campaigns can resemble bureaucratic structures (Weber 1922; Follett 1926), in which strategic decisionmaking authority rarely moves outside the inner circle of political consultants, especially during campaign crises. As the case studies demonstrate, campaigns are not as rigid as bureaucracies. Implementers can be involved in making strategic decisions, especially if they have strong relationships with candidates. Political professionals in the field must also implement crisis-management decisions, not unlike Lipsky's (1980) "street-level bureaucrats." This book also uncovers links between

political campaigns and high-reliability organizations (HROs), which are designed to prevent crises from occurring in high-technology settings. For example, airplane crashes and nuclear meltdowns never occur for one reason alone. Instead, they occur when small malfunctions combine to create a massive system failure. According to Charles Perrow (1984), when dealing with complex ("tightly coupled") technical systems like airplanes, aircraft carriers, and power plants, massive crises are eventually inevitable. Perrow refers to this phenomenon as "normal accidents," which are the product of "tightly coupled" systems and high technology. HROs emerge to prevent high-technology disasters by taking normally hierarchical, bureaucratic organizations (such as the flight deck of an aircraft carrier) and transforming them into "flat" organizations during crises, in which one's technical ability to save the organization becomes more important than rank (La Porte and Consolini 1991; Pfeiffer 1989). Political campaigns are not high-tech endeavors in the same vein as power plants and airplanes, but there are interesting similarities between the "death by a thousand paper cuts" analogy many political professionals used when describing the complexity of campaign crises and cumulative system failures seen in the HRO literature. Campaign crises are rarely explained by one event. Even crises that *result* from one event (such as Paul Wellstone's death) are mitigated or exacerbated by a complex array of other factors inside and outside the campaign.

3. Emphasis in original.

4. For a preliminary discussion of political professionals' views on the BCRA's effects on campaigns, see Bauer (2006).

5. Boyda lost a 2008 reelection bid.

6. On consultants seeking office during the 2009 elections in Virginia, see, e.g., Somashekhar (2009), Toeplitz (2009), and Vargas (2009).

7. For example, political consultant Lyn Nofziger served as a communications adviser during the Ronald Reagan administration.

8. Plouffe's position suggests that the distinction between strategists and implementers (examined in Chapter 4) could be more semantic than substantive if the manager is an experienced consultant. Readers will recall that this was also true for both sides of the 2000 Senate race in Washington State (although Republican Tony J. Williams was the "campaign director" rather than the "manager").

9. Gorton's 9/11 Commission service dates come from the Congressional Biographical Directory, available at http://bioguide.congress.gov/scripts/biodisplay.pl?index =G000333; accessed November 4, 2008. The commission was formally known as the National Commission on Terrorist Attacks Upon the United States.

10. See the court's opinion in *Coleman v. Franken*, A09-697, released June 30, 2009, at http://www.courts.state.mn.us/opinions/sc/current/OPA090697-6030.pdf.

Methodological Appendix

This book argues that existing research on campaign crises relies on an inverted perspective by considering final decisions that result from scandals, such as entering or withdrawing from races, but pays little or no attention to the critical decisions that political professionals make as crises unfold. The existing literature also focuses exclusively on scandals rather than campaign crises, which often include events that go well beyond scandals. To address this gap in the literature, the book examines how political professionals describe and think about crises and how crises affect campaign organizations, strategies, and tactics.

In the broadest sense, elite decisions are the unit of analysis. *Elite decisions* include strategic choices made by political consultants and others whom the data identify as key campaign strategists (i.e., political consultants, campaign managers, etc.). Elite decisions can include political professionals' thinking about campaign crises. Specifically, the two theory-building chapters explore how, through their decisions, political professionals define campaign crises (Chapter 2) and describe how crises affect campaign organizations (Chapter 3) and how crises affect subsequent strategic outcomes. Chapters 4–7 apply the lessons learned from Chapters 2 and 3 to four case studies of US Senate campaigns.

This book employs a mixed methodology combining qualitative and quantitative analysis. Original, in-depth interview data with senior political professionals are the heart of the analysis. The interview data are primarily presented in narrative form, highlighting the project's emphasis on grounded theory and descriptive research. Some of the interview data are also coded and analyzed using descriptive statistics. Archival media coverage and political advertising data from the Wisconsin Advertising Project

(Goldstein, Franz, and Ridout 2002; Goldstein and Rivlin 2005) supplement the case-study interviews.

Methodological Foundations

Grounded theory is central to the book. Through grounded theory, political professionals can explain campaign crises as they see them, illuminating a theoretically important but unexplored area of electoral politics (Glaser and Strauss 1967; see also Rubin and Rubin 1995; King, Keohane, and Verba 1994). "Thick description" (Geertz 1973) is also essential for giving political professionals the leeway to think and talk at length about how they view crises and crises' impacts on campaigns. Like other works that take broad, exploratory approaches (Faucheux and Herrnson 2001; Faucheux and Herrnson 2002; Fenno 1973; Fenno 1978; Kolodny 1998), this book's key goal is to reveal a largely untouched area of campaign politics and to lay the foundation for future research. However, future explanation cannot occur without a strong foundation. Like Robin Kolodny (1998, xiii), "I do not see this study as the end of inquiry but rather the beginning, and hope that other scholars will flesh out the skeleton I have constructed."

Accordingly, findings throughout this book demonstrate the value of letting the data speak for themselves. Robert Yin (1994; 2003) warns against employing quantitative-style hypotheses in exploratory qualitative and case-study research. Especially in unexplored territory, an "imperfect fit" between research design, theory, and data often emerges (King, Keohane, and Verba 1994, 13). Consequently, although this book can inform future hypotheses, it does not include hypothesis-testing.

Theoretical Generalizability

The interview methodology was designed around analytical generalizability (sometimes called "theoretical generalizability") rather than statistical generalizability (Yin 1994; 2003). Because we know so little about campaign crises, allowing political professionals to think and talk at length creates a better scholarly and applied understanding of campaign crises and how they affect modern campaigns. According to Herbert and Irene Rubin (1995, 1), "Qualitative interviewing is a way of finding out what others feel and think about their worlds. Through qualitative interviews you can understand experiences and reconstruct events in which you did not participate. Through what you hear and learn, you can extend your intellectual and emotional reach across time, class, race, sex and geographical division."

The emphasis on "encouraging people to describe their worlds in their own terms" (Rubin and Rubin 1995, 2) is especially important to understanding the relatively closed world of professional politics. This "thick description" (Geertz 1973) is "rooted in the interviewees' firsthand experience [and] forms the material that researchers gather up, synthesize, and analyze as part of hearing the meaning of data" (Rubin and Rubin 1995, 8).

Research Design: The Interviews

Most of this book relies on two sets of in-depth interviews with experienced political professionals. The first round focuses on theoretically generalizable data about campaign crises. The second applies the theory developed in the first set of interviews to four case studies.[1] Both sets of interviews (which, as discussed below, were largely with different people) rely on "semistructured" (also known as "focused") interviews, in which the researcher guides the interview with a specific topic and set of questions. Despite the semistructured design, this method also encourages flexibility, which allows interviewees to shift the discussion based on their expertise (Rubin and Rubin 1995, 5).

The interviews also draw on two other kinds of qualitative inquiries: topical interviews and oral histories. Topical interviews focus on "events or processes" (Rubin and Rubin 1995, 6). The elite-interview data resemble topical interviews by exploring general crisis-management techniques in the first-round interviews and specific crisis-management decisions in the case studies. Topical elite interviews are particularly appropriate because they "trace a process or how a particular decision was made" (Rubin and Rubin 1995, 29–30) and because discussions of campaign crises inevitably involve references to specific cases and the strategic decisions surrounding those cases.[2] Similarly, the case studies can be classified as oral histories of particular campaigns.

Storytelling also plays a major role in this book. Importantly, it is focused storytelling designed to illuminate theoretically generalizable data. As Rubin and Rubin (1995, 231) explain, "Stories, as [qualitative researchers] use the term, are refined versions of events that may have been condensed or altered to make a point indirectly. Narratives are straightforward efforts to answer the question, 'What happened?' But a story is often thought out in advance and designed to make a point, usually one that cannot be made in a direct way." The first-round interviews emphasize answers to general questions about crises. Those answers sometimes included stories. The case studies concentrate on the stories of crises within particular campaigns. Both kinds of answers help reinforce each other. This approach ensures that the project provides something more academically rigorous than simply a collection of stories, but it is not so rigid as to exclude the political drama behind crises.

The First-Round Interviews

The first set of interviews (the first-round interviews) is devoted to building theory about campaign crises. The interviews provide exploratory data about crises and crisis management in House and Senate campaigns. These thirty-seven in-depth interviews establish, for the first time in the scholarly community, how experienced political professionals from both parties define campaign crises.[3] The first-round interviews provide a foundation for understanding what campaign crises are, how political professionals think about them, how they believe crises affect campaigns, and how congressional campaigns manage crises.

Given the time limitations inherent in elite interviewing (Rubin and Rubin 1995), the interview format was more structured than some grounded theory work or Richard Fenno's (1978) "soak and poke" method, for example. Interview questions were designed to solicit interpretive responses (Rubin and Rubin 1995, 33–35) that allow political professionals to consider crises in detail. Political professionals were encouraged to interject their own analysis and suggestions for additional directions. The final product is a focused, yet flexible, exploration of crises and crisis management in House and Senate campaigns.

The Case-Study Interviews

The case-study (second-round) interviews provide an in-depth understanding of crises and crisis management in four US Senate races from the 2000 and 2002 election cycles. These include the 2002 contests in Georgia, Minnesota, and New Jersey and the 2000 race in Washington State. Chapter 4 discusses case selection, introduces the case studies, and reviews the Georgia race. The case studies explore three important themes in each race: (1) how political professionals defined crises in each race; (2) how crises affected each campaign organization; and (3) what strategic and tactical decisions campaign officials made in battling campaign crises. These three themes follow the book's two theory-building chapters (developed during the first-round interviews).

The Interview Questions

Because the first-round interviews provide a baseline for understanding crises, asking the same set of questions was important to the extent that time allowed. Occasionally questions had to be omitted or combined due to time constraints. Even in interviews in which the entire battery of questions could not be asked, the same major themes were always covered. The case-study interviews were more flexible than the first-round interviews. In the case-study interviews, political professionals were asked the same basic set of questions to compare perspectives on which events represented campaign crises, how those crises affected the campaign, and how the campaign responded. However, the case-study interviews were also tailored to individuals' specific jobs, relationships, and perspectives. The generic interview instrument used in the first-round and case-study interviews appears at the end of this appendix.

The First-Round Interview Sample

Because this book explores decisionmaking during campaign crises, finding experienced political professionals was paramount. The literature reviewed in Chapters 1 and 3 establishes that political consultants are the major strategic actors in congressional campaigns, which is why their views are such an integral part of the data. Because of the focus on theory-building, the first-round interviews relied on a two-stage purposive ("snowball") sampling method. This method initially relied on contacts between the American University Center for Congressional and Presidential Studies' Campaign Management Institute and the consulting industry, including the American Association of Political Consultants. Many of the senior consultants generated from these contacts represented the most active and prominent firms working in congressional politics. Sampling emphasized experienced general consultants, media consultants, and pollsters because they play lead roles in setting campaign strategy and managing crises. Party officials and campaign managers were also included. To reduce selection bias, political professionals who participated in interviews were asked to recommend experienced colleagues for future interviews (the second stage of the sample).[4]

Every effort was made to interview equal numbers of various professional groups (e.g., media consultants, pollsters, etc.) and to strike a balance between Democrats and Republicans. The top priority was selecting professionals likely to produce the richest data. This meant choosing people who had the most diverse and relevant experience.[5] Most interview subjects were political consultants holding the rank of principal or vice president in major firms actively engaged in providing strategic advice to US House and Senate candidates. The dataset also contains interviews with experienced campaign managers, party campaign committee officials, and senior congressional staff. Additional information on the interview pool appears in Table A.1.

Table A.1　**First-Round Interviews: Professional Demographics**

Professional Specialization	Democrats (N)	Republicans (N)	Total (N)
Election attorneys	0	1	1
Congressional staff[a]	4	3	7
General consultants	1	2	3
Media consultants	5	3	8
Members of Congress[b]	1	1	2
Opposition researchers	1	1	2
Party officials[c]	4	4	8
Pollsters	3	3	6
Total	19	18	37

Notes: Includes position at time of interview or most recent professional position.
a. Refers to senior staff such as chief of staff and communications director.
b. Former senior campaign staffer and senior congressional staff.
c. Refers to senior staff. Titles remain confidential at interview subjects' request.

The sampling method provided a balanced pool and assembled a dataset of remarkable professional experience. Of the first-round interviewees, 17 (46.9 percent) were identified through the first stage of the sample, while 20 (54.1 percent) were referrals from other interviewees. The sample also achieved partisan balance with 19 Democrats and 18 Republicans (51.4 percent and 48.6 percent, respectively). The sampling method was also highly effective. Fifty-three political professionals were asked to participate in first-round interviews. Fourteen never responded; two declined. The 37 successfully completed interviews represent an affirmative response rate of 69.8 percent.

Sampling Bias

The focus on theoretical generalizability reduces selection-bias concerns from the snowball sampling. That is, expertise is more important in building theory than is statistical randomness. Quite simply, a random sample would not have done this book justice. Field-test interviews confirmed that political professionals were unwilling to provide thorough answers (or sometimes participate in interviews at all) without trusted verification of the author's identity and objectives. Throughout the interviews, several political professionals volunteered that they would not have participated without personal recommendations from colleagues. This made random sampling impractical.[6]

Sample Size

The interview sample drew upon a narrow population: political professionals possessing a wealth of crisis-management experience. The literature on campaign strategy and the data uncovered in this project also make it clear that the political professionals, on whom this book focuses, especially political consultants, play the lead role during campaign crises. Therefore, the data should be highly externally valid. Although a larger sample would be preferable, consistency across interviews suggested that a larger sample would not have produced substantially different results.

Selecting the Case Studies

In the first-round interviews, two questions gave interviewees the opportunity to reflect on cases involving campaign crises. One asked political professionals to describe a House or Senate race (preferably between the 1998 and 2002 election cycles) in which some kind of crisis occurred. These examples could be based on personal experience or general knowledge. Another asked for recommendations of recent examples of campaign crises worth considering as case studies. Political professionals were encouraged to recommend cases that covered the themes discussed in the first-round interviews.

From dozens of possibilities, the final case studies included the 2000 race in Washington State and the 2002 races in Georgia, New Jersey, and Minnesota. Each race represents various dimensions of the typology of campaign crises. Chapter 4 explains other priorities behind case selection. In choosing the case studies, some may suspect "selecting on the dependent variable" (King, Keohane, and Verba 1994) because each case involved crises. However, it would be a mistake to think of crisis as a "dependent variable" in this project. For crisis to be a dependent variable, the focus would have to be on factors (independent variables) *causing* campaign crises. This is not really the case; instead, the focus is on elite decisionmaking during crises. The selected cases were most likely to exhibit the traits needed to develop a theory of campaign crises, including illustrating the typology of campaign crises.

The Case-Study Interview Sample

Case-study data sources included interviews with senior decisionmakers from each campaign (consultants, managers, etc.), local and specialized media reports, and political advertising data made available through nationaljournal.com, the Campaign Media Analysis Group, and the University of Wisconsin's Wisconsin Advertising Project. The Wisconsin Advertising Project data (Goldstein, Franz, and Ridout 2002; Goldstein and

Rivlin 2005) provided detailed storyboards, scripts, and broadcast information for television political advertising that aired during each race.[7]

Background research established the decisionmaking "subsystem" surrounding strategic crisis management inside each campaign.[8] Initially, case-study interviewees were identified using the annual "winners and losers" edition of *Campaigns and Elections* (now *Politics*) magazine, a trade journal for political professionals that lists political consulting firms employed by political campaigns. Additional background information came from media accounts of each race.[9] This research provided a preliminary list of potential interview sources and questions. Early case-study interviewees played the major role in identifying other interviewees. Whenever possible, interviews for each case began with a senior consultant or the campaign manager, which invariably facilitated access to the rest of the team.

The four Senate races included ten individual campaigns. Political professionals agreed that nine of those campaigns (all except Frank Lautenberg's in New Jersey) experienced their own substantial crises or exploited those of opponents. Given the focus on strategic decisionmakers, the number of interviews for each race was intentionally limited, ranging from three to eight interviews per individual campaign (not race), depending on whether or not the campaign involved substantial crises. This number does not include additional interviews with party officials who supported multiple campaigns. Although the numbers are small, the interviews included most of the political professionals involved in each campaign's strategic crisis management.

The Complete Interview Dataset

The combined dataset of first-round and case-study sessions included 106 interviews. That total includes seven field-test interviews conducted early in the project. An additional background interview with a political journalist was also conducted early in the project. These eight interviews were not included in the core dataset used in the preceding chapters because of the preliminary nature of the investigation at the time those interviews were conducted. This left 98 substantive sessions used in the working dataset for this book, including 76 interviews with different people.[10] There was a total of 37 first-round interviews and 61 case-study interviews. The author conducted all the interviews. Most first-round interviews occurred between May and December 2003. The case-study interviews occurred mostly between January and August 2004. A few remaining interviews were conducted in 2005.

Whenever possible, interviews were conducted in person. However, many political professionals preferred to speak by telephone. Political professionals not based in the Washington, D.C., area were interviewed by telephone. There was no evidence of significant differences in interview quality in either setting. Individual sessions ranged from about twenty minutes to almost three hours. The average session lasted about forty-five minutes. The transcribed interviews included a total of 55,552 lines of data (text), from which the quotations are taken.

Each session began with an explanation of the project and how the data would be used. Political professionals were then asked if they consented to be named and quoted in the written product. Political professionals are named whenever possible. Many asked that their identities remain confidential. This is especially true in the case studies, where professional relationships can be particularly sensitive. Confidential sources specified their own generic labels, such as "Republican pollster" or "strategist inside the Cantwell campaign." The generic interview instruments follow.

Conclusion

This book relies primarily on in-depth interviews with experienced political professionals. Two sets of interviews work together to establish general theories about campaign crises and to consider that theory against four case studies. The first-round interviews established what campaign crises are, how they affect campaigns, and what strategies and tactics campaigns employ when managing campaign crises. The second round of interviews (the case-study interviews) examined how the first-round findings hold up when considering crisis management in four US Senate contests. The case studies were selected to reflect the variety found in the typology of campaign crises. Media coverage and political advertising data supplement the interview data in the case studies. The methodology produces an unusually detailed and unique account of political professionals' world as they see it. Although most of the analysis is qualitative, quantitative analysis reveals general patterns in the first-round interviews.

Generic First-Round
Interview Instrument

Consent Questions

[The following questions were asked after providing background information about the project.]

A1. Do you have any questions about what I have just told you about the project and are you comfortable proceeding with the interview?

A2. Do you object if I tape record and take notes?

A3. Would you like your identity or your firm's identity to remain confidential in the final narrative?

A4. [If confidentiality is requested] How would you like me to identify you in the text (e.g., "senior source," etc.)?

Screen/Demographics

A. Have you provided strategic advice to any US House or Senate campaign between 1998 and the present?

B. What year did you accept your first paid campaign job?

C. Very briefly, how would you describe your current professional position?

D. How long have you held that position?

E. Approximately how many US House and Senate campaigns have you worked on in your career? A specific number would be helpful.

   F. Have you ever worked as a campaign manager in a congressional campaign? If so, how recently and how often?

   G. What is your age?

Substantive Questions

1. I'd like to ask you to think about your experiences with campaign crises. For this project, I'm tentatively defining crises as *political events which could cause substantial vote loss or credibility problems for the campaign.* But, I'd like to know what crisis means to you. What does "campaign crisis" mean to you, or what kinds of events come to mind compared with routine campaign events?

2. Do crises always have to involve scandals?

3. Which people/positions in and around campaigns typically play leadership roles during campaign crises?

4. How does the decisionmaking environment differ during campaign crises compared with routine campaign decisions or events? For example, are there different people involved; is the timing different, etc.?

5. Could you give me an example of a campaign between 1998 and the present, if possible, with which you are familiar that had some sort of crisis and describe how the campaign responded?

6. How do campaigns successfully avoid crises?

7. Do you think there is a standard set of response options for campaign crises, or are there certain responses or processes that you would always or never recommend?

8. When crises occur, what is your top duty as a political consultant— is it to the candidate individually, to the campaign overall, to your firm, etc.?
   [*Question 8 was asked of political consultants; alternative questions were substituted for nonconsultants.*]

9. In your experience, what role do ethics play in decisionmaking during campaign crises?

10. What do you think is the biggest popular or academic misconception about how political consultants behave or what their role is in campaign crises?
   [*"Political consultant" was substituted with the relevant title if the interview subject was not being interviewed in a consultant capacity.*]

11. When campaign crises occur, how common is it that political parties would play a major strategic role in crisis management?
12. When campaign crises occur, how common is it that interest groups would play a major strategic role in crisis management?

Concluding Questions

C1. Could you recommend other consultants or others involved in campaigns that might be willing to participate in an interview like this one?
C2. Do you have any recommendations for House or Senate races between 1998 and 2002 which might be worth looking into as possible case studies?
   PROBE: May I use your name as a reference?
C3. Do you know a few people who worked on that race who might be willing to be interviewed?
   PROBE: May I use your name as a reference?
C4. If necessary, would you be willing to participate in a brief follow-up interview sometime in the next few months?
C5. You've been very generous with your time. Are there any questions which I did not ask but should have, or is there anything you would like to add?

Generic Case-Study (Second-Round) Interview Instrument

Consent Questions

[The following questions were asked after providing background information about the project.]

    A. Do you have any questions about the project as I have just described it to you?

    B. Do you object if I tape record and take notes?

    C. Would you like your identity to remain confidential in the final product?

    D. [If confidentiality is requested] How would you like me to identify you in the text (e.g., senior source, etc.)?

General Questions

[Begin by offering crisis definition used to begin first-round interviews, but stressing that the subject is free to disagree with that characterization.]

    1. Based on your general campaign experiences, not even necessarily talking about this race, what do you think of when you think about campaign "crises"? What does that term mean to you or what kinds of events come to mind?

   2a. Based on the description you just gave about what crises are, what events, if any, for the [*opposing*] campaign would you classify as a crisis?

2b. Why do you feel those events should be classified as crises?

3a. What events, if any, in the [*employing*] campaign would you classify as a crisis?

3b. Why do you feel those events should be classified as crises?

4. In your opinion, who made up the strategic decisionmaking team in your campaign?

5. On either side, how, if at all, do you think the crises you mentioned a moment ago changed the outcome of the race?

6. How did those crises affect the campaign as an organization? For example, when crisis occurred, did the decisionmaking team change; did the campaign become distracted from planned business, etc.?

7. How, if at all, did the campaign's relationship with the media change during the campaign?

8. If you could ask [the opposing campaign team] about one or two strategic decisions they made during this race, what would you like to ask, and why are you most curious about those questions?

Case-Specific Questions

[*Case-specific questions varied by interviewee. Questions focused on clarifying individual crises, specifics about individuals' roles within the campaign, and strategies and tactics. These themes are consistent with the data presented in Chapters 2 and 3.*]

Concluding Questions

C1. Do you have any suggestions about which other people who participated in the campaign might be willing to participate in an interview like this one?

C2. May I use your name as a reference and tell those people that we have discussed the race?

C3. Do you have updated contact information for those people?

C4. You have been very generous with your time. Are there any questions which I should have asked but did not, or is there anything you would like to add?

Appendix Notes

1. Together, the first-round interviews and case-study interviews help triangulate the findings (Jick 1979). The two components of the interview data (the generalizable inter-

views and the case studies) also resemble Lin's (1998) commitment to unifying positivist and interpretivist approaches. Positivist approaches concentrate on identifying general patterns, whereas interpretivist approaches identify causal relationships within cases. For counterarguments, see King, Keohane, and Verba (1994) and Lincoln and Guba (1985).

2. For a discussion of qualitative interview types, see Rubin and Rubin (1995, 26–31).

3. Interviews were solicited until findings became predictable and a rough balance in party and professional specialization was achieved. The thirty-interview threshold also increases reliability in analyzing the data with basic statistics. Although not included in the analysis, eight field-test interviews were also conducted, bringing the total first-round N to 43.

4. During the first round, potential interviewees were first approached with a letter, followed by e-mail or telephone calls. Later in the research, e-mail became the primary source of solicitation because of its effectiveness and speed.

5. Therefore, although in using a snowball sample the author adopted some techniques similar to network analysis, the aim was not to select interviewees based on the most frequent number of recommendations (DeGregorio 1997). For example, although only one consultant recommended interviewing a particular colleague, the fact that the colleague was a prominent former Democratic Congressional Campaign Committee official who had previously worked on several major campaigns made the colleague an attractive interview subject. Dulio (2001; 2004) discusses the weakness in basing consultant research on frequency of mentions or reputation alone.

6. Because this book is about enhancing the scholarly understanding of campaign crises based on input from experienced political professionals, it also would have made little sense to conduct a random interview sample and hope that the respondents' experiences in crisis management would be as thorough as those of a group of seasoned political professionals who are regularly exposed to diverse campaign experiences, including crises. Even without a statistically generalizable sample, the broad agreement displayed across the first-round and case-study interviews, and across party lines and professional specializations, suggests that the understanding of campaign crises reported here represents political professionals in general.

7. See Chapter 1 for required disclaimers associated with the Wisconsin Advertising Project data.

8. On policy subsystems, see Jones (1982), Redford (1969), and Thurber (1996). On related discussions of issue networks and iron triangles, see Jordan (1981), Kingdon (1984), and Mills (1957).

9. At minimum, this included reading local print media coverage, in addition to reviewing individual political profiles in sources such as *National Journal's Almanac of American Politics*. The *Washington Post, The New York Times, Roll Call, The Hill*, and The Associated Press state and local wire reports and local newspapers for each case were also consulted. Applicable newspapers were identified via searches in the LexisNexis Academic Universe archive. All media sources that appeared likely to cover the race were included in the LexisNexis Academic Universe search. In cases in which known major news sources were unavailable or contained only sparse coverage, the Westlaw electronic news archive provided supplemental coverage.

10. Twenty-two of the ninety-eight official sessions were multiple interviews with the same person. In most cases, these twenty-two sessions were continuations of prior interviews that had to be limited due to time. In a few cases, multiple (usually no more than two) interviews were conducted with the same person in both the first-round and case-study settings.

References

Abbe, Owen G., and Paul S. Herrnson. n.d. "Adversaries or Allies? Campaign Professionals and Political Parties in the States." Unpublished manuscript. Center for American Politics and Citizenship, University of Maryland.

Abramowitz, Alan I., and Jeffrey A. Segal. 1992. *Senate Elections.* Ann Arbor: University of Michigan Press.

Agresti, Alan, and Barbara Finlay. 1997. *Statistical Methods for the Social Sciences.* 3rd ed. Upper Saddle River, NJ: Prentice Hall.

Aldrich, John. 1985. *Why Parties? The Origin and Transformation of Political Parties in America.* Chicago: University of Chicago Press.

Ansolabehere, Stephen, David Brady, and Morris Fiorina. 1992. "The Vanishing Marginals and Electoral Responsiveness." *British Journal of Political Science* 22(1): 21–38.

Applebome, Paul. 2008. "With G.O.P. Congressman's Loss, a Moderate Tradition Ends in New England." *The New York Times,* November 6, late edition, A26; at http://www.lexisnexis.com; accessed November 10, 2008.

The Associated Press. "'96 Torricelli Worker Admits Illegal Donation." *The New York Times,* December 2, 1999, B18.

Bailey, Holly. 2008. "No Prize to the Noble Loser." *Newsweek* 152(16), October 20; at http://www.lexisnexis.com; accessed November 10, 2008.

Bailey, Michael A., Ronald A. Faucheux, Paul S. Herrnson, and Clyde Wilcox, eds. 2001. *Campaigns and Elections: Contemporary Case Studies.* Washington, DC: CQ Press.

Banducci, Susan A., and Jeffrey A. Karp. 1994. "Electoral Consequences of Scandal and Reapportionment in the 1992 House Elections." *American Politics Quarterly* 22(1): 3–26.

Barnard, Chester I. [1938] 1997. "Informal Organizations and Their Relation to Formal Organizations." In *The Classics of Public Administration.* 4th ed. Ed. Jay M. Schafritz and Albert C. Hyde. Fort Worth, TX: Harcourt Brace, 95–99.

Barone, Michael, and Richard E. Cohen. 2003. *The Almanac of American Politics 2004.* Washington, DC: National Journal Group.

Bauer, Robert F. 2006. "A Report from the Field: Campaign Professionals on the First Election Cycle under the Bipartisan Campaign Reform Act." *Election Law Journal* 5(2): 105–120.

Baxter, Tom. 2001. "Eyed by GOP, Cleland Braces for Tough '02 Race." *Atlanta Journal Constitution*, April 10; at http://web.lexisnexis.com; accessed May 11, 2005.

———. 2002. "Election Ploy Boomerangs in Louisiana." *Atlanta Journal-Constitution*, December 6; at http://web.lexisnexis.com; accessed May 12, 2005.

Bennett, George. 2008. "Mahoney Admits to 'Multiple' Affairs." *Palm Beach Post* (Florida), October 18; at http://www.palmbeachpost.com/news/content/local_news/epaper/2008/10/17/1017mahoney.htm; accessed May 31, 2009.

Black, Eric. 2002. "13 Days: Behind the Scenes of Two Campaigns in One Extraordinary Election." *Star Tribune* (Minneapolis), November 10, metro edition; at http://web.lexisnexis.com; accessed May 25, 2005.

Blalock, Hubert M., Jr. 1979. *Social Statistics.* 2nd ed. New York: McGraw Hill.

Born, Richard. 1990. "The Shared Fortunes of Congress and Congressmen: Members May Run, but They Can't Hide." *Journal of Politics* 52(4): 1223–1241.

Bradshaw, Joel C. 2004. "Who Will Vote for You and Why: Designing Campaign Strategy and Message." In *Campaigns and Elections American Style.* 2nd ed. Ed. James A. Thurber and Candice J. Nelson. Boulder: Westview, 37–56.

Brewer, Sarah E. 2003. "Gender and Political Vocation: Women Campaign Consultants." Ph.D. diss. American University.

Bridgmon, Phillip Brandon. 2002. "Presidential Scandal, Impeachment Politics, and U.S. House Elections: Strategies and Choices in 1998 and 2000." Ph.D. diss. The University of Alabama.

Brophy-Baermann, Michelle Desiree. 1995. "Rubber Representatives? The Electoral Consequences of the 1992 House Bank Scandal." Ph.D. diss. The University of Iowa.

Brown, Lara Michelle. 2001. "The Character of Congress: Scandals in the United States House of Representatives, 1966–1996." Ph.D. diss. University of California, Los Angeles.

Bryant, Jay. 2004. "Paid Media Advertising: Political Communication from the Stone Age to the Present." In *Campaigns and Elections American Style.* 2nd ed. Ed. James A. Thurber and Candice J. Nelson. Boulder: Westview, 90–108.

Burton, Michael John, and Daniel M. Shea. 2001. *Campaign Craft: The Strategies, Tactics, and Art of Political Campaign Management.* 2nd ed. Westport, CT: Praeger.

———. 2003. *Campaign Mode: Strategic Vision in Congressional Elections.* Lanham, MD: Rowman and Littlefield.

Burrell, Barbara C. 1994. *A Woman's Place Is in the House: Campaigning for Congress in the Feminist Era.* Ann Arbor: University of Michigan Press.

Campbell, Colton C., and Nicol Rae. 2003. *Impeaching Clinton.* Lawrence: University Press of Kansas.

Carson, Jamie L. 2005. "Strategy, Selection, and Candidate Competition in U.S. House and Senate Elections." *Journal of Politics* 67(1): 1–28.

CBS News. 2008. "The Inner Circle." *60 Minutes.* Transcript, November 9; at http://www.lexisnexis.com; accessed November 10, 2008.

Chestnut, Beatrice Marie. 1996. "The Narrative Construction of Iran-Contra: The Failure of Congress and the Press to Hold Reagan Accountable." Ph.D. diss. Northwestern University.

Chong, Dennis. 1993. "How People Think, Reason, and Feel About Rights and Liberties." *American Journal of Political Science* 37(3): 897–899.

Cleland, Max. 1980. *Strong at the Broken Places*. Lincoln, VA: Chosen Books.

Cohen, David M. 1998. "Amateur Government." *Journal of Public Administration Research and Theory* 8(4): 450–497.

Congressional Record. 2002. 107th Cong., 2nd sess. "Senate Ethics Committee Investigation of Senator Robert Torricelli." Statement by Mr. Torricelli. US Senate, *Congressional Record*, July 30, S7564–S7565; at http://thomas.loc.gov; accessed May 20, 2005.

Connelly, Joel. 2000a. "Gorton Seeks Greener Image in 2000 Race: Here and Nationally, He's an Environmental Mover." *Seattle Post-Intelligencer*, September 8, final edition, A1; at http://seattlepi.nwsource.com; accessed July 19, 2005.

———. 2000b. "State GOP Gets Money from Firm Linked to Okanogan Mine." *Seattle Post-Intelligencer*, October 23, final edition, A1; at http://seattlepi.nwsource.com; accessed July 19, 2005.

Constantini, Edmond. 1990. "Political Women and Political Ambition: Closing the Gender Gap." *American Journal of Political Science* 34(3): 741–770.

The Cook Political Report. 2000. "2000 Senate Rankings." Washington, DC: National Journal, August 9.

Corrado, Anthony, David B. Magleby, and Kelly D. Patterson, eds. 2006. *Financing the 2004 Elections*. Washington, DC: Brookings Institution Press.

DeGregorio, Christine A. 1997. *Networks of Champions: Leadership, Access, and Advocacy in the U.S. House of Representatives*. Ann Arbor: University of Michigan Press.

Dewar, Helen. 2002. "For Wellstone, Iraq Vote Is Risk but Not a Choice: Principles May Be Costly in November." *Washington Post*, October 9, final edition, A08; at http://web.lexisnexis.com; accessed May 28, 2005.

Dimock, Michael A., and Gary C. Jacobson. 1995. "Checks and Choices: The House Bank Scandal's Impact on Voters in 1992." *Journal of Politics* 57(3): 1143–1159.

Doyle, Kenneth P. 2009. "Judge Backs Dismissal of Stevens Case, Orders Probe of Top Prosecutors' Conduct." *Daily Report for Executives*, April 8, A1.

Dulio, David A. 2001. "For Better or Worse? How Political Consultants Are Changing Elections in the United States." Ph.D. diss. American University.

———. 2004. *For Better or Worse? How Political Consultants Are Changing Elections in the United States*. Albany: State University of New York Press.

Dulio, David A., and R. Sam Garrett. 2007. "Organizational Strength and Campaign Professionalism in State Parties." In *The State of the Parties: The Changing Role of Contemporary American Parties*. 5th ed. Ed. John C. Green and Daniel J. Coffey. Lanham, MD: Rowman and Littlefield.

Dulio, David A., and Candice J. Nelson. 2005. *Vital Signs: Perspectives on the Health of American Campaigning*. Washington, DC: Brookings Institution Press.

Dulio, David A., and James A. Thurber. 2003. "The Symbiotic Relationship Between Political Parties and Political Consultants: Partners Past, Present, and Future." In

The State of the Parties: The Changing Role of Contemporary American Parties. 4th ed. Ed. John C. Green and Rick Farmer. Lanham, MD: Rowman and Littlefield.

Edsall, Thomas B. 2001. "Lawmaker Tries to Explain Remark; Rep. Chambliss, a Senate Hopeful, Commented on Muslims." *Washington Post*, November 21, final edition, A02; at http://web.lexisnexis.com; accessed May 13, 2005.

Eilperin, Juliet. 2008. "Those up for Reelection Have Explaining to Do: A Midwestern Republican Who Voted Against the Plan Is Blasted for 'Inaction' by Opponent." *Washington Post*, October 1, home edition, A10.

Eversley, Melanie. 2001. "Cleland Tours Lithonia in Bid for New Senate Term." *Atlanta Journal-Constitution*, April 17, home edition; at http://web.lexisnexis.com; accessed May 11, 2005.

Ezra, Marni, and Candice J. Nelson. 2004. "Do Campaigns Matter?" In *Campaigns and Elections American Style*. 2nd ed. Ed. James A. Thurber and Candice J. Nelson. Boulder: Westview, 223–234.

Faucheux, Ronald A. 2002. *Running for Office: The Strategies, Techniques, and Messages Modern Political Candidates Need to Win Elections.* New York: M. Evans.

Faucheux, Ronald A., and Paul S. Herrnson, eds. 2001. *The Good Fight: How Political Candidates Struggle to Win Elections Without Losing Their Souls.* Washington, DC: Campaigns and Elections.

———. 2002. *Campaign Battle Lines: The Practical Consequences of Crossing the Line Between What's Right and What's Not in Political Campaigning.* Washington, DC: Campaigns and Elections.

Fenno, Richard F., Jr. 1973. *Congressmen in Committees.* Boston: Little, Brown.

———. 1978. *Home Style: House Members in Their Districts.* Boston: Little, Brown.

———. 1992. *When Incumbency Fails: The Senate Career of Mark Andrews.* Washington, DC: CQ Press.

———. 1996. *Senators on the Campaign Trail: The Politics of Representation.* Norman: University of Oklahoma Press.

Fiorina, Morris P. 1977. "The Case of the Vanishing Marginals: The Bureaucracy Did It." *American Political Science Review* 71(1): 177–181.

Follett, Mary Parker. [1926] 1997. "The Giving of Orders." In *The Classics of Public Administration*. 4th ed. Ed. Jay M. Schafritz and Albert C. Hyde. Fort Worth, TX: Harcourt Brace, 53–60.

Garrett, R. Sam. 2003. "Concepts, Campaigns, and Crises: How Political Professionals Conceptualize and Define Electoral Crisis." Presented at the symposium "Political Campaigning and Elections: Organization, Consultants and Issues," held in conjunction with the annual meeting of the Northeastern Political Science Association, Philadelphia.

———. 2004a. "Congressional Campaign Crises and the Candidate-Centered Campaign." Presented at the annual meeting of the Southern Political Science Association, New Orleans.

———. 2004b. "Understanding Crises and Crisis-Management in House and Senate Campaigns." Presented at the annual meeting of the American Political Science Association, Chicago.

———. 2005. "'Adrenalized Fear': Crisis-Management in U.S. House and Senate Campaigns." Ph.D. diss. American University.

————. 2006a. "Concepts, Crises, and Campaigns: How Political Professionals Define Electoral 'Crisis.'" *Journal of Political Marketing* 5(1/2): 127–148.

————. 2006b. "Reconsidering Campaign Leadership, Political Professionals, and Campaign Crises." Presented at the annual meeting of the Southern Political Science Association, Atlanta.

Garrett, R. Sam, Paul S. Herrnson, and James A. Thurber. 2006. "Perspectives on Campaign Ethics." In *The Electoral Challenge: Theory Meets Practice*. Ed. Stephen C. Craig. Washington, DC: CQ Press, 203–224.

Garrett, R. Sam, James A. Thurber, A. Lee Fritschler, and David H. Rosenbloom. 2006. "Assessing the Impact of Bureaucracy Bashing by Electoral Campaigns." *Public Administration Review* 66(2): 228–240.

Geertz, Clifford. 1973. "Thick Description: Toward an Interpretive Theory of Culture." In *The Interpretation of Cultures*. Ed. Clifford Geertz. New York: Basic Books, 3–30.

Gilens, Martin. 2001. "Political Ignorance and Collective Policy Preferences." *American Political Science Review* 95(2): 369–379.

Glaser, Barney, and Anselm Strauss. 1967. *The Discovery of Grounded Theory*. Chicago: Aldine.

Goidel, Robert K., and Donald A. Gross. 1994. "A Systems Approach to Campaign Finance in U.S. House Elections." *American Politics Quarterly* 22(2): 125–153.

Goldenberg, Edie N., and Michael W. Traugott. 1984. *Campaigning for Congress*. Washington, DC: CQ Press.

Goldstein, Kenneth, Michael Franz, and Travis Ridout. 2002. "Political Advertising in 2000." Combined file [dataset]. Final release. Madison, WI: Department of Political Science at the University of Wisconsin–Madison and the Brennan Center for Justice at New York University.

Goldstein, Kenneth, and Joel Rivlin. 2005. "Political Advertising in 2002." Combined file [dataset]. Final release. Madison, WI: The Wisconsin Advertising Project, the Department of Political Science at the University of Wisconsin–Madison.

Green, John C., and Daniel J. Coffey, eds. 2007. *The State of the Parties*. 5th ed. Lanham, MD: Rowman and Littlefield.

Groseclose, Timothy, and Keith Krehbiel. 1994. "Golden Parachutes, Rubber Checks, and Strategic Retirements from the 102nd House." *American Journal of Political Science* 38(1): 75–99.

Hamburger, Martin. 2000. "Lessons from the Field: A Journey into Political Consulting." In *Campaign Warriors: Political Consultants in Elections*. Ed. James A. Thurber and Candice J. Nelson. Washington, DC: Brookings Institution Press, 53–64.

Heclo, Hugh. 1977. *A Government of Strangers: Executive Politics in Washington*. Washington, DC: Brookings Institution Press.

Hernandez, Raymond, and David W. Chen. "Now a Lobbyist, an Ex-Senator Uses Campaign Money." *The New York Times*, August 27, 2007; at http://www.nytimes.com; accessed November 10, 2008.

Herrnson, Paul S. 1988. *Party Campaigning in the 1980s*. Cambridge: Harvard University Press.

————. 1992. "Campaign Professionalism and Fundraising in Congressional Elections." *Journal of Politics* 54(3): 859–870.

————. 1998. "Interest Groups, PACs, and Campaigns." In *The Interest Group Connection: Electioneering, Lobbying, and Policymaking in Washington.* Ed. Paul S. Herrnson, Ronald G. Shaiko, and Clyde Wilcox. Chatham, NJ: Chatham House, 37–51.

————. 2000a. *Congressional Elections: Campaigning and at Home in Washington.* 3rd ed. Washington, DC: CQ Press.

————. 2000b. "Hired Guns and House Races: Campaign Professionals in House Elections." In *Campaign Warriors: Political Consultants in Elections.* Ed. James A. Thurber and Candice J. Nelson. Washington, DC: Brookings Institution Press, 65–90.

————. 2004. *Congressional Elections: Campaigning and at Home in Washington.* 4th ed. Washington, DC: CQ Press.

Holbrook, Thomas M. 1996. *Do Campaigns Matter?* Thousand Oaks, CA: Sage.

Hrebenar, Ronald J., Matthew J. Burbank, and Robert C. Benedict. 1999. *Political Parties, Interest Groups, and Political Campaigns.* Boulder: Westview.

Inouye, Daniel K., Pat Roberts, Blanche Lincoln, George Voinovich, Jack Reed, and Craig Thomas. 2002. Letter of Admonition to Robert G. Torricelli. July 30. U.S. Senate Select Committee on Ethics; at http://ethics.senate.gov/downloads /pdffiles/torricelli.pdf; accessed May 20, 2005.

Jacobellis v. Ohio. 1964. 378 U.S. 184.

Jacobson, Gary C. 1987. "The Marginals Never Vanished: Incumbency and Competition in Elections to the U.S. House of Representatives, 1952–82." *American Journal of Political Science* 31(1): 126–141.

————. 2001. *The Politics of Congressional Elections.* 5th ed. New York: Addison Wesley/Longman.

Jacobson, Gary C., and Michael A. Dimock. 1994. "Checking Out: The Impact of Bank Overdrafts on the 1992 House Elections." *American Journal of Political Science* 38(3): 601–624.

Jacobson, Gary C., and Samuel Kernell. 1983. *Strategy and Choice in Congressional Elections.* 2nd ed. New Haven: Yale University Press.

Jamieson, Kathleen Hall, Paul Waldman, and Susan Sherr. 2000. "Eliminate the Negative? Categories of Analysis for Political Advertisements." In *Crowded Airwaves: Campaign Advertising in Elections.* Ed. James A. Thurber, Candice J. Nelson, and David A. Dulio. Washington, DC: Brookings Institution Press, 44–64.

Janis, Irving L. 1982. *Groupthink: Psychological Studies of Policy Decisions and Fiascoes.* Rev. ed. Boston: Houghton Mifflin.

Jasperson, Amy. 2004. "The Perfect Storm of Politics: Media and Advertising During the 2002 Senate Campaign(s) in Minnesota." In *Lights, Camera, Campaign! Media, Politics, and Political Advertising.* Ed. David A. Schultz. New York: Peter Lang, 149–187.

Jick, Todd D. 1979. "Mixing Qualitative and Quantitative Methods: Triangulation in Action." *Administrative Science Quarterly* 24(4): 602–611.

Johnson, Dennis W. 2000. "The Business of Political Consulting." In *Campaign Warriors: Political Consultants in Elections.* Ed. James A. Thurber and Candice J. Nelson. Washington, DC: Brookings Institution Press, 37–52.

————. 2001. *No Place for Amateurs: How Political Consultants Are Reshaping American Democracy.* New York: Routledge.

————. 2007. *No Place for Amateurs: How Political Consultants Are Reshaping American Democracy.* 2nd ed. New York: Routledge.

Jones, Charles O. 1982. *The United States Congress: People, Place, and Policy.* Homewood, IL: Dorsey.

Jordan, Grant. 1981. "Iron Triangles, Woolly Corporatism, and Elastic Nets: Images of the Policy Process." *Journal of Public Policy* 1(1): 95–123.

Joshi, Jitendra. 2008. "Obama and McCain Strategists Are Worlds Apart." Agence France Presse wire report, October 27; at http://www.lexisnexis.com; accessed November 10, 2008.

Kane, Paul. 2008. "Ted Stevens Loses Battle for Alaska Senate Seat." *Washington Post,* November 19, home edition, A1.

Katz, Daniel, and Robert L. Kahn. [1966] 1997. "Organizations and the Systems Concept." In *The Classics of Public Administration.* 4th ed. Ed. Jay M. Schafritz and Albert C. Hyde. Fort Worth, TX: Harcourt Brace, 209–219.

Kazee, Thomas A. 1980. "The Decision to Run for the U.S. Congress: Challenger Attitudes in the 1970s." *Legislative Studies Quarterly* 5(1): 79–100.

Kernell, Samuel. 1997. *Going Public: New Strategies in Presidential Leadership.* 3rd ed. Washington, DC: CQ Press.

Key, V. O., Jr., with the assistance of Milton C. Cummings Jr. 1966. *The Responsible Electorate: Rationality in Presidential Voting, 1936–1960.* New York: Vintage.

King, Gary, Robert O. Keohane, and Sidney Verba. 1994. *Designing Social Inquiry: Scientific Inquiry in Qualitative Research.* Princeton: Princeton University Press.

Kingdon, John W. 1984. *Agendas, Alternatives, and Public Policies.* Boston: Little, Brown.

Kinnard, Meg. 2002. "Chambliss Ad Features Saddam, Bin Laden." National Journal Ad Spotlight, October 15, 2002; at http://nationaljournal.com; accessed May 11, 2005.

Kinney, David. 2002a. "GOP Candidates Zero in on Torricelli—But They're Taking Shots at Each Other, Too." Newark *Star-Ledger,* April 7, New Jersey edition (final), 021; at http://wawa.starledger.com; accessed July 19, 2005.

————. 2002b. "Millionaire Outruns Rivals in Cash Race for Senate—Forrester Uses Own Money in GOP Primary." Newark *Star-Ledger,* April 16, New Jersey edition (final), 021; at http://wawa.starledger.com; accessed July 19, 2005.

————. 2002c. "Senate Candidacy Takes a Hard Hit—Republicans Have Made Ethics a Top Issue in Their Efforts to Beat Democrat Torricelli." Newark *Star-Ledger,* April 19, news edition (final), 026; at http://wawa.starledger.com/texis; accessed July 19, 2005.

————. 2002d. "'Not Your Conventional Politician.' What Made Forrester Run? Moral Outrage, for One." Newark *Star-Ledger,* October 13, news edition (final), 001; at http://wawa.starledger.com; accessed July 19, 2005.

Kocieniewski, David. 2002. "Appeals Court Orders Letter on Torricelli Released." *The New York Times,* September 21, late edition (final), B6.

Kocieniewski, David, with Tim Golden. 2002. "Charges Ruled Out as U.S. Concludes Torricelli Inquiry." *The New York Times,* January 4, late edition (final), A1; at http://web.lexisnexis.com; accessed May 20, 2005.

Kocieniewski, David, and Iver Peterson. 2002. "Senate Race in New Jersey Is on as Courts Reject G.O.P. Appeals." *The New York Times,* October 8, late edition (final), A1; at http://web.lexisnexis.com; accessed May 23, 2005.

Kolodny, Robin. 1998. *Pursuing Majorities: Congressional Campaign Committees in American Politics*. Norman: University of Oklahoma Press.

———. 2000. "Electoral Partnerships: Political Consultants and Political Parties." In *Campaign Warriors: Political Consultants in Elections*. Ed. James A. Thurber and Candice J. Nelson. Washington, DC: Brookings Institution Press, 110–132.

Krasno, Jonathan S. 1994. *Challengers, Competition, and Reelection: Comparing Senate and House Elections*. New Haven: Yale University Press.

Kumar, Kavita, Dane Smith, and Patricia Lopez. 2002. "Memorial Service: One Last Rally: Victims Remembered with Cheers and Tears; Republicans Decry Service as Political." *Star Tribune* (Minneapolis), October 30, metro edition, 1S; at http://web.lexisnexis.com; accessed May 27, 2005.

Langley, Monica. 2008. "As Economic Crisis Peaked, Tide Turned Against McCain." *The Wall Street Journal*, November 5, A1.

La Porte, Todd, and R. Consolini. 1991. "Working in Practice but Not in Theory: Theoretical Challenges of High-Reliability Organizations." *Public Administration Research and Theory* 1(1): 19–47.

La Raja, Raymond J. 2008. *Small Change: Money, Political Parties, and Campaign Finance Reform*. Ann Arbor: University of Michigan Press.

Larocca, Roger. 2004. "Strategic Diversion in Political Communication." *Journal of Politics* 66(2): 469–491.

Lau, Richard R., and Gerald M. Pomper. 2004. *Negative Campaigning: An Analysis of U.S. Senate Elections*. Lanham, MD: Rowman and Littlefield.

Layton, Lyndsen. 2008. "Kansas Congresswoman Isn't Capitalizing on Her (D)." *Washington Post*, October 31, A5.

Lee, Frances E., and Bruce I. Oppenheimer. 1999. *Sizing Up the Senate: The Unequal Consequences of Equal Representation*. Chicago: University of Chicago Press.

Lin, Ann Chih. 1998. "Bridging Positivist and Interpretivist Approaches to Qualitative Methods." *Policy Studies Journal* 26(1): 162–180.

Lincoln, Yvonna S., and Egon G. Guba. 1985. *Naturalistic Inquiry*. Newbury Park, CA: Sage.

Lipsky, Michael. 1980 [1997]. "Street-Level Bureaucracy: The Critical Role of Street-Level Bureaucrats." In *The Classics of Public Administration*. 4th ed. Ed. Jay M. Schafritz and Albert C. Hyde. Fort Worth, TX: Harcourt Brace, 401–408.

Livingston, Steven G., and Sally Friedman. 1993. "Reexamining Theories of Congressional Retirement: Evidence from the 1980s." *Legislative Studies Quarterly* 18(2): 231–253.

Lizza, Ryan. 2008. "How Obama Won." *The New Yorker*, November 17; at http://www.newyorker.com; accessed November 10, 2008.

Loomis, Burdett, and Michael Struemph. 2003. "Organized Interests, Lobbying, and the Industry of Politics: A First-Cut Overview." Paper presented at the annual meeting of the Midwest Political Science Association, Chicago.

———. 2004. "Growing Larger, Going Abroad, Getting Acquired: D.C. Lobbying as an Industry and a Cash-Flow Source." Paper presented at the annual meeting of the Southern Political Science Association, New Orleans.

Lough, Todd Allen. 1998. "The Effects of Scandal on Elections for the United States House of Representatives: 1976–1994." Ph.D. diss. Loyola University of Chicago.

Luntz, Frank I. 1988. *Candidates, Consultants, and Campaigns: The Style and Substance of American Electioneering.* New York: Basil Blackwell.

Magleby, David B., Kelly D. Patterson, and James A. Thurber. 2002. "Campaign Consultants and Responsible Party Government." In *Responsible Partisanship? The Evolution of American Parties Since 1950.* Ed. John C. Green and Paul S. Herrnson. Lawrence: University Press of Kansas.

Maisel, L. Sandy, and Darrell M. West. 2004. *Running on Empty? Political Discourse in Congressional Elections.* Lanham, MD: Rowman and Littlefield.

Mark, David. 2006. *Going Dirty: The Art of Negative Campaigning.* Lanham, MD: Rowman and Littlefield.

Mayhew, David R. 1974. *Congress: The Electoral Connection.* New Haven: Yale University Press.

McCurley, Carl, and Jeffery J. Mondak. 1995. "Inspected by #1184063113: The Influence of Incumbents' Competence and Integrity in U.S. House Elections." *American Journal of Political Science* 39(4): 864–885.

Medvic, Stephen K. 2000. "Professionalization in Congressional Campaigns." In *Campaign Warriors: Political Consultants in Elections.* Ed. James A. Thurber and Candice J. Nelson. Washington, DC: Brookings Institution Press, 91–109.

———. 2001. *Political Consultants in U.S. Congressional Elections.* Columbus: Ohio State University Press.

———. 2003. "Notes on a Theory of Professional Campaign Activity." Prepared for presentation at the symposium "Political Campaigning and Elections: Organization, Consultants, and Issues" at the annual meeting of the Northeastern Political Science Association, Philadelphia.

Miller, Dale E., and Stephen K. Medvic. 2002. "Civic Responsibility or Self-Interest?" In *Shades of Gray: Perspectives on Campaign Ethics.* Ed. Candice J. Nelson, David A. Dulio, and Stephen K. Medvic. Washington, DC: Brookings Institution Press, 18–38.

Mills, C. Wright. 1957. *The Power Elite.* New York: Oxford University Press.

Mondak, Jeffery J. 1995. "Competence, Integrity, and the Electoral Success of Congressional Incumbents." *Journal of Politics* 57(4): 1043–1069.

Monroe, J. P. 2001. *The Political Party Matrix: The Persistence of Organization.* Albany: State University of New York Press.

Napolitan, Joseph. 1972. *The Election Game and How to Win It.* Garden City, NJ: Doubleday.

National Public Radio. 2008. "How Obama Mapped out His Path to Power." *All Things Considered.* Transcript, November 5; at http://www.lexisnexis.com; accessed November 10, 2008.

National Transportation Safety Board. 2003. "Loss of Control and Impact with Terrain, Aviation Charter, Inc. Raytheon (Beechcraft) King Air A100, N41BE, Eveleth, Minnesota." October 25, 2002, Aircraft Accident Report. NTSB/AAR-03/03, PB2003-910493, Notation 7602. Adopted November 18.

Nelson, Candice J. 1994. "Women's PACs in the Year of the Woman." In *The Year of the Woman: Myths and Realities.* Ed. Elizabeth Addell Cook, Sue Thomas, and Clyde Wilcox. Boulder: Westview, 181–196.

———. 1998. "The Money Chase: Partisanship, Committee Leadership Change, and PAC Contributions in the House of Representatives." In *The Interest Group Con-*

nection: Electioneering, Lobbying, and Policymaking in Washington. Ed. Paul S. Herrnson, Ronald G. Shaiko, and Clyde Wilcox. Chatham, NJ: Chatham House, 52–64.

Nelson, Candice J., David A. Dulio, and Stephen K. Medvic, eds. 2002. *Shades of Gray: Perspectives on Campaign Ethics.* Washington, DC: Brookings Institution Press.

Nelson, Candice J., Stephen K. Medvic, and David A. Dulio. 2002. "Hired Guns or Gatekeepers of Democracy?" In *Shades of Gray: Perspectives on Campaign Ethics.* Ed. Candice J. Nelson, David A. Dulio, and Stephen K. Medvic. Washington, DC: Brookings Institution Press, 75–97.

New Webster's Dictionary and Roget's Thesaurus. 1992. New York: Book Essentials.

Nimmo, Dan. 1970. *The Political Persuaders: The Techniques of Modern Election Campaigns.* Englewood Cliffs, NJ: Prentice Hall.

Perrow, Charles. 1984. *Normal Accidents.* New York: Basic Books.

Peters, John G., and Susan Welch. 1978. "Political Corruption in America: A Search for Definitions and a Theory." *American Political Science Review* 72(3): 974–984.

———. 1980. "The Effects of Charges of Corruption on Voting Behavior in Congressional Elections." *American Political Science Review* 74(3): 697–708.

Peters, Ronald M., Jr. 1999. "Institutional Context and Leadership Style: The Case of Newt Gingrich." In *Old Minority or New Majority? The Impact of Republicans on Congress.* Ed. Colton C. Campbell and Nicol C. Rae. Lanham, MD: Rowman and Littlefield, 43–67.

Peterson, David A., and Paul A. Djupe. 2005. "When Primary Campaigns Go Negative: The Determinants of Campaign Negativity." *Political Research Quarterly* 58(1): 45–54.

Petracca, Mark P. 1989. "Political Consultants and Democratic Governance." *PS: Political Science and Politics* 22(1): 11–14.

Pfeiffer, John. 1989. "The Secret of Life at the Limits: Cogs Become Big Wheels." *Smithsonian* 20(4): 38–51.

Public Broadcasting Service. 2008. "The Choice 2008." *Frontline.* Transcript, October 22; at http://www.pbs.org; accessed November 11, 2008.

Rackaway, Chapman, Michael Smith, and Kevin Anderson. 2004. "The Eulogy Effect Redux: A Study of Campaign News Coverage After a Candidate Has Died." Presented at the annual meeting of the Western Political Science Association, Portland, Oregon.

Redford, Emmette S. 1969. *Democracy in the Administrative State.* New York: Oxford University Press.

Roberds, Stephen C. 1997. "Sex, Money and Deceit: Incumbent Scandals in U.S. House and Senate Elections, 1974–1990." Ph.D. diss. University of Missouri–St. Louis.

Rodeffer, Mark H. 2002a. "New Jersey GOP Mocks Senate Switch." National Journal Ad Spotlight, October 11; at http://nationaljournal.com; accessed May 25, 2005.

———. 2002b. "Coleman Back on TV; Mondale Launches Ad." National Journal Ad Spotlight, November 1, 2002; at http://nationaljournal.com; accessed May 27, 2005.

Romano, Lois. 2009. "The Adviser in the 'Lucky Office.'" *Washington Post,* February 13, A15.

Rosen, Yereth. 2008. "Alaska Sen. Stevens Concedes Defeat." Reuters wire report, November 20; at http://www.washingtonpost.com; accessed November 20, 2008.

Rosenbloom, David Lee. 1973. *The Election Men: Professional Campaign Managers and American Democracy.* New York: Quadrangle Books.

The Rothenberg Political Report. 2000. "The Rothenberg Political Report." October 27.

Rubin, Herbert J., and Irene S. Rubin. 1995. *Qualitative Interviewing: The Art of Hearing Data.* Thousand Oaks, CA: Sage.

Sabato, Larry J. 1981. *The Rise of Political Consultants: New Ways of Winning Elections.* New York: Basic Books.

Salisbury, Robert H., and Paul Johnson, with John P. Heinz, Edward O. Laumann, and Robert L. Nelson. 1989. "Who You Know Versus What You Know." *American Journal of Political Science* 33(4): 175–195.

Savage, Randall. 2001. "Chambliss Spokesman Blames Democrats, Media for Controversy." *Macon Telegraph*, A1; at http://web2.westlaw.com; accessed May 13, 2005.

Schafritz, Jay M., and Albert C. Hyde. 1997. *The Classics of Public Administration.* 4th ed. Fort Worth, TX: Harcourt Brace.

Scheufele, Dietram A. 2001. "Democracy for Some? How Political Talk Informs and Polarizes the Electorate." In *Communication in U.S. Elections: New Agendas.* Ed. Roderick P. Hart and Daron R. Shaw. Lanham, MD: Rowman and Littlefield, 19–32.

Schiller, Wendy J. 2000. *Partners and Rivals: Representation in U.S. Senate Delegations.* Princeton: Princeton University Press.

Schmidt, Susan, and James V. Grimaldi. 2001. "Torricelli and the Money Man: N.J. Senator Had Symbiotic Relationship with Executive." *Washington Post*, May 13, A01; at http://www.washingtonpost.com; accessed May 19, 2005.

Schmitt, Richard B. 2008. "Corruption Conviction Doesn't Daunt Stevens." *Los Angeles Times*, October 28, A1; at http://www.lexisnexis.com; accessed November 13, 2008.

Schouten, Fredreka. 2008. "Hagan Takes Republican Seat of Dole." *USA Today*, November 5, A12; at http://www.lexisnexis.com; accessed November 13, 2008.

Sears, David O. 2001. "The Role of Affect in Symbolic Politics." In *Citizens and Politics: Perspectives from Political Psychology.* Ed. J. H. Kuklinski. New York: Cambridge University Press.

Sellers, Patrick J. 1998. "Strategy and Background in Congressional Campaigns." *American Political Science Review* 92(1): 159–171.

Shah, Dhavan. 2001. "The Collision of Convictions: Value Framing and Value Judgments." In *Communication in U.S. Elections: New Agendas.* Ed. Roderick P. Hart and Daron R. Shaw. Lanham, MD: Rowman and Littlefield, 55–74.

Shea, Daniel M., and Michael John Burton. 2006. *Campaign Craft: The Strategies, Tactics, and Art of Political Campaign Management.* 3rd ed. Westport, CT: Praeger.

Sherman, Ted, and Robert Cohen. 2001. "Torricelli Stays on Offensive: Senator Raises Funds While He Belittles Probe." Newark *Star-Ledger*, February 25, news edition (final), 001; at http://wawa.starledger.com; accessed July 19, 2005.

Skinner, Richard M. 2005. "Do 527's Add up to a Party? Thinking About the 'Shadows' of Politics." Presented at the annual meeting of the Midwest Political Science Association, Chicago.

———. 2007. *More Than Money: Interest Group Action in Congressional Elections.* Lanham, MD: Rowman and Littlefield.

Smith, James T. 2002. "The Institutionalization of Politics by Scandal and the Effect on the American View of Government." Ph.D. diss. University of Nebraska.

Smith, Michael A., Chapman Rackaway, and Kevin Anderson. 2002. "The Eulogy Effect: Candidate Death and Its Effect on Media Coverage in a U.S. Senate Campaign." Presented at the annual meeting of the Southwest Political Science Association, New Orleans.

Somashekar, Sandhya. 2009. "Former Campaign Staffers Launch Their Own Bids." *Washington Post*, May 25, B1.

Star Tribune (Minneapolis). 2002. "Straying from Memorial to Rally." October 31, metro edition, 22A; at http://web.lexisnexis.com; accessed May 27, 2005.

Stewart, Charles III. 1994. "Let's Fly a Kite: Causes and Consequences of the House Bank Scandal." *Legislative Studies Quarterly* 19: 521–535.

Strother, Raymond D. 2003. *Falling Up: How a Redneck Helped Invent Political Consulting*. Baton Rouge: Louisiana State University Press.

Taylor, Steven. 2004. "Political Culture and African Americans' Forgiveness of Elected Officials." Presented at the annual meeting of the Northeastern Political Science Association, Boston.

Tharpe, Jim. 2002. "VFW Endorses Chambliss; Veterans Split on Cleland." *Atlanta Journal-Constitution*, October 10, home edition (with correction appended); at http://web.lexisnexis.com; accessed May 13, 2005.

Thompson, Krissah Williams. 2008. "Those up for Reelection Have Explaining to Do: A Southern Democrat Who Voted for the Plan Begins Addressing Some Angry Constituents." *Washington Post*, October 1, home edition, A10.

Thurber, James A. 1996. "Political Power and Policy Subsystems in American Politics." In *Agenda for Excellence: Administering the State*. Ed. B. Guy Peters and Bert A. Rockman. Chatham, NJ: Chatham House, 76–104.

———. 1998. "The Study of Campaign Consultants: A Subfield in Search of Theory." *PS: Political Science and Politics* 31(2): 145–149.

———. 2000. "Introduction to the Study of Campaign Consultants." In *Campaign Warriors: Political Consultants in Elections*. Ed. James A. Thurber and Candice J. Nelson. Washington, DC: Brookings Institution Press, 1–9.

———, ed. 2001. *The Battle for Congress: Consultants, Candidates, and Voters*. Washington, DC: Brookings Institution Press.

Thurber, James A., and Candice J. Nelson, eds. 2000. *Campaign Warriors: Political Consultants in Elections*. Washington, DC: Brookings Institution Press.

———. 2004. *Campaigns and Elections American Style*. 2nd ed. Boulder: Westview.

Thurber, James A., Candice J. Nelson, and David A. Dulio. 2000. "Portrait of Campaign Consultants." In *Campaign Warriors: Political Consultants in Elections*. Ed. James A. Thurber and Candice J. Nelson. Washington, DC: Brookings Institution Press, 10–36.

Toeplitz, Shira. 2009. "Shop Talk." *Roll Call*, February 12, 11.

United Press International. 2008. "Scandal-Plagued Democrat Loses in Fla." Wire report, November 5; at http://www.lexisnexis.com; accessed November 10, 2008.

Van Riper, Paul P. 1997. "Some Deep Anomalies in the History of U.S. Public Administration." *Public Administration Review* 57(3): 218–222.

Vargas, Theresa. 2009. "Democrat a Mix of Showmanship, Political Savvy." *Washington Post*, May 28, B1.

Vogel, Kenneth P. 2008. "Axelrod Mulls Huge Pay Cut, Opening Books." *Politico*, November 12; at http://www.politico.com; accessed November 12, 2008.

Waismel-Manor, Israel. 2005. "Making Up Their Minds: Knowledge, Learning and Decision-Making Among Campaign Consultants." Ph.D. diss. Cornell University.

Weber, Max. [1922] 1997. "Bureaucracy." In *The Classics of Public Administration*. 4th ed. Ed. Jay M. Schafritz and Albert C. Hyde. Fort Worth, TX: Harcourt Brace, 37–43.

Webster's II New Riverside Dictionary, Revised Edition. 1996. Office ed. Boston: Houghton Mifflin.

Welch, Susan, and John R. Hibbing. 1997. "The Effects of Charges of Corruption on Voting Behavior in Congressional Elections, 1982–1990." *Journal of Politics* 59(1): 226–239.

Whaley, John. 2003. "The Evolution and Maintenance of Ethics Regimes in Congress." Ph.D. diss. American University.

White House, The. 2009. "President Obama Announces More Key Administration Posts." Office of the Press Secretary, press release, May 21; at http://www.whitehouse.gov/the_press_office/President-Obama-Announces-More-Key-Administration-Posts-5-21-09/; accessed May 31, 2009.

Wilcox, Clyde. 1987. "The Timing of Strategic Decisions: Candidacy Decisions in 1982 and 1984." *Legislative Studies Quarterly* 12(4): 565–572.

Wilson, Woodrow. [1887] 1997. "The Study of Administration." In *The Classics of Public Administration*. 4th ed. Ed. Jay M. Schafritz and Albert C. Hyde. Fort Worth, TX: Harcourt Brace, 14–26.

Yachin, Jennifer, and Paul Singer. 2008. "Scandalized Lawmakers Face Voters." *Roll Call*, November 4 (November 5); at http://www.lexisnexis.com; accessed November 10, 2008.

Yin, Robert K. 1994. *Case Study Research: Design and Methods*. 2nd ed. Thousand Oaks, CA: Sage.

———. 2003. *Case Study Research: Design and Methods*. 3rd ed. Thousand Oaks, CA: Sage.

Index

Abramoff, Jack, 2
Academic perspective of campaigns, 3–4
Ace Transcription, x
Advertising: Cantwell criticisms of Gorton amendment, 147–148, 150–151, 152, 156(n8); Cantwell's image, 146; Chambliss's geographical advantage, 89–90; Chambliss's perspective of advertising as crisis, 82–85; Coleman's strategic response to Wellstone's death, 128–130; "11 Times" ad, 70, 72–73, 82–85, 86, 91(n1), 93(n33); Forrester's criticisms of Torricelli's ethics, 98; North Carolina Senate race, 174; political advertising as crises in Cleland-Chambliss race, 72–75; Republicans' attempts to link Lautenberg to Torricelli, 116–117; ten-second ad campaign targeting Cleland, 74–75; Torricelli-Lautenberg ballot switch, 112; Torricelli's "Fighter" ad, 103–104, 107, 118(n8); Wellstone-Mondale transition, 132–133; Wisconsin Advertising Project, 15(n11). *See also* Media
Age: effectiveness and status of campaign managers, 50–51
Allen, Diane, 97
American Association of Political Consultants (AAPC), 181

American Battle Monuments Commission, 173
American University (AU), ix–x, 181
Andrews, Jim, 122
Ashcroft, John, 127
Attack crises: Cantwell-Gorton race, 34–35; partisan differences and use of the attack frame, 28(tables), 29(table), 40(n27), 170–171; political professionals defining campaign crises, 22(table), 24–25; prevalence of, 160; professional demographics and defining crisis, 27–28, 29(table); race-baiting accusation in Chambliss campaign, 75–78; typology of campaign crises, 34, 35
Axelrod, David, 99, 171, 172
Ayres, Whit, 41, 49–50

Backus, Jenny, ix, 25, 31–32, 50, 57
Bainwol, Mitch, 108, 126
Ballot switch, 108, 110–114, 166
Bank scandal, US House of Representatives, 11, 19
Barkley, Dean, 133, 172–173
Barnes, Matthew, 108
Barnes, Roy, 71, 76, 78, 80, 90, 91, 141
Battle Mountain Gold, 143–144, 146–148
Baxter, Tom, 90–91
Bea, Keith, xi
Begich, Mark, 174

About the Book

How do sleepy congressional campaigns become heated battles? What happens behind the scenes during pivotal moments? Sam Garrett explores the dynamic process of electioneering by focusing on the insights and activities of political professionals: the consultants, party officials, staff, and others who make a career out of campaigning. As his analysis makes clear, how these experts handle crises—be they real, imagined, or manufactured by or for the competition—often shapes electoral outcomes.

R. Sam Garrett received his Ph.D. in political science from American University's School of Public Affairs in 2005, where he has served as a visiting and adjunct faculty member. He also serves as a research fellow at AU's Center for Congressional and Presidential Studies. Garrett works as an analyst in American national government at the Congressional Research Service, Library of Congress. Originally from suburban St. Louis, he is a former Presidential Management Fellow. He and his wife, Karen, live in Washington, D.C.